THE ROUGH GUIDE

GREEK

PHRASEBOOK

Compiled by

LEXUS

www.roughguides.com

Credits

Compiled by Lexus with Costas Panayotakis
Lexus Series Editor: Sally Davies
Rough Guides Reference Director: Andrew Lockett
Rough Guides Series Editor: Mark Ellingham

First edition published in 1995.
Reprinted in 1996 and 1998.
Revised in 1999.
This updated edition published in 2006 by
Rough Guides Ltd,
80 Strand, London WC2R 0RL
345 Hudson St, 4th Floor, New York 10014, USA
Email: mail@roughguides.co.uk.

Distributed by the Penguin Group.

Penguin Books Ltd, 80 Strand, London WC2R 0RL
Penguin Putnam, Inc., 375 Hudson Street, NY 10014, USA
Penguin Group (Australia), 250 Camberwell Road, Camberwell,
Victoria 3124, Australia
Penguin Books Canada Ltd, 10 Alcorn Avenue, Toronto,
Ontario, Canada M4V 1E4
Penguin Group (New Zealand), Cnr Rosedale and Airborne Roads,
Albany, Auckland, New Zealand

Typeset in Bembo and Helvetica to an original design by Henry Iles.
Printed in Italy by LegoPrint S.p.A

British Library Cataloguing in Publication Data
A catalogue for this book is available from the British Library.

ISBN 13: 978-1-84353-629-1
ISBN 10: 1-84353-629-3

The publishers and authors have done their best to ensure the
accuracy and currency of all information in The Rough Guide Greek
Phrasebook however, they can accept no responsibility for any loss
or inconvenience sustained by any reader using the book.

Online information about Rough Guides can be found at our
website www.roughguides.com

CONTENTS

Introduction

The Rough Guide Greek phrasebook is a highly practical introduction to the contemporary language. Laid out in clear A-Z style, it uses key-word referencing to lead you straight to the words and phrases you want – so if you need to book a room, just look up 'room'. The Rough Guide gets straight to the point in every situation, in bars and shops, on trains and buses, and in hotels and banks.

The main part of the Rough Guide is a double dictionary: English-Greek then Greek-English. Before that, there's a section called **Basic Phrases** and to get you involved in two-way communication, the Rough Guide includes, in this new edition, a set of **Scenario** dialogues illustrating questions and responses in key situations such as renting a car and asking directions. You can hear these and then download them free from **www.roughguides. com/phrasebooks** for use on your computer or MP3 player.

Forming the heart of the guide, the **English-Greek** section gives easy-to-use transliterations of the Greek words wherever pronunciation might be a problem. Throughout this section, cross-references enable you to pinpoint key facts and phrases, while asterisked words indicate where further information can be found in a section at the end of the book called **How the Language Works**. This section sets out the fundamental rules of the language, with plenty of practical examples. You'll also find here other essentials like numbers, dates, telling the time and basic phrases. The **Greek-English** section is in two parts: a dictionary, arranged phonetically, of all the words and phrases you're likely to hear (starting with a section of slang and colloquialisms); then a compilation, arranged by subject, of various signs, labels, instructions and other basic words you may come across in print or in public places.

Near the back of the book too the Rough Guide offers an extensive **Menu Reader**. Consisting of food and drink sections (each starting with a list of essential terms), it's indispensable whether you're eating out, stopping for a quick drink, or browsing through a local food market.

καλό ταξίδι!
kalo taxithi!
have a good trip!

Basic
Phrases

Basic Phrases

yes
ναί
neh

no
όχι
okhi

OK
εντάξει
endaxi

hello
χαίρετε
khereteh

good morning
καλημέρα
kalimera

good evening
καλησπέρα
kalispera

good night
καληνύχτα
kalinikhta

goodbye
αντίο
andio

hi
γειά
ya

see you
γειά, θα τα πούμε
ya, тна ta poomeh

please
παρακαλώ
parakalo

thank you
ευχαριστώ
efkharisto

yes, please
ναί, παρακαλώ
neh, parakalo

no thank you
όχι, ευχαριστώ
okhi, efkharisto

excuse me, please (to attract
   attention, to get past someone)
συγγνώμη, παρακαλώ
signomi, parakalo

sorry!
συγγνώμη!
signomi!

pardon? (sorry?, what did you
   say?)
ορίστε;
oristeh?

8

what did you say?
πώς είπατε;
pos ipateh?

I don't understand
δεν καταλαβαίνω
then katalaveno

do you speak English?
μιλάτε Αγγλικά;
milateh Anglika?

I don't speak Greek
δεν μιλάω Ελληνικά
then milo Elinika

please speak more slowly
παρακαλώ, μιλάτε πιό αργά;
parakalo, milateh pio arga?

could you repeat that?
το ξαναλέτε αυτό, σας
   παρακαλώ;
to xanaleteh afto, sas parakalo?

please write it down
μου το γράφετε, παρακαλώ;
moo to grafeteh, parakalo?

I would like ...
θα ήθελα ...
тнa iтнela ...

can I have ...?
μπορώ να έχω ...;
boro na ekho ...?

how much is it?
πόσο κάνει;
poso kani?

cheers!
εις υγείαν!
is iyian!

where is/are the ...?
πού είναι ...;
poo ineh ...?

Scenarios

download these scenarios as MP3s from:

1. Accommodation

is there an inexpensive hotel you can recommend?
▶ υπάρχει κάποιο φτηνό ξενοδοχείο που μπορείτε να μου συστήσετε;
[iparkhi kapio ftino xenothokhio poo boriteh na moo sistiseteh?]

λυπάμαι, φαίνεται ότι είναι όλα κλεισμένα ◀
[lipameh, feneteh oti ineh ola klismena]
I'm sorry, they all seem to be fully booked

---

can you give me the name of a good middle-range hotel?
▶ μπορείτε να μου πείτε το όνομα ενός ξενοδοχείου μεσαίας κατηγορίας;
[boriteh na moo piteh to onoma enos xenothokhioo meseas katigorias?]

δώστε μου να δω: θέλετε να είστε στο κέντρο της πόλης; ◀
[thosteh moo na tho; THeleteh na isteh sto kendro tis polis?]
let me have a look; do you want to be in the centre?

---

if possible
▶ αν είναι δυνατό
[an ineh thinato]

θα σας πείραζε να είστε λίγο έξω από την πόλη; ◀
[THa sas pirazeh na isteh ligo exo apo tin poli?]
do you mind being a little way out of town?

---

not too far out
▶ όχι πολύ μακριά
[okhi poli makria]

where is it on the map?
▶ πού είναι στον χάρτη;
[poo ineh ston kharti?]

can you write the name and address down?
▶ μπορείτε να μου γράψετε το όνομα και τη διεύθυνση;
[boriteh na moo grapseteh to onoma keh ti di-efTHinsi?]

I'm looking for a room in a private house
▶ ψάχνω για ένα δωμάτιο σε πανσιόν
[psakhno ya ena thomatio seh pansion]

ScanCnaG##e# 2. Banks

bank account	ο τραπεζικός λογαριασμός	[o trapezikos logariasmos]
to change money	αλλάζω χρήματα	[alazo khrimata]
cheque	μιά επιταγή	[mia epitayi]
to deposit	κάνω κατάθεση	[kano kataτhesi]
euro	ένα ευρώ	[ena evro]
pin number	ο κωδικός	[o kothikos]
pound	η λίρα Αγγλίας	[i lira anglias]
to withdraw	κάνω ανάληψη	[kano analipsi]

can you change this into euros?
▶ μπορείτε να αλλάξετε αυτά σε ευρώ;
[boriteh na alaxeteh afta seh evro?]

πώς θέλετε τα χρήματα; ◀
[pos τheleteh ta khrimata?]
how would you like the money?

small notes
▶ χαρτονομίσματα μικρής αξίας
[khartonomismata mikris axias]

big notes
▶ χαρτονομίσματα μεγάλης αξίας
[khartonomismata megalis axias]

do you have information in English about opening an account?
▶ έχετε πληροφορίες στα Αγγλικά για να ανοίξω έναν λογαριασμό;
[ekheteh plirofories sta Anglika ya na anixo enan logariasmo?]

ναι, τι είδος λογαριασμού θέλετε; ◀
[neh, ti ithos logariasmoo τheleteh?]
yes, what sort of account do you want?

I'd like a current account
▶ θα ήθελα έναν τρεχοντα λογαριασμό
[τha iτhela enan trekhonda logariasmo]

το διαβατήριό σας, παρακαλώ ◀
[to thiavatirio sas, parakalo]
your passport, please

can I use this card to draw some cash?
▶ μπορώ να κάνω ανάληψη μετρητών με αυτή την κάρτα;
[boro na kano analipsi metriton me afti tin karta?]

πρέπει να πάτε στο ταμείο ◀
[prepi na pateh sto tamio]
you have to go to the cashier's desk

I want to transfer this to my account at National Bank
▶ θέλω να μεταφέρω αυτά στον λογαριασμό μου στην Εθνική Τράπεζα
[τhelo na metafero afta ston logariasmo moo stin Eτhniki Trapeza]

εντάξει, αλλά θα πρέπει να σας χρεώσουμε για το τηλεφώνημα ◀
[endaxi, ala τha prepi na sas khreosoomeh ya to tilefonima]
OK, but we'll have to charge you for the phonecall

14

download these scenarios as MP3s from:

3. Booking a room

shower	το ντους	[to doos]
telephone in the room	το τηλέφωνο στο δωμάτιο	[to tilefono sto thomatio]
payphone in the lobby	το καρτοτηλέφωνο στη ρεσεψιόν	[to kartotilefono sti resepsion]

do you have any rooms?
▶ έχετε δωμάτια;
[ekheteh thomatia?]

▶ για πόσα άτομα;
[ya posa atoma?]
for how many people?

for one/for two
▶ για ένα/για δύο
[ya ena/ya thio]

▶ ναι, έχουμε ελεύθερα δωμάτια
[neh, ekhoomeh elefThera thomatia]
yes, we have rooms free

▶ για πόσα βράδυα;
[ya posa vrathia?]
for how many nights?

just for one night
▶ μόνο για ένα βράδυ
[mono ya ena vrathi]

how much is it?
▶ πόσο κάνει;
[poso kani?]

▶ ενενήντα ευρώ με λουτρό και εβδομήντα ευρώ χωρίς λουτρό ◀
[eneninda evro meh lootro keh evthominda evro khoris lootro]
90 euros with bathroom and 70 euros without bathroom

does that include breakfast?
▶ αυτό περιλαμβάνει και πρωινό;
[afto perilamvani keh pro-ino?]

can I see a room with bathroom?
▶ μπορώ να δω ένα δωμάτιο με λουτρό;
[boro na tho ena thomatio meh lootro?]

ok, I'll take it
▶ εντάξει, θα το κλείσω
[endaxi, THa to kliso]

when do I have to check out?
▶ πότε πρέπει να κάνω 'check-out';
[poteh prepi na kano 'check-out'?]

is there anywhere I can leave luggage?
▶ μπορώ να αφήσω τις αποσκευές μου κάπου;
[boro na afiso tis aposkeves moo kapoo?]

www.roughguides.com/phrasebooks

15

4. Car hire

automatic	το αυτόματο	[to aftomato]
full tank	το γεμάτο τεπόζιτο	[to yemato tepozito]
manual	το σειριακό	[to siriako]
rented car	το νοικιασμένο αυτοκίνητο	[to nikiasmeno aftokinito]

I'd like to rent a car
- θα ήθελα να νοικιάσω ένα αυτοκίνητο
[THa iThela na nikiaso ena aftokinito]

για πόσο καιρό ◀
[ya poso kero?]
for how long?

two days | I'll take the ...
- για δύο ημέρες | - θα πάρω το ...
[ya thio imeres] | [THa paro to ...]

is that with unlimited mileage?
- έχει απεριόριστο αριθμό χιλιομέτρων;
[ekhi aperioristo arithmo khiliometron?]

ναι ◀
[neh]
it is

παρακαλώ, μπορώ να δω την άδεια οδήγησης; ◀
[parakalo, boro na tho tin athia othiyisis?]
can I see your driving licence, please?

και το διαβατήριό σας ◀
[keh to thiavatirio sas]
and your passport

is insurance included?
- περιλαμβάνεται η ασφάλεια;
[perilamvaneteh i asfalia?]

ναι, αλλά πρέπει να πληρώσετε τα πρώτα εκατό ευρώ ◀
[neh, ala prepi na pliroseteh ta prota ekato evro]
yes, but you have to pay the first 100 euros

μπορείτε να δώσετε εγγύηση εκατό ευρώ; ◀
[boriteh na thoseteh engi-isi ekato evro?]
can you leave a deposit of 100 euros?

and if this office is closed, where do I leave the keys?
- και αν αυτό το γραφείο είναι κλειστό, πού μπορώ να αφήσω τα κλειδιά;
[keh an afto to grafio ineh klisto, poo boro na afiso ta klithia?]

τα ρίχνετε σε αυτό το κουτί ◀
[ta riKHneteh se afto to kooti]
you drop them in that box

5. Communications

ADSL modem	το μόντεμ ADSL	[to modem ADSL]
at	παπάκι	[papaki]
dial-up modem	το μόντεμ αναλογικής τηλεφωνίας	[to modem analo-yikis tilefonias]
dot	τελεία	[telia]
Internet	το 'Internet'	[to 'Internet']
mobile (phone)	το κινητό	[to kinito]
password	ο κωδικός	[o kothikos]
telephone socket adaptor	ο αντάπτορας για πρίζα τηλεφώνου	[o adaptoras ya priza tilefonoo]
wireless hotspot	η περιοχή για ασύρματο 'internet'	[i periokhi ya asirmato 'internet']

is there an Internet café around here?
▶ υπάρχει 'Internet café' εδώ γύρω;
[iparkhi 'Internet café' etho yiro?]

can I send email from here?
▶ μπορώ να στείλω 'email' από εδώ;
[boro na stilo 'email' apo etho?]

where's the at sign on the keyboard?
▶ πού είναι το παπάκι στο πληκτρολόγιο;
[poo ineh to papaki sto pliktrolo-yio?]

can you switch this to a UK keyboard?
▶ μπορείτε να αλλάξετε αυτό σε βρετανικό πληκτρολόγιο;
[boriteh na alaxeteh afto seh vretaniko pliktrolo-yio?]

can you help me log on?
▶ μπορείτε να με βοηθήσετε να κάνω είσοδο;
[boriteh na meh vo-iTHiseteh na kano isotho?]

can you put me through to ...?
▶ μπορείτε να με συνδέσετε με το ...;
[boriteh na meh sintheseteh meh to ...?]

I'm not getting a connection, can you help?
▶ δεν πιάνω γραμμή, μπορείτε να βοηθήσετε;
[then piano grami, boriteh na vo-iTHiseteh?]

where can I get a top-up card for my mobile?
▶ πού μπορώ να πάρω μια κάρτα ανανέωσης για το κινητό μου;
[poo boro na paro mia karta ananeosis ya to kinito moo?]

zero	five
μηδέν	πέντε
[mithen]	[pendeh]
one	six
ένα	έξι
[ena]	[exi]
two	seven
δύο	επτά
[thio]	[epta]
three	eight
τρία	οχτώ
[tria]	[okhto]
four	nine
τέσσερα	εννιά
[tesera]	[enia]

6. Directions

hi, I'm looking for Panepistimiou Street
> γειά σας, ψάχνω την οδό Πανεπιστημίου
[ya sas, psakhno ya tin otho Panepistimioo]

hi,
Panepistimiou
Street, do you
know where
it is?
γειά σας, η οδός
Πανεπιστημίου
ξέρετε πού
είναι;
[ya sas, i othos
Panepistimioo
xereteh poo
ineh?]

λυπάμαι, δεν την έχω ακουστά ◄
[lipameh, then tin ekho akoosta]
sorry, never heard of it

hi, can you tell me where Panepistimiou Street is?
> γειά σας, μπορείτε να μου πείτε πού είναι η οδός
Πανεπιστημίου;
[ya sas, boriteh na moo piteh poo ineh i othos
Panepistimioo?]

είμαι και εγώ ξένος εδώ ◄
[imeh keh ego xenos etho]
I'm a stranger here too

where?   which direction?
πού   προς ποια κατεύθυνση
[poo?]   [pros pia katefthinsi?]

> στη γωνία   > αριστερά στα δεύτερα φανάρια
[sti gonia]   [aristera sta theftera fanaria]
around the corner   left at the second traffic lights

> κατόπιν, είναι ο πρώτος δρόμος στα δεξιά
[katopin ineh o protos thromos sta thexia]
then it's the first street on the right

αμέσως μετά	επόμενος	μετά το...	παραπέρα
[amesos meta]	[epomenos]	[meta to ...]	[parapera]
just after	next	past the ...	further
απέναντι από	ευθεία	μπροστά	πίσω
[apenandi apo]	[efthia]	[brosta]	[piso]
opposite	straight ahead	in front of	back
στα αριστερά			στρίβω
[sta aristera]			[strivo]
on the left	κοντά	η οδός	turn off
εκεί	[konda]	[i othos]	στα δεξιά
[eki]	near	street	[sta thexia]
over there			on the right

7. Emergencies

accident	το ατύχημα	[to atikhima]
ambulance	το πρώτων βοηθειών	[to proton vo-iTHion]
consul	ο πρόξενος	[o proxenos]
embassy	η πρεσβεία	[i presvia]
fire brigade	η πυροσβεστική	[i pirosvestiki]
police	η αστυνομία	[i astinomia]

help!
▶ βοήθεια!
[vo-iTHia]

can you help me?
▶ μπορείτε να με βοηθήσετε;
[boriteh na meh vo-iTHiseteh?]

please come with me! it's really very urgent
▶ ελάτε, παρακαλώ μαζί μου! είναι πραγματικά πολύ επείγον
[elateh, parakalo, mazi moo! ineh pragmatika poli epigon]

I've lost (my keys)
▶ έχασα (τα κλειδιά μου)
[ekhasa (ta klithia moo)]

(my car) is not working
▶ (το αυτοκίνητό μου) δεν λειτουργεί
[(to aftokinito moo) then litooryi]

(my purse) has been stolen
▶ έκλεψαν (το πορτοφόλι μου)
[eklepsan (to portofoli moo)]

I've been mugged
▶ με λήστεψαν
[meh listepsan]

πώς σας λένε; ◀
[pos sas leneh?]
what's your name?

χρειάζεται να δω το διαβατήριό σας ◀
[khriazeteh na tho to thiavatirio sas]
I need to see your passport

I'm sorry, all my papers have been stolen
▶ λυπάμαι, μου έκλεψαν όλα τα στοιχεία ταυτότητας
[lipameh, moo eklepsan ola ta stikhia taftotitas]

8. Friends

hi, how're you doing?
▶ γειά σου, τι κάνεις;
[ya soo, ti kanis?]

καλά, και εσύ; ◀
[kala, keh esi?]
OK, and you?

yeah, fine
▶ ναι, ωραία
[neh, orea]

not bad
▶ όχι άσχημα
[okhi askhima]

d'you know Mark?
▶ ξέρεις τον Μάρκ;
[xeris ton Mark?]

and this is Hannah
▶ και αυτή είναι η Χάννα
[keh afti ineh i khana]

ναι, γνωριζόμαστε ◀
[neh, gnorizomasteh]
yeah, we know each other

where do you know each other from?
▶ από που γνωρίζεστε;
[apo poo gnorizesteh?]

συναντηθήκαμε στο σπίτι του Γιάννη ◀
[sinandiTHikameh sto spiti too Yani]
we met at Yanis' place

that was some party, eh?
▶ πολύ ωραίο πάρτυ, ε;
[poli oreo parti, eh?]

το καλύτερο ◀
[to kalitero]
the best

are you guys coming for a beer?
▶ έρχεστε για μιά μπύρα;
[erkhesteh ya mia bira?]

▶ 'cool', πάμε
['cool', pameh]
cool, let's go

▶ όχι, θα συναντήσω τη Μαρία
[okhi, THa sinandiso ti Maria]
no, I'm meeting Maria

see you at Yanis' place tonight
▶ τα λέμε στο σπίτι του Γιάννη απόψε
[ta lemeh sto spiti too Yani apopseh]

τα λέμε ◀
[ta lemeh]
see you

20

9. Health

I'm not feeling very well
▶ δεν αισθάνομαι πολύ καλά
[then esTHanomeh poli kala]

can you get a doctor?
▶ μπορείτε να φέρετε έναν γιατρό;
[boriteh na fereteh enan yatro?]

▶ πού πονάει;   it hurts here
[poo pona-i?]   ▶ πονάει εδώ
where does it hurt?   [pona-i etho]

▶ πονάει συνεχώς;   it's not a constant pain
[pona-i sinekhos?]   ▶ δεν πονάει συνεχώς
is the pain constant? [then pona-i sinekhos]

can I make an appointment?
▶ μπορώ να κλείσω ένα ραντεβού;
[boro na kliso ena randevoo?]

can you give me something for ...?
▶ μπορείτε να μου δώσετε κάτι για ...;
[boriteh na moo thoseteh kati ya ...?]

yes, I have insurance
▶ ναι, έχω ασφάλεια
[neh, ekho asfalia]

antibiotics	το αντιβιοτικό	[to andiviotiko]
antiseptic ointment	η αντισηπτική αλοιφή	[i andisiptiki alifi]
cystitis	η κυστίτιδα	[i kistititha]
dentist	ο/η οδοντίατρος	[o/i othondiatros]
diarrhoea	η διάρροια	[i thiari-a]
doctor	ο γιατρός	[o yatros]
hospital	το νοσοκομείο	[to nosokomio]
ill	άρρωστος	[arostos]
medicine	το φάρμακο	[to farmako]
painkillers	τα παυσίπονα	[ta pafsipona]
pharmacy	το φαρμακείο	[to farmakio]
to prescribe	γράφω συνταγή	[grafo sinda-yi]
thrush	η στοματίτιδα	[i stomatitida]

10. Language difficulties

a few words | λίγες λέξεις | [liyes lexis]
interpreter | ο/η διερμηνέας | [o/i thi-ermineas]
to translate | μεταφράζω | [metafrazo]

η πιστωτική σας κάρτα δεν έγινε δεκτή ◀
[i pistotiki sas karta then eyineh thekti]
your credit card has been refused

---

what, I don't understand; do you speak English?
▶ τι; δεν καταλαβαίνω, μιλάτε Αγγλικά;
[ti? then katalaveno; milateh Anglika?]

αυτή δεν ισχύει ◀
[afti then iskhi-i]
this isn't valid

---

could you say that again?
▶ μπορείτε να το ξαναπείτε αυτό;
[boriteh na to xanapiteh afto?]

slowly
▶ αργά
[arga]

I understand very little Greek
▶ καταλαβαίνω πολύ λίγα Ελληνικά
[katalaveno poli liga Elinika]

I speak Greek very badly
▶ δεν μιλάω καθόλου καλά Ελληνικά
[then milao katHoloo kala Elinika]

δεν μπορείτε να πληρώσετε με αυτή την κάρτα ◀
[then boriteh na pliroseteh meh afti tin karta]
you can't use this card to pay

▶ καταλαβαίνετε;
[katalaveneteh?]
do you understand?

sorry, no
▶ όχι, λυπάμαι
[okhi, lipameh]

---

is there someone who speaks English?
▶ μιλάει κανείς εδώ Αγγλικά;
[mila-i kanis etho Anglika?]

---

oh, now I understand
▶ α, τώρα καταλαβαίνω
[ah, tora katalaveno]

is that ok now?
▶ είναι εντάξει τώρα;
[ineh endaxi tora?]

---

11. Meeting people

hello
▶ γειά σας
[ya sas]

γειά σας, με λένε Κατερίνα ◀
[yasas, meh leneh Katerina]
hello, my name's Katerina

Graham, from England, Thirsk
▶ με λένε Graham και είμαι από το Thirsk στην Αγγλία
[meh leneh Graham keh imeh apo to Thirsk stin Anglia]

δεν το ξέρω, που βρίσκεται; ◀
[then to xero, poo vrisketeh?]
don't know that, where is it?

not far from York, in the North; and you?
▶ όχι μακριά από το York στον Βορρά, και εσύ;
[okhi makria apo to York ston vora; keh esi?]

εγώ είμαι από τη Θεσσαλονίκη; είσαι εδώ μόνος σου; ◀
[ego imeh apo ti THesaloniki; iseh etho monos soo?]
I'm from Thessaloniki; here by yourself?

no, I'm with my wife and two kids
▶ όχι, είμαι με τη γυναίκα μου και τα δύο μου παιδιά
[okhi, imeh meh ti yineka moo keh ta thio moo pethia]

what do you do?   είμαι στους υπολογιστές ◀
▶ τι δουλειά κάνεις;   [imeh stoos ipolo-yistes]
[ti thoolia kanis?]   I'm in computers

me too
▶ κι εγώ επίσης
[ki ego episis]

here's my wife now
▶ να και η γυναίκα μου
[na keh i yineka moo]

χαίρω πολύ ◀
[khero poli]
nice to meet you

12. Post offices

airmail	αεροπορικώς	[a-eroporikos]
post card	η κάρτα	[i karta]
post office	το ταχυδρομείο	[to takhithromio]
stamp	το γραμματόσημο	[to gramatosimo]

what time does the post office close?
▶ τί ώρα κλείνει το ταχυδρομείο;
[ti ora klini to takhithromio?]

τις καθημερινές στις 5 ◀
[tis kaTHimerines stis pendeh]
five o'clock weekdays

is the post office open on Saturdays?
▶ είναι ανοιχτά το ταχυδρομείο το Σάββατο;
[ineh anikhta to takhithromio to Savato?]

μέχρι το μεσημέρι ◀
[mekhri to mesimeri]
until midday

I'd like to send this registered to England
▶ θα ήθελα να στείλω αυτό συστημένο στην Αγγλία
[THa iTHela na stilo afto sistimeno stin Anglia]

βεβαίως, κάνει 10 ευρώ ◀
[veveos, kani theka evro]
certainly, that will cost 10 euros

and also two stamps for England, please
▶ και δύο γραμματόσημα για την Αγγλία, παρακαλώ
[keh thio gramatosima ya tin Anglia, parakalo]

do you have some airmail stickers?
▶ έχετε αυτοκόλλητα `Αεροπορικώς`;
[ekheteh aftokolita 'a-eroporikos'?]

do you have any mail for me?
▶ έχετε γράμματα για μένα;
[ekheteh gramata ya mena?]

γράμματα	[gramata]	letters
δέματα	[themata]	parcels
εξωτερικού	[exoterikoo]	international
εσωτερικού	[esoterikoo]	domestic
ποστ-ρεστάντ	[post-restant]	poste restante

13. Restaurants

bill	menu	table
ο λογαριασμός	ο κατάλογος	το τραπέζι
[o logariasmos]	[o katalogos]	[to trapezi]

can we have a non-smoking table?
▶ μπορούμε να έχουμε ένα τραπέζι για μη-καπνιστές;
[boroomeh na ekhoomeh ena trapezi ya mi-kapnistes?]

there are two of us
▶ είμαστε δύο άτομα
[imasteh thio atoma]

there are four of us
▶ είμαστε τέσσερα άτομα
[imasteh tesera atoma]

what's this?
▶ τί είναι αυτό;
[ti ineh afto?]

είναι ένα είδος ψαριού ◀
[ineh ena ithos psarioo]
it's a type of fish

είναι μιά τοπική σπεσιαλιτέ ◀
[ineh mia topiki spesialiteh]
it's a local speciality

ελάτε μέσα και θα σας δείξω ◀
[elateh mesa keh THa sas thixo]
come inside and I'll show you

we would like two of these, one of these, and one of those
▶ θα θέλαμε δύο από αυτά, ένα από αυτά και ένα από εκείνα
[THa THelameh thio apo afta, ena apo afta keh ena apo ekina]

▶ και τί θα πιείτε;
[keh ti THa pi-iteh?]
and to drink?

red wine
▶ κόκκινο κρασί
[kokino krasi]

white wine
▶ λευκό κρασί
[lefko krasi]

a beer and two orange juices
▶ μία μπύρα και δύο πορτοκαλάδες
[mia bira keh thio portokalathes]

some more bread please
▶ ακόμη λίγο ψωμί, παρακαλώ
[akomi ligo psomi, parakalo]

▶ σας άρεσε το γεύμα;
[sas areseh to yevma?]
how was your meal?

excellent!, very nice!
▶ έξοχο!, πολύ νόστιμο!
[exokho!, poli nostimo!]

▶ τίποτα άλλο;
[tipota alo?]
anything else?

just the bill thanks
▶ μόνο τον λογαριασμό, ευχαριστώ
[mono ton logariasmo, efkharisto]

14. Shopping

μπορώ να σας βοηθήσω; ◄
[boro na sas vo-iTHiso?]
can I help you?

can I just have a look around?
► μπορώ να κοιτάξω μόνο γύρω;
[boro na kitaxo mono yiro?]

yes, I'm looking for ...
ναι, ψάχνω για ...
[neh, psakhno ya ...]

how much is this?
► πόσο κάνει αυτό;
[poso kani afto?]

τριάντα δύο ευρώ ◄
[trianda thio evro]
thirty-two euros

OK, I think I'll have to leave it; it's a little too expensive for me
► εντάξει, νομίζω ότι δεν θα το πάρω; είναι λίγο ακριβό για μένα
[endaxi, nomizo oti then THa to paro; ineh ligo akrivo ya mena]

αυτό πως σας φαίνεται; ◄
[afto pos sas feneteh?]
how about this?

can I pay by credit card?
► μπορώ να πληρώσω με πιστωτική κάρτα;
[boro na pliroso meh pistotiki karta?]

it's too big
► είναι πολύ μεγάλο
[ineh poli megalo]

it's too small
► είναι πολύ μικρό
[ineh poli mikro]

it's for my son – he's about this high
► είναι για τον γιό μου – είναι περίπου τόσο ψηλός
[ineh ya ton yo moo – ineh peripoo toso psilos]

► θέλετε τίποτα άλλο;
[THeleteh tipota alo?]
will there be anything else?

that's all thanks
► μόνο αυτό, ευχαριστώ
[mono afto, efkharisto]

make it twenty euros and I'll take it
► θα το πάρω αν μου το δώσετε για 20 ευρώ
[THa to paro an moo to thoseteh ya ikosi evro]

fine, I'll take it
► ωραία, θα το πάρω
[orea, THa to paro]

αλλαγές	[ala-yes]	to exchange
ανοιχτά	[anikhta]	open
εκπτώσεις	[ekptosis]	sale
κλειστά	[klista]	closed
ταμείο	[tamio]	cash desk

15. Sightseeing

art gallery	η πινακοθήκη	[i pinakoTHiki]
bus tour	η ξενάγηση με λεωφορείο	[i xenayisi meh leoforio]
city centre	το κέντρο της πόλης	[to kendro tis polis]
closed	κλειστά	[klista]
guide	ο/η ξεναγός	[o/i xenagos]
museum	το μουσείο	[to moosio]
open	ανοιχτός	[anikhtos]

I'm interested in seeing the old town

▶ Θα με ενδιέφερε να δω την παλιά πόλη
[THa meh enthiefereh na tho tin palia poli]

are there guided tours?

▶ υπάρχουν ξεναγήσεις;
[iparkhoon xenayisis?]

λυπάμαι, είναι όλα κλεισμένα ◀
[lipameh, ineh ola klismena]
I'm sorry, it's fully booked

how much would you charge to drive us around for four hours?

▶ πόσα θα χρεώσετε για να μας πάτε βόλτα για τέσσερις ώρες;
[posa THa khreoseteh ya na mas pateh volta ya teseris ores?]

can we book tickets for the concert here?

▶ μπορούμε να κλείσουμε εδώ εισιτήρια για το κονσέρτο;
[boroomeh na klisoomeh etho isitiria ya to konserto?]

▶ ναι, σε τι όνομα;
[neh, seh ti onoma?]
yes, in what name?

▶ ποιά πιστωτική κάρτα;
[pia pistotiki karta?]
which credit card?

where do we get the tickets?

▶ πού θα πάρουμε τα εισιτήρια;
[poo tha paroomeh ta isitiria?]

θα τα πάρετε στην είσοδο ◀
[THa ta pareteh stin isotho]
just pick them up at the entrance

is it open on Sundays?

▶ είναι ανοικτά την Κυριακή;
[ineh anikta tin Kiriaki?]

how much is it to get in?

▶ πόσο κάνει η είσοδος;
[poso kani i isothos?]

are there reductions for groups of 6?

▶ υπάρχει έκπτωση για ομάδα έξι ατόμων;
[iparkhi ekptosi ya omatha exi atomon?]

that was really impressive!

▶ αυτό ήταν πραγματικά εντυπωσιακό!
[afto itan pragmatika endiposiako!]

16. Trains

to change trains	αλλάζω τρένο	[alazo treno]
platform	η πλατφόρμα	[i platforma]
return	ένα εισιτήριο με επιστροφή	[ena isitirio meh epistrofi]
single	ένα εισιτήριο απλό	[ena isitirio aplo]
station	ο σταθμός	[o staTHmos]
stop	η στάση	[i stasi]
ticket	ένα εισιτήριο	[ena isitirio]

how much is ...?
▶ πόσο κάνει ...;
[poso kani ...?]

a single, second class to ...
▶ ένα εισιτήριο απλό, δεύτερη θέση για ...
[ena isitirio aplo, thefteri THesi ya ...]

two returns, second class to ...
▶ δύο εισιτήρια με επιστροφή, δεύτερη θέση για ...
[thio isitiria meh epistrofi, thefteri THesi ya ...]

for today
▶ για σήμερα
[ya simera]

for tomorrow
▶ για αύριο
[ya avrio]

for next Tuesday
▶ για την άλλη Τρίτη
[ya tin ali Triti]

θέλετε να κρατήσετε θέση; ◀
[THeleteh na kratiseteh THesi?]
do you want to make a seat reservation?

πρέπει να αλλάξετε στη Λαμία ◀
[prepi na alaxeteh sti Lamia]
you have to change at Lamia

what time is the last train to Corinth?
▶ τι ώρα είναι το τελευταίο τρένο για την Κόρινθο;
[ti ora ineh to telefteo treno ya tin KorinTHo?]

is this seat free?
▶ είναι ελεύθερη αυτή η θέση;
[ineh elefTHeri afti i THesi?]

excuse me, which station are we at?
▶ με συγχωρείτε, σε ποιό σταθμό είμαστε;
[meh sinkhoriteh, seh pio staTHmo imasteh?]

is this where I change for Thessaloniki?
▶ εδώ πρέπει να αλλάξω τρένο για τη Θεσσαλονίκη;
[etho prepi na alaxo treno ya ti THesaloniki?]

English

→

Greek

a, an* enas, mia, ena
about: about 20 peripoo ikosi
  it's about 5 o'clock ineh yiro
  stis pendeh
  a film about Greece ena ergo
  ya tin Elatha
above pano apo
abroad sto exoteriko
absolutely! (I agree) apolitos!
accelerator to gazi
accept thekhomeh
accident to thistikhima
  there's been an accident
  eyineh ena thistikhima
accommodation i thiamoni
accurate akrivis
ache o ponos
  my back aches pona-i i plati
  moo
across: across the road
  apenandi sto thromo
adapter to polaplo
  (for voltage change) i briza taf
address i thi-efrhinsi
  what's your address? pia ineh
  i thi-efrhinsi soo?
address book i adzenda ton
  thi-efrhinseon
admission charge timi isothoo
adult (man/woman) o enilikos/i
  eniliki
advance: in advance
  prokatavolika
aeroplane to a-eroplano
after meta
  after you meta apo sas

after lunch meta apo to
  yevma
afternoon apo-yevma
  in the afternoon kata to apo-
  yevma
  this afternoon afto to apo-
  yevma
aftershave i kolonia meta to
  xirisma
aftersun cream to galaktoma
  ya ton ilio
afterwards meta
again xana
against enandion
age i ilikia
ago: a week ago prin apo mia
  evthomatha
  an hour ago prin apo mia ora
agree: I agree simfono
AIDS to AIDS
air o a-eras
  by air a-eroporikos
air-conditioning o klimatismos
airmail: by airmail
  a-eroporikos
airmail envelope o
  a-eroporikos fakelos
airport to a-erothromio
  to the airport, please sto
  a-erothromio, parakalo
airport bus to leoforio
  a-erothromi-oo
aisle seat thesi thipla sto
  thiathromo
alarm clock to xipnitiri
Albania i Alvania
Albanian (adj) Alvanikos
alcohol to alko-ol
alcoholic inopnevmatothis

all: all the boys ola ta agoria
all the girls ola ta koritsia
all the men oli i andres
all the women oles i yinekes
all of it olokliro
all of them ola afta
that's all, thanks afta ineh ola,
efkharisto
allergic: I'm allergic to ... imeh
aleryikos meh ...
allowed: is it allowed?
epitrepeteh?
all right endaxi
I'm all right imeh endaxi
are you all right? (adj) iseh
endaxi?
(pol) esis endaxi?
almond to amigthalo
almost skhethon
alone monos
alphabet to alfavito
see page 209
already ithi
also episis
although an keh
altogether sinolika
always panda
am*: I am imeh
am: at seven am stis efta pro
mesimvrias
amazing (surprising)
ekpliktikos
(very good) thavmasios
ambulance to asTHenoforo
call an ambulance! kalesteh
ena asTHenoforo!
America i Ameriki
American (adj) Amerikanikos
I'm American (man/woman)
imeh Amerikanos/
Amerikana
among anamesa
amount to poso
(money) ta khrimata
amp: a 13-amp fuse mia
asfalia thekatria amper
amphitheatre to
amfiтнeatro
Ancient Greece i arkhea
Elatha
Ancient Greek ta arkhea
Elinika
and keh
angry тнimomenos
animal to zo-o
ankle o astragalos
anniversary (wedding) i epetios
too gamoo
annoy: this man's annoying
me aftos o andras meh
enokhli
annoying enokhlitikos
another alos, ali, alo
can we have another room?
boroomeh na ekhoomeh ena
alo thomatio?
another beer, please ali mia
bira, parakalo
antibiotics to andiviotiko
antihistamine to andi-
istaminiko farmako
antique: is it an antique? ineh
antika?
antique shop to paleopolio
antiseptic to andisiptiko
any: have you got any bread/
tomatoes? ekheteh psomi/
domates?

dialogue

do you have any change?
ekhis katнoloo psila?
sorry, I don't have any
lipameh, then ekho
katнoloo

anybody kanis
does anybody speak English?
mila-i kanis Anglika?
there wasn't anybody there
then itan kanis eki
anything otithipoteh

dialogues

anything else? tipoteh alo?
nothing else, thanks
tipoteh, efkharisto

would you like anything to
drink? тнa тнelateh na pi-
iteh kati?
I don't want anything,
thanks then тнelo tipoteh,
efkharisto

apart from ektos apo
apartment to thiamerisma
appendicitis i skoliko-ithitis
appetizer to proto piato
appetizers ta orektika
aperitif to aperitif
apology i signomi
apple to milo
appointment to
randevoo

dialogue

good afternoon, sir, how
can I help you? kalispera
sas, kiri-eh, pos boro na sas
vo-iтнiso?
I'd like to make an
appointment тнa iтнela na
kliso ena randevoo
what time would you like?
ti ora тнeleteh? ·
three o'clock tris i ora
I'm afraid that's not
possible; is four o'clock
all right? fovameh oti afto
then yineteh; boriteh stis
teseris?
yes, that will be fine neh,
poli kala
the name was ...? to
onoma sas?

apricot to verikoko
April o Aprilios
archaeology i arkheoloyia
are*: we are imasteh
  you are isteh
  thoy are ineh
area i periokhi
area code o kothikos ariтнmos
arm to kheri
arrange: will you arrange it for
us? тнa to kanonisis ya mas?
arrival i afixi
arrive ftano
  when do we arrive? poteh
  ftanoomeh?
  has my fax arrived yet?
  eftaseh to fax moo?

we arrived today ftasameh simera
art i tekhni
art gallery i pinakoтнiki
artist (man/woman) o kalitekhnis/i kalitekhnitha
as: as big as ... megalo san ...
  as soon as possible oso pio grigora yineteh
ashtray to tasaki, to stokhto-thokhio
ask roto
  I didn't ask for this then zitisa afto
  could you ask him to ...? boris na too pis na ...?
asleep: she's asleep kimateh
aspirin i aspirini
asthma i asтнma
astonishing ekpliktikos
at: at the hotel sto xenothokhio
  at the station sto staтнmo
  at six o'clock stis exi i ora
  at Yanni's stoo Yanni
Athens i Aтнina
athletics o aтнlitismos
attractive elkistikos
aubergine i melidzana
August o Avgoostos
aunt i тнia
Australia i Afstralia
Australian (adj) Afstralezikos
  I'm Australian (man/woman) imeh Afstralos/Afstraleza
automatic (adj) aftomatos
  (car) to aftomato aftokinito
automatic teller i mikhani ya metrita

autumn to fтнinoporo
  in the autumn sto fтнinoporo
avenue i leoforos
average (not good) metrio
  on average kata meson oro
awake: is he awake? ineh xipnios?
away: go away! fiyeh
  is it far away? ineh poli makria?
awful apesios
axle o axonas

B

baby to moro
baby food i pethiki trofi
baby's bottle to bibero
baby-sitter i baby-sitter
back (of body) i plati
  (back part) piso
  at the back sto piso meros
  can I have my money back? boro na ekho ta lefta moo piso?
  to come/go back epistrefo, yirizo piso
backache ponos stin plati
bacon to bacon
bad kakos
  a bad headache enas askhimos ponokefalos
badly askhima
bag i tsanda
  (suitcase) i valitsa
baggage i aposkeves
baggage check o khoros filaxis aposkevon

baggage claim anazitisi
aposkevon
bakery o foornaris
balcony to balkoni
 a room with a balcony ena
 thomatio meh balkoni
bald falakros
ball (large) i bala
 (small) to balaki
ballet to baleto
banana i banana
band (musical) to singrotima
bandage o epithesmos
Bandaid® to lefkoplast
bank i trapeza
bank account o trapezikos
 logariasmos
bar to bar
 a bar of chocolate mia
 sokolata
barber's to koorio
basket to kalaтни
basketball to basketball, i
 kalaтнosferisi
bath to banio
 can I have a bath? boro na
 kano ena banio?
bathroom to lootro, to banio
 with a private bathroom meh
 ithiotiko lootro
bath towel i petseta too
 banioo
battery i bataria
bay o kolpos
be* imeh
beach i paralia
beach mat i psaтна
beach umbrella i ombrela
beans ta fasolia

green beans ta fasolakia
runner beans ta fasolakia
 freska
broad beans ta kookia
beard ta yenia
beautiful oreos
because epithi
 because of ... exetias ...
bed to krevati
 I'm going to bed now pao ya
 ipno tora
bed and breakfast thomatio
 meh pro-ino
bedroom to ipnothomatio
beef to moskhari
beer i bira
 two beers, please thio bires,
 parakalo
before prin
begin arkhizo
 when does it begin? poteh
 arkhizi?
beginner (man/woman) o
 arkharios/i arkharia
beginning: at the beginning
 kat arkhas
behind piso
 behind me apo piso moo
beige bez
believe pistevo
belly-dancing to tsifteteli
below apo kato
belt i zoni
bend (in road) i strofi
berth (on ship) i klini
beside: beside the ... thipla
 sto ...
best aristos
better kaliteros

better than ... kaliteros apo ...
are you feeling better?
esthaneseh kalitera?
between metaxi
beyond pera apo
bicycle to pothilato
big megalos
  too big poli megalo
  it's not big enough then ineh
  arketa megalo
bike to pothilato
  (motorbike) to mikhanaki
bikini to bikini
bill o logariasmos
  (US) to khartonomisma
  could I have the bill, please?
  boro na ekho ton logariasmo,
  parakalo?
bin o skoopithotenekes
bin liners i sakoola skoopithion
bird to pooli
biro® to stilo
birthday ta yenethlia
  happy birthday! khronia pola!
biscuit to biskoto
bit: a little bit ligo
  a big bit ena megalo komati
  a bit of ... ligo apo ...
  a bit expensive ligo akrivo,
  akrivootsiko
bite (by insect) to tsibima
  (by dog) i thagonia
bitter (taste etc) pikros
black mavros
blanket i kooverta
bleach (for toilet) to Harpik®
bless you! ya soo!
blind tiflos
blinds ta pantzooria

blister i fooskala
blocked (road, pipe)
  frakarismenos
  (sink) voolomenos
block of flats i polikatikia
blond xanthos
blood to ema
  high blood pressure ipsili
  pi-esi ematos
blouse i blooza
blow-dry to khtenisma
  I'd like a cut and blow-dry
  tha ithela kopsimo keh
  khtenisma
blue bleh
  blue eyes galana matia
blusher i poothra
boarding house i pansion
boarding pass i karta
  epivivaseos
boat (small) to ka-iki
  (for passengers) to plio
body to soma
boil (verb) vrazo
boiled egg to vrasto avgo
boiler o vrastiras
bone to kokalo
bonnet (of car) to kapo
book to vivlio
  (verb) klino
  can I book a seat? boro na
  kliso mia thesi?

dialogue

I'd like to book a table for
two tha ithela na kliso ena
trapezi ya thio atoma
what time would you like

it booked for? ti ora to
THeleteh?
half past seven stis efta
keh misi
that's fine endaxi
and your name? to onoma
sas, parakalo?

bookshop to vivliopolio
bookstore to vivliopolio
boot (footwear) i bota
  (of car) to port-bagaz
border (of country) ta sinora
bored: I'm bored vari-emeh
boring varetos
born: I was born in
  Manchester yeniTHika sto
  Manchester
  I was born in 1960 yeniTHika
  to 1960 (khilia eniakosia
  exinda)
borrow thanizomeh
  may I borrow ...? boro na
  thanisto ...?
both keh i thio
bother: sorry to bother you
  signomi poo sas enokhlo
bottle to bookali
  a bottle of house red ena
  bookali kokino spitiko krasi
bottle-opener to anikhtiri
bottom (of person) o kolos
  at the bottom of the hill sto
  vaTHos too lofoo
  at the bottom of the road sto
  telos too thromoo
box to kooti
box office to tamio
boy to agori

boyfriend o filos
bra to sooti-en
bracelet to vrakhioli
brake to freno
  (verb) frenaro
brandy to koniak
bread to psomi
  white bread to aspro psomi
  brown bread to mavro psomi
  wholemeal bread to starenio
  psomi
break (verb) spao
  I've broken the ... espasa to ...
  I think I've broken my wrist
  nomizo oti espasa ton karpo
  moo
break down (car) paTHeno
  vlavi
  I've broken down khalaseh to
  aftokinito moo
breakdown (car) i vlavi
breakdown service i vlaves
  aftokiniton
breakfast to pro-ino
break-in: I've had a break-in
  meh listepsan
breast to stiTHos
breathe anapneo
breeze to aeraki
bridge (over river) i yefira
brief sindomos
briefcase o khartofilakas
bright (light etc) fotinos
  bright red khtipitos kokinos
brilliant (idea, person)
  katapliktikos
bring ferno
  I'll bring it back later THa to
  fero piso argotera

Britain i Vretania
British Vretanikos
brochure to prospektoos
broken spasmenos
  it's broken ineh spasmeno
bronchitis i vronkhititha
brooch i karfitsa
broom i skoopa
brother o athelfos
brother-in-law o gambros
brown kafeh
  brown hair kastana malia
  brown eyes kastana matia
bruise i melania
brush i voortsa
  (for hair) i voortsa ya ta malia
  (artist's) to pinelo
bucket o koovas
buffet car to boofeh
buggy (for child) to pethiko
  amaxaki
building to ktirio
bulb (light bulb) i lamba
Bulgaria i Voolgaria
Bulgarian (adj) Voolgarikos
bumper o profilaktiras
bunk i kooketa
bureau de change Sinalagma
burglary i thiarixi
burn (noun) to kapsimo
  (verb) keo
burnt: this is burnt afto ineh
  kameno
burst: a burst pipe mia
  spasmeni solina
bus to leoforio
  what number bus is it to ...? ti
  ariTHmo ekhi to leoforio
  ya ...?

when is the next bus to
...? poteh ineh to epomeno
leoforio ya ...?
what time is the last bus? ti
ora ineh to telefteo leoforio?
could you let me know when
we get there? boriteh na moo
to piteh, otan ftasoomeh eki?

dialogue

does this bus go to ...?
piyeni afto to leoforio
sto ...?
no, you need a number ...
okhi, prepi na pareteh to
leoforio ariTHmos ...

business i thooli-es
bus station to praktorio
leoforion, o staTHmos
leoforion
bus stop i stasi leoforioo
bust (sculpture) i protomi
(measurement) to stiTHos
busy (restaurant etc)
polisikhnastos
I'm busy tomorrow imeh
apaskholimenos avrio
but ala
butcher's o khasapis
butter to vootiro
button to koobi
buy agorazo
where can I buy ...? poo boro
na agoraso ...?
by: by bus/car meh to
leoforio/aftokinito
written by ... grameno apo ...

by the window thipla sto paraтнiro
by the sea konda sti тнalasa
by Thursday prin apo tin Pempti
bye yasoo

C

cabbage to lakhano
cabin (on ship) i kabina
cable car to teleferik
café i kafeteria, to kafenio
cagoule to athiavrokho
cake to cake
cake shop to zakharoplastio
call fonazo
  (to phone) tilefono
  what's it called? pos to leneh?
  he/she is called ... ton/tin leneh ...
  please call a doctor seh parakalo, tilefoniseh seh ena yatro
  please give me a call at 7.30 am tomorrow seh parakalo, tilefoniseh moo avrio to pro-i stis efta keh misi
  please ask him to call me seh parakalo, pes too na moo tilefonisi
call back: I'll call back later тнa xanaтнo argotera
  (phone back) тнa seh paro piso
call round: I'll call round tomorrow тнa peraso avrio
camcorder i mikhani lipseos

camera i fotografiki mikhani
camera shop to katastima fotografikon ithon
camp (verb) kataskinono
  can we camp here? boroomeh na kataskinosoomeh etho?
camping gas to igra-erio
campsite to kambing
can to kooti, i konserva
  a can of beer mia bira seh kooti
can: can you ...? boriteh na ...?
  can I have ...? boro na ekho ...?
  I can't ... then boro ...
Canada o Kanathas
Canadian Kanathezikos
  I'm Canadian (man/woman) imeh Kanathos/Kanatheza
canal to kanali
cancel akirono
candies i karameles
candle to keri
canoe to kano
canoeing kano kano
can-opener to anikhtiri
cap (hat) to kapelo
  (of bottle) to kapaki
car to aftokinito
  by car meh to aftokinito
carafe i karafa
  a carafe of house white, please mia karafa aspro spitiko krasi, parakalo
caravan to trokhospito
caravan site topoтнesia ya trokhospita

carburettor to karbirater
card (birthday etc) i karta
here's my (business) card
oristeh, i karta moo
cardigan i zaketa
cardphone i tilekarta
careful prosektikos
  be careful! prosekheh!
caretaker o/i epistatis
car ferry to feri-bot
car hire enikiasis aftokiniton
car park to parking
carpet to khali
  (fitted) i moketa
carriage (of train) to vagoni
carrier bag i sakoola
carrot to karoto
carry metafero
carry-cot to port-beh-beh
carton i koota
carwash to plindirio
  aftokiniton
case (suitcase) i valitsa
cash ta metrita
  will you cash this for me? THa
  moo to exaryiroseteh?
cash desk to tamio
cash dispenser i mikhani ya
  metrita
cashier o/i tamias
cassette i kaseta
cassette recorder to
  kasetofono
castle to kastro
casualty department Protes
  Vo-iTHi-es
cat i gata
catch piano
  where do we catch the bus

  to ...? apo poo THa paroomeh
  to leoforio?
cathedral o kaTHethrikos naos
Catholic (adj) katholikos
cauliflower to koonoopithi
cave i spilia
ceiling to tavani
celery to selino
cellar (for wine) to kelari
cemetery to nekrotafio
Centigrade* Kelsioo
centimetre* ena ekatosto
central kendrikos
central heating i kendriki
  THermansi
centre to kendro
  how do we get to the city
  centre? pos THa pameh sto
  kendro?
cereal ta cornflakes
certainly sigoora
  certainly not fisika okhi
chair i karekla
champagne i sampania
change (money) ta resta
  (verb: money, trains) alazo
  can I change this for ...? boro
  na alaxo afto ya ...?
  I don't have any change then
  ekho psila
  can you give me change for
  a 5,000 drachma note?
  boriteh na moo khalaseteh
  pendeh khiliathes thrakhmes?

dialogue

  do we have to change
  (trains)? prepi na

alaxoomeh treno?
yes, change at Corinth/no,
it's a direct train neh,
alaxteh stin Korintho/
okhi, piyeni katefthian

changed: to get changed
  alazo rookha
chapel to eklisaki
charge i timi, i thapani
  (verb) khreono
charge card i pistotiki karta
cheap ftinos
  do you have anything
  cheaper? ekheteh tipoteh
  ftinotero?
check (verb) epalithevo
  (US: cheque) i epitayi
see cheque
  (US: bill) o logariasmos
see bill
  could you check the ...,
  please? boriteh na elenxeteh
  to ..., parakalo?
checkbook to karneh epitagon
check-in to check-in
check in kano check-in
  where do we have to check
  in? poo prepi na kanoomeh
  check-in?
cheek (on face) to magoolo
cheerio! yasoo!
cheers! (toast) stin iya sas!, is
  iyian!
cheese to tiri
chemist's to farmakio
cheque i epitayi
  do you take cheques?
  perneteh epitayes?

cheque book to karneh
  epitagon
cheque card i karta
  epitagon
cherry to kerasi
chess to skaki
chest to stithos
chewing gum i tsikhla
chicken to kotopoolo
chickenpox i anemovloyia
child to pethi
  children ta pethia
child minder i dada
children's pool i pisina ton
  pethion
children's portion i pethiki
  meritha
chin to pigooni
china i porselani
Chinese (adj) Kinezikos
chips i tiganites patates
chocolate i sokolata
  milk chocolate i sokolata
  galaktos
  plain chocolate sokolata sketi
  a hot chocolate i zesti
  sokolata, mia sokolata rofima
choose thialego
Christian name to mikro
  onoma
Christmas ta khristooyena
  Christmas Eve i paramoni ton
  khristooyenon
  merry Christmas! kala
  khristooyena!
church i eklisia
cicada o tzitzikas
cider cider
cigar to pooro

cigarette to tsigaro
cigarette lighter o anaptiras
cinema o kinimatografos, to sinema
circle o kiklos
(in theatre) o exostis
city i poli
city centre to kendro tis polis
clean (adj) kaтнaros
can you clean these for me?
moo pleneteh afta?
cleaning solution (for contact lenses) to kaтнaristiko thialima
cleansing lotion to galaktoma kaтнarismoo
clear kaтнaros
(obvious) profanis
clever exipnos
cliff o apotomos vrakhos
climbing i orivasia
cling film to na-ilon
clinic i kliniki
cloakroom i gardaroba
clock to rolo-i
close klino

dialogue

what time do you close? ti ora klineteh?
we close at 8 pm on weekdays and 6 pm on Saturdays klinoomeh stis okto to vrathi tis kaтнimerines keh stis exi to apoyevma ta Savata
do you close for lunch?

klineteh ya mesimeriano fayito?
yes, between 1 and 3.30 pm
neh, apo ti mia mekhri tis tris keh misi

closed klistos
cloth (fabric) to ifasma
(for cleaning etc) to pani
clothes ta rookha
clothes line i aplostra
clothes peg to mandalaki
cloud to sinefo
cloudy sinefiasmenos
clutch to debrayaz, o siblektis
coach (bus) to poolman
(on train) to vagoni
coach station o staтнmos iperastikon leoforion
coach trip to taxithi meh poolman
coast i akti
on the coast stin akti
coat (long coat) to palto
(jacket) to sakaki
coathanger i kremastra
cockroach i katsaritha
cocoa to kakao
coconut i karitha
code (for phoning) o kothikos
what's the (dialling) code for Athens? pios ineh o kothikos ya tin Aтнina?
coffee o kafes
two Greek coffees, please
thio Elinikoos kafethes, parakalo
coin to kerma

Coke® i koka-kola
cold krios
 I'm cold kriono
 I have a cold imeh kriomenos
collapse: he's collapsed
 katarefseh
collar o yakas
collect paralamvano
 I've come to collect ... ilTHa
 ya na paro ...
collect call tilefono collect
college to koleyio
colour to khroma
 do you have this in other
 colours? to ekheteh seh ala
 khromata?
colour film to enkhromo
 film
comb i khtena
come erkhomeh

dialogue

 where do you come from?
 apo poo iseh?
 I come from Edinburgh
 imeh apo to Ethimvoorgo

come back epistrefo
 I'll come back tomorrow THa
 epistrepso avrio
come in beno mesa
comfortable (chair) anapaftikos
 (clothes) anetos
 (room, hotel) volikos
compact disc to compact disc
company (business) i eteria
compartment (on train) to
 koopeh

compass i pixitha
complain paraponoomeh
complaint to parapono
 I have a complaint ekho ena
 parapono
completely telios
computer o ipolo-yistis
concert i sinavlia
concussion i thiasisi engefaloo
conditioner (for hair) to
 kondisioner
condom to profilaktiko
conference to sinethrio
confirm epiveveono
congratulations! sinkharitiria!
connecting flight sinthesi ptisis
connection (travel) i sinthesi
conscious sinesTHanomenos
constipation i thiskiliotis
consulate to proxenio
contact erkhomeh seh epafi
contact lenses i faki epafis
contraceptive (pill) to
 andisiliptiko
 (condom) to profilaktiko
convenient volikos
 that's not convenient then
 meh volevi
convent to monastiri
cook (verb) ma-yirevo
 not cooked misopsimeno
cooker i koozina
cookie to biskoto
cooking utensils ta ma-yirika
 skevi
cool throseros
Corfu i Kerkira
cork o felos
corkscrew to anikhtiri

corner: on the corner sti gonia
  in the corner sti gonia
cornflakes ta cornflakes
correct (right) sostos
corridor o thiathromos
cosmetics ta kalindika
cost (verb) stikhizo
  how much does it cost? poso kani?
cot i koonia
cotton to vamvaki
cotton wool to vamvaki
couch o kanapes
couchette i kooketa
cough o vikhas
cough medicine to farmako ya ton vikha
could: could you ...? boriteh na ...?
  could I have ...? boro na ekho ...?
  I couldn't ... then boroosa na ...
country (nation) i khora
  (countryside) i exokhi
countryside i exokhi
couple (man and woman) to zevgari
  a couple of ... thio apo ...
courgette to kolokiтнaki
courier o/i sinothos
course (main course etc) to piato
  of course veveh-a
  of course not fisika okhi
cousin (male/female) o xathelfos/i xathelfi
cow i a-yelatha
crab to kavoori

cracker to krakeraki
craft shop to ergastiri
crash i sigroosi
  I've had a crash trakara
crazy trelos
cream (on milk, in cake) i krema
  (lotion) i krema thermatos
  (colour) krem
creche o pethikos staтнmos
credit card i pistotiki karta

dialogue

can I pay by credit card? boro na pliroso meh pistotiki karta?
which card do you want to use? ti karta тнeleteh na khrisimopi-iseteh?
yes, sir endaxi, kiri-eh
what's the number? ti ariтнmo ekhi?
and the expiry date? keh poteh ineh i imerominia lixeos?

Crete i Kriti
crisps ta tsips
crockery ta piatika
crossing (by sea) to тнalasio taxithi
crossroads to stavrothromi
crowd o kosmos
crowded yematos kosmo
crown (on tooth) i korona
cruise i krooazi-era
crutches i pateritses
cry (weep) kleo

(shout) fon**a**zo
cucumber to ag**oo**ri
cup to flidz**a**ni
a cup of ..., please **e**na
flidz**a**ni ..., parakal**o**
cupboard to dool**a**pi
cure i тнerap**i**a
curly sgoor**o**s, katsar**o**s
current to r**e**vma
curtains i koort**i**nes
cushion to maxil**a**raki
custom to **e**тнimo
Customs to Tel**o**nio
cut to k**o**psimo
(verb) k**o**vo
I've cut myself k**o**pika
cutlery ta makherop**i**roona
cycling i pothil**a**sia
cyclist o/i pothil**a**tis
Cyprus i K**i**pros

D
=

dad o bab**a**s
daily катнimerin**a**
damage (verb) katastr**e**fo
damaged katastraf**i**keh
I'm sorry, I've damaged this
lip**a**meh, to kh**a**lasa
damn! na p**a**ri i or**y**i!
damp (adj) igr**o**s
dance o khor**o**s
(verb) khor**e**vo
would you like to dance?
тн**e**lis na khor**e**psoomeh?
dangerous epik**i**nthinos
Danish than**o**s
dark (adj: colour) skotin**o**s

(hair) m**a**vros
it's getting dark skotini**a**zi
date*: what's the date today?
p**o**so **e**khi o m**i**nas s**i**mera?
let's make a date for next
Monday as sinandiтн**oo**meh
tin ep**o**meni theft**e**ra
dates (fruit) i khoorm**a**thes
daughter i k**o**ri
daughter-in-law i n**i**fi
dawn i av**y**i
at dawn tin av**y**i
day i m**e**ra
the day after tin ep**o**meni
m**e**ra
the day after tomorrow
meтн**a**vrio
the day before tin pro-
ig**oo**meni m**e**ra
the day before yesterday
pr**o**khtes
every day k**a**тнeh m**e**ra
all day **o**li tin im**e**ra
in two days' time met**a** ap**o**
th**i**o m**e**res
day trip to tax**i**thi aftн**i**mer**o**n
dead peтнam**e**nos, nekr**o**s
deaf koof**o**s
deal (business) i simfon**i**a
it's a deal simfon**i**sameh,
end**a**xi
death o тнan**a**tos
decaffeinated coffee o kaf**e**s
khor**i**s kaf**e**-ini
December o thek**e**mvrios
decide apofas**i**zo
we haven't decided yet then
ekh**oo**meh apof**a**sisi ak**o**ma
decision i ap**o**fasi

deck (on ship) to katastroma
deckchair i politHrona, i sez long
deduct afero
deep vaтHis
definitely oposthipoteh
 definitely not seh kamia periptosi
degree (qualification) to ptikhio
delay i katHisterisi
deliberately epitithes
delicatessen ta delicatessen
delicious nostimotatos
deliver thianemo
delivery (of mail) i thianomi, i parathosi
demotic i dimotiki
Denmark i thania
dental floss to othondiko nima
dentist o/i othondiatros

dialogue

> it's this one here afto etho ineh
> this one? afto?
> no, that one okhi, ekino
> here? etho?
> yes neh

dentures i masela
deodorant to aposmitiko
department to tmima
department store to megalo katastima
departure i anakhorisi
departure lounge i eтHoosa anakhoriseos

depend: it depends exartateh
 it depends on ... exartateh apo ...
deposit (as security) i kataтHesi
 (as part payment) i prokatavoli
description i perigrafi
dessert to glikisma
destination o pro-orismos
develop anaptiso
 (a film) emfanizo

dialogue

> could you develop these films? boriteh na emfaniseteh afta ta film?
> when will they be ready? poteh тнa ineh etima?
> tomorrow afternoon avrio to apoyevma
> how much is the four-hour service? poso kani i emfanisi seh teseris ores?

diabetic (man/woman) o thiavitikos/i thiavitiki
 diabetic foods i thiavitiki trofi
dial (verb) kalo, perno ariтHmo
dialling code o kothikos ariтHmos
diamond to thiamandi
diaper i pana
diarrhoea i thiaria
diary to imerolo-yio
dictionary to lexiko
didn't
 see not
die peтHeno

diesel i dizel

diet i thi-eta

  I'm on a diet kano thi-eta

  I have to follow a special diet
prepi na kano ithiki thi-eta

difference i thiafora

  what's the difference? pia
ineh i thiafora?

different thiaforetikos

  this one is different afto etho
ineh thiaforetiko

  a different table ena alo
trapezi

difficult thiskolos

difficulty i thiskolia

dinghy to zodiak®

dining room i trapezaria

dinner (evening meal) to
thipno

  to have dinner tro-o
vrathino

direct (adj) kat-efтніan

  is there a direct train? iparkhi
kat-efтніan treno
ya ...?

direction i katefтнinsi

  which direction is it? pros ta
poo ineh?

  is it in this direction? ineh
pros afti tin katefтнinsi?

directory enquiries i
plirofori-es

dirt i vroma

dirty vromikos

disabled anapiros

  is there access for the
disabled? iparkhi prosvasi ya
toos anapiroos?

disappear exafanizomeh

it's disappeared exafanistikeh

disappointed apogo-
itevmenos

disappointing apogo-iteftiko

disaster i katastrofi

disco i diskotek

discount i ekptosi

  is there a discount? kaneteh
ekptosi?

disease i arostia

disgusting a-ithiastikos

dish (meal) to piato
(bowl) to bol

dishcloth i patsavoora

disinfectant to apolimandiko

disk (for computer) i thisketa

disposable diapers i khartines
panes

disposable nappies i khartines
panes

distance i apostasi

  in the distance eki kato

distilled water apestagmeno
nero

district i sinikia

disturb enokhlo

diversion (detour) i parakampsi

diving board i zanitha vootias

divorced: I'm divorced
(man/woman) khorismenos/
khorismeni

dizzy: I feel dizzy zalizomeh

do kano

  what shall we do? ti тнa
kanoomeh?

  how do you do it? pos to
kaneteh?

  will you do it for me? boriteh
na moo to kaneteh?

dialogues

how do you do? ti kaneteh?

nice to meet you kharika ya ti gnorimia

what do you do? ti thoolia kaneteh?

I'm a teacher, and you? imeh thaskalos, ki esis?

I'm a student imeh fititis

what are you doing this evening? ti THa kaneteh apopseh?

we're going out for a drink; do you want to join us? THa pameh ya ena poto – THeleteh na elTHeteh mazi mas?

do you want cream? THeleteh krema?

I do, but she doesn't ego neh, ekini, omos, okhi

doctor o/i yatros

we need a doctor khriazomasteh enan yatro

please call a doctor seh parakalo, kaleseh enan yatro

dialogue

where does it hurt? poo ponateh?

right here akrivos etho

does that hurt more? sas pona-i afto pio poli?

yes neh

take this to a chemist thosteh afto seh ena farmaki-o

document to engrafo

dog o skilos

doll i kookla

domestic flight ptisi esoterikoo

donkey o ga-itharos

don't! mi!

don't do that! min to kanis afto!

(stop) stamata!

see not

door i porta

doorman o THiroros

double thiplo

double bed to thiplo krevati

double room to thiplo thomatio

doughnut to donat

down kato

down here etho kato

put it down over there valeh to eki kato

it's down there on the right vrisketeh eki kato sta thexia

it's further down the road ineh ligo parakato

downmarket (restaurant etc) ftinos

downstairs kato

dozen mia doozina

half a dozen misi doozina

drain o okhetos

draught beer varelisia bira

draughty: it's draughty kani revma

drawer to sirtari

drawing to skhethio
dreadful friktos
dream to oniro
dress to forema
dressed: to get dressed dinomeh
dressing (for cut) i gaza
(for salad) to lathoxitho
dressing gown i roba
drink to poto
(verb) pino
a cold drink to anapsiktiko
can I get you a drink? boro na seh keraso kanena poto?
what would you like (to drink)? ti THa THelateh na pi-iteh?
no thanks, I don't drink okhi, efkharisto, then pino
I'll just have a drink of water THa paro monon ena potiri nero
drinking water to posimo nero
is this drinking water? ineh posimo afto to nero?
drive othiga-o
we drove here othiyisameh etho
I'll drive you home THa seh pao spiti
driver o/i othigos
driving licence i athia othiyiseos, to thiploma othiyiseos
drop: just a drop, please (of drink) poli ligo, parakalo
drug to farmako
drugs (narcotics) ta narkotika
drunk (adj) meTHismenos

drunken driving methismeno othiyima
dry (adj) stegnos
(wine) xiros
dry-cleaner to stegno-kaTHaristirio
duck i papia
due: he was due to arrive yesterday eprokito na ftasi khtes
when is the train due? poteh ftani to treno?
dull (pain) exasTHenimenos
(weather) moondos
(boring) varetos
dummy (baby's) i pipila
during kata ti thiarkia
dust i skoni
dusty skonismeno
dustbin o skoopithodenekes
duty-free (goods) ta aforolo-yita
duty-free shop to katastima aforolo-yiton
duvet to paploma

E

each kaTHeh
how much are they each? poso ekhi to kaTHena?
ear to afti
earache: I have earache ekho pono sto afti
early noris
early in the morning noris to pro-i
I called by earlier perasa pro-

Ea

igoomenos
earrings ta skoolarikia
east i anatoli
  in the east stin anatoli
Easter to Paskha
Easter Sunday i Kiriaki too
  Paskha
easy efkolos
eat tro-o
  we've already eaten, thanks
  fagameh ithi, efkharisto
eau de toilette i kolonia
EC i eok
economy class tooristiki THesi
egg to avgo
  hard-boiled egg avgo
  sfikhto
  fried egg tiganito avgo
eggplant i melidzana
either: either ... or ... i ... i ...
  either of them opio naneh
elastic to lastikho
elastic band to lastikhaki
elbow o angonas
electric ilektrikos
electrical appliances ilektrikes
  siskeves
electric fire i ilektriki somba
electrician o ilektrologos
electricity to ilektriko revma
elevator to asanser
else: something else kati alo
  somewhere else kapoo aloo

dialogue

would you like anything
else? THa THelateh tipoteh
alo?

no, nothing else, thanks
okhi, tipoteh alo,
efkharisto

e-mail to e-mail
embassy i presvia
emergency i ektakti anangi
  this is an emergency! ineh
  epigon!
emergency exit i exothos
  kinthinoo
empty (adj) athios
end to telos
  (verb) teliono
  at the end of the street sto
  telos too thromoo
  when does it end? poteh
  telioni?
engaged (toilet, telephone)
  katilimenos
  (to be married: man/woman)
  aravoniasmenos/
  aravoniasmeni
engine (car) i mikhani too
  aftokinitoo
England i Anglia
English ta Anglika
  I'm English (man/woman) imeh
  Anglos/Anglitha
  do you speak English?
  milateh anglika?
enjoy: to enjoy oneself
  thiaskethazo

dialogue

how did you like the film?
pos soo fanikeh to ergo?
I enjoyed it very much;

did you enjoy it? moo areseh para poli; esena soo areseh?

enjoyable efkharistos
enlargement (of photo) i me-yenthisi
enormous terastios
enough arketa
 there's not enough then iparkhi arketo
 it's not big enough then ineh arketa megalo
 that's enough ftani, arki
entrance i isothos
envelope o fakelos
epileptic (man/woman) o epiliptikos/i epiliptiki
equipment o exoplismos
error to lathos
especially ithika
essential vasikos, aparetitos
 it is essential that ... ineh aparetito na ...
EU Evropa-iki Enosi
euro to evro
Eurocheque to Eurocheque
Eurocheque card i karta Eurocheque
Europe i Evropi
European (adj) Evropa-ikos
European Union Evropa-iki Enosi
even: even the Greeks akoma keh i Elines
 even if ... akoma ki an ...
evening to vrathi
 this evening simera to vrathi
 in the evening to vrathi

evening meal to thipno
eventually telika
ever poteh

dialogue

have you ever been to Crete? ekheteh pa-i poteh stin Kriti?
yes, I was there two years ago neh, imoon eki prin apo thio khronia

every katheh
 every day katheh mera
everyone oli
everything katheh ti
everywhere pandoo
exactly! akrivos!
exam to thiagonisma
example to parathigma
 for example parathigmatos kharin
excellent exokhos
 excellent! exokha!
except ektos
excess baggage to ipervaro
exchange rate sinalagmatiki isotimia
exciting sinarpastikos
excuse me (to get past) signomi (to get attention) parakalo (to say sorry) meh sinkhoriteh
exhaust (pipe) i exatmisi
exhausted (tired) exandlimenos
exhibition i ekthesi
exit i exothos
 where's the nearest exit? poo ineh i plisi-esteri exothos?

expect perimeno

expensive akrivos

experienced embiros

explain exigo

can you explain that? boris na moo to exiyisis?

express mail to katepigon

express train to treno express

extension (telephone) i sinthesi tilefonoo

could you get me extension 221, please? meh sintheh-eteh meh to 221 (thiakosia ikosi ena), parakalo?

extension lead i pro-ektasi

extra: can we have an extra chair? boroomeh na ekhoomeh mia karekla akoma?

do you charge extra for that? khreoneteh epipleon ya afto?

extraordinary asiniTHistos

extremely ipervolika

eye to mati

will you keep an eye on my suitcase for me? THa moo to prosekheteh?

eyebrow pencil to molivi ya ta frithia

eye drops i stagones ya ta matia

eyeglasses (US) ta yialia

eyeliner to eyeliner

eye make-up remover to galaktoma kaTHarismoo

eye shadow i skia mation

F

face to prosopo

factory to ergostasio

Fahrenheit* vaTHmi Farena-it

faint (verb) lipoTHimao

she's fainted lipoTHimiseh

I feel faint esTHanomeh lipoTHimia

fair (funfair) to paniyiri

(trade) i ekTHesi

(adj) thikeos

fairly arketa

fake i apomimisi

fall to fTHinoporo

see autumn

fall (verb) pefto

she's had a fall epeseh

false pseftikos

family i iko-yenia

famous thiasimos

fan (electrical) o anemistiras

(hand held) i ventalia

(sports) o/i opathos

fan belt to vendilater

fantastic fandastikos

far makria

dialogue

is it far from here? ineh makria apo etho?

no, not very far okhi, okhi keh poli makria

well how far? poso makria, thilathi?

it's about 20 kilometres

ineh peripoo ikosi
khiliometra

fare i timi too isitirioo
farm to agroktima
fashionable tis mothas
fast grigoros
fat (person) pakhis
  (on meat) to lipos
father o pateras
father-in-law o peтнeros
faucet i vrisi
fault to elatoma
  sorry, it was my fault signomi,
  itan sfalma moo
  it's not my fault then fteo
  ego
faulty elatomatikos
favourite agapimenos
fax to fax
  (verb: person) stelno fax seh ...
  (document) stelno seh fax
February o Fevrooarios
feel esтнanomeh
  I feel hot zestenomeh
  I feel unwell then
  esтнanomeh kala
  I feel like going for a walk
  ekho orexi na pao mia volta
  how are you feeling? pos
  esтнaneseh?
  I'm feeling better
  esтнanomeh kalitera
felt-tip pen o markathoros
fence o fraktis
fender o profilaktiras
ferry to feri bot
festival to festival
fetch pa-o na fero

I'll fetch him тнa pa-o na ton
fero
will you come and fetch me
later? тнa elтнis na meh paris
argotera?
feverish empiretos
few: a few liyi, liyes, liga
  a few days liyes meres
fiancé o aravoniastikos
fiancée i aravoniastikia
field to khorafi
fight o agonas
figs ta sika
fill yemizo
fill in yemizo
  do I have to fill this in? prepi
  na to yemiso?
fill up yemizo telios
  fill it up, please yemisteh tin,
  parakalo
filling (in cake, sandwich) i yemisi
  (in tooth) to sfra-yisma
film to film

dialogue

do you have this kind of
film? okheteh totio film?
yes – how many
exposures? neh – meh
poses stasis?
36 trianda-exi

film processing i emfanisi too
film
filter coffee o kafes filtroo
filter papers ta filtra ya
kafeh
filthy vromeros

find vrisko
  I can't find it then to vrisko
  I've found it to vrika
find out anakalipto
  could you find out for me?
  boris na maTHis?
fine (weather) oreos
  (punishment) to prostimo

dialogues

how are you? ti kanis?
I'm fine thanks mia khara,
efkharisto

is that OK? afto ineh
endaxi?
that's fine thanks ineh mia
khara, efkharisto

finger to thakhtilo
finish teliono
  I haven't finished yet then
  ekho teliosi akomi
  when does it finish? poteh
  telioni?
fire: fire! pirkaya!
  can we light a fire here?
  boroomeh na anapsoomeh
  fotia etho?
  it's on fire pireh fotia
fire alarm o sinayermos
  pirkayas
fire brigade i pirosvestiki
  ipiresia
fire escape i exothos pirkayas
fire extinguisher o pirosvestiras
first protos
  I was first imoon protos

at first stin arkhi
the first time i proti fora
first on the left protos sta
  aristera
first aid i protes vo-iTHi-es
first aid kit to kooti proton
  vo-iTHi-on
first class (travel etc) proti THesi
first floor to proto patoma
  (US) to iso-yio
first name to onoma
fish to psari
fisherman o psaras
fishing village to psarokhori
fishmonger's to psarathiko
fit (attack) i prosvoli
  it doesn't fit me then moo
  khora-i
fitting room to thokimastirio
fix ftiakhno
  (arrange) kanonizo
  can you fix this? boris na to
  ftiaxis?
fizzy meh anTHrakiko
flag i simea
flannel to sfoogari
flash (for camera) to flas
flat (apartment) to thiamerisma
  (adj) epipethos
  I've got a flat tyre me epiaseh
  lastikho
flavour i gefsi
flea o psilos
flight i ptisi
flight number ariTHmos ptisis
flippers ta vatrakhopethila
flood i plimira
floor (of room) to patoma
  (of building) o orofos

on the floor sto patoma
florist o anthopolis
flour to alevri
flower to looloothi
flu i gripi
fluent: he speaks fluent Greek
mila-i aptesta elinika
fly i miga
(verb) peto
can we fly there? boroomeh
na pameh eki a-eroporikos?
fly in peta-o pros
fly out peta-o apo
fog i omikhli
foggy: it's foggy ekhi omikhli
folk dancing i thimotiki khori
folk music i thimotiki moosiki
follow akolootho
follow meh akolootha meh
food to fa-yito
food poisoning trofiki
thilitiriasi
food shop/store to bakaliko
foot* to pothi
on foot meh ta pothia
football (game) to pothosfero
(ball) i bala
football match o pothosferikos
agonas
for ya
do you have something
for ...? (headache/diarrhoea etc)
ekheteh kati ya ...?

dialogues

who's the moussaka for?
ya pion ineh o moosakas?
that's for me ya mena

and this one? ki afto etho?
that's for her afto ineh ya
ekini

where do I get the bus for
Akropolis? apo poo tha
paro to leoforio ya tin
Akropoli?
the bus for Acropolis
leaves from Stathiou Street
to leoforio ya tin Akropoli
fevyi apo tin Otho
Stathioo

how long have you been
here for? poso kero iseh
etho pera?
I've been here for two
days, how about you?
vriskomeh etho pera etho
keh thio meres, esi?
I've been here for a week
vriskomeh etho pera etho
keh mia vthomatha

forehead to metopo
foreign xenos
foreigner (man/woman) o xenos/
i xeni
forest to thasos
forget xekhno
I forget xekhno
I've forgotten xekhasa
fork (for eating) to pirooni
(in road) i thiaklathosi
form (document) i etisi
formal (dress) episimos
fortnight to theka-
penthimero

fortunately eftikhos

forward: could you forward my mail? boriteh na moo stileteh ta gramata moo?

forwarding address i thi-efтнinsi apostolis

foundation cream krema prosopoo ya makiyaz

fountain i piyi

foyer to foyer

fracture to katagma

free eleftнeros

(no charge) thorean

is it free of charge? ineh thorean?

freeway i eтнniki othos

freezer i katapsixi

French (adj) galikos

(language) ta galika

French fries i tiganites patates

frequent sikhnos

how frequent is the bus to Corinth? kaтнeh poteh ekhi leoforio ya tin Korinтнo?

fresh (weather, breeze) throseros

(fruit etc) freskos

fresh orange o freskos khimos portokali

Friday i Paraskevi

fridge to psiyio

fried tiganismenos

fried egg to tiganito avgo

friend (male/female) o filos/i fili

friendly filikos

from apo

when does the next train from Patras arrive? poteh ftani to epomeno treno apo tin Patra?

from Monday to Friday apo

theftera os Paraskevi

from next Thursday apo tin ali Pempti

dialogue

where are you from? apo poo iseh?
I'm from Slough imeh apo to Sla-oo

front to mbrostino meros

in front mbrosta

in front of the hotel mbrosta apo to xenothokhio

at the front sto mbrostino meros

frost i pagonia, o pa-yetos

frozen pagomenos

frozen food i katepsiymeni trofi

fruit ta froota

fruit juice o khimos frooton

fry tiganizo

frying pan to tigani

full yematos

it's full of ... ineh yemato meh ...

I'm full khortasa

full board fool pansion

fun: it was fun kala itan, kanameh kefi

funeral i kithia

funny (strange) paraxenos

(amusing) astios

furniture ta epipla

further parapera

it's further down the road ineh akoma parakato

dialogue

how much further is it to
Piraeus? poso ineh akomi
mekhri ton Pirea?
about 5 kilometres yiro sta
pendeh khiliometra

fuse i asfalia
 the lights have fused
 ka-ikaneh ta fota
fuse box to kooti meh tis
 asfali-es
fuse wire to sirma asfalias
future to melon
 in future sto melon

G

gallon* ena galoni
game (cards etc) to pekhnithi
 (match) o agonas
 (meat) to kiniyi
garage (for fuel) to venzinathiko
 (for repairs) to sineryio
 (for parking) to garaz
garden o kipos
garlic to skortho
gas to gazi
gas cylinder (camping gas) i
 fiali gazi
gasoline i venzini
gas permeable lenses i
 imiskliri faki epafis
gas station to venzinathiko
gate i avloporta
 (at airport) i exothos
gay (adj) omofilofilos

gay bar to gay bar
gears i takhitita
gearbox to kivotio takhititon
gear lever o levi-es takhititon
general yenikos
gents (toilet) i too-aleta ton
 anthron
genuine (antique etc)
 afтнendikos
German (adj) Yermanikos
 (language) ta Yermanika
German measles i eriтнra
Germany i Yermania
get (fetch) perno
 will you get me another one,
 please? тна moo paris alo
 ena, parakalo?
 how do I get to ...? pos boro
 na pao sto ...?
 do you know where I can get
 them? mipos xereteh poo
 boro na vro tetia?

dialogue

can I get you a drink? na
seh keraso kanena poto?
no, I'll get this one, what
would you like? okhi, ego
kernao afti ti fora; ti тна
iтнeles?
a glass of red wine ena
potiri kokino krasi

get back (return) epistrefo
get in (arrive) ftano
get off kateveno
 where do I get off? poo тна
 katevo?

get on (to train etc) aneveno
get out (of car etc) vyeno
get up (in the morning) sikonomeh
gift to thoro
gift shop katastima thoron, ithi thoron
gin to tzin
  a gin and tonic, please ena tzin meh tonik, parakalo
girl to koritsi
girlfriend i filenatha
give thino
  can you give me some change? boriteh na moo thoseteh psila?
  I gave it to him to ethosa seh afton
  will you give this to ...? to thinis afto ston ...?

dialogue

how much do you want for this? posa THelis ya afto?
10,000 drachmas theka khiliathes thrakhmes
I'll give you 7,000 drachmas soo thino efta khiliathes

give back epistrefo, thino piso
glad efkharistimenos
glass (material) to yali
  (tumbler, wine glass) to potiri
  a glass of wine ena potiri krasi
glasses ta yalia
gloves ta gandia
glue i kola
go pao

we'd like to go to the ... theloomeh na pameh sto ...
where are you going? poo pateh?
where does this bus go? poo pa-i afto to leoforio?
let's go! pameh
she's gone (left) efiyeh
where has he gone? poo piyeh aftos?
I went there last week piga eki tin perasmeni evthomatha
hamburger to go khamboorger ya to spiti
go away fevgo
go away! fiyeh!
go back (return) epistrefo
go down (the stairs etc) kateveno
go in beno
go out (in the evening) v-yeno
  do you want to go out tonight? theleteh na pateh exo apopseh?
go through thiaskhizo, pao thia mesoo
go up (the stairs etc) aneveno
goat i katsika
goat's cheese to katsikisio tiri
God o THEos
goggles i maska
gold o khrisos
golf to golf
golf course to yipetho golf
good kalos
  good! kala!
  it's no good (product etc) afto then ineh kalo
  (not worth trying) then ofeli

goodbye ya khara, adio
good evening kalispera
Good Friday i Megali
 Paraskevi
good morning kalimera
good night kalinikhta
goose i khina
got: we've got to ... prepi
 na ...
 have you got any ...? ekheteh
 katholoo ...?
government i kivernisi
gradually siga-siga
grammar i gramatiki
gram(me) ena gramario
granddaughter i egoni
grandfather o papoos
grandmother i ya-ya
grandson o egonos
grapefruit to grapefruit
grapefruit juice o khimos
 grapefruit
grapes ta stafilia
grass to khortari, to grasithi
grateful evgnomon
gravy o zomos too kreatos
great (excellent) poli kalo
 that's great! iperokha!
 it's a great success ineh
 megali epitikhia
Great Britain i Megali Vretania
Greece i Elatha
greedy akhortagos
Greek (adj) Elinikos
 (language) ta Elinika
 (man) o Elinas
 (woman) i Elinitha
 the Greeks i Elines
Greek coffee Elinikos kafes

Greek-Cypriot (adj)
 Elinokiprios
Greek Orthodox Elinikos
 Orthothoxos
green prasinos
green card (car insurance) i
 asfalia ya othiyisi sto exoteriko
greengrocer's o manavis
grey grizos
grill i psistaria
grilled psitos sti skhara
grocer's to bakaliko
ground to ethafos
 on the ground sto ethafos
ground floor to iso-yio
group to groop
guarantee i engi-isi
 is it guaranteed? ineh engi-
 imeno?
guest (man/woman) o
 filoxenoomenos/i
 filoxenoomeni
guesthouse i pansion
guide o/i xenagos
guidebook o tooristikos
 othigos
guided tour i xenayisi
guitar i kithara
gum (in mouth) to oolo
gun (pistol) to pistoli
 (rifle) to oplo
gym to yimnastirio

H

hair ta malia
hairbrush i voortsa ya malia,
 i khtena

haircut (man's) to **koo**rema
  (woman's) to ko**psi**mo
hairdresser's to komo**ti**rio
  (men's) to koo**ri**o
hairdryer to pisto**la**ki
hair gel o a**fros** ma**li**on
hairgrips ta piastra**ki**a
  ma**li**on
hair spray to spray ya
  ta ma**li**a
half mi**sos**
  half an hour mi**si o**ra
  half a litre mi**so li**tro
  about half that peri**poo** to
  mi**so** a**po** af**to**
half board demi-pansi**on**
half-bottle mi**so** boo**ka**li
half fare mi**so** isi**ti**rio
half price miso**ti**mis
ham to zam**bon**
hamburger to kham**boor**ger
hammer to **sfi**ri
hand to **khe**ri
handbag i **tsan**da
handbrake to khi**ro**freno
handkerchief to man**di**li
  (paper) to khartoman**di**lo
handle to khe**roo**li
hand luggage to sakvooa-**yaz**
hang-gliding i anemopo**ri**a
hangover o pono**ke**falos
  I've got a hangover **e**kho
  pono**ke**falos
happen sim**ve**ni
  what's happening? ti
  sim**ve**ni?
  what has happened? ti
  si**ne**vi?
happy eftikhis**me**nos

  I'm not happy about this then
  imeh efkharistime**nos** meh
  af**to**
harbour to li**ma**ni
hard skli**ros**
  (difficult) **this**kolos
hard-boiled egg to **sfikh**to
  av**go**
hard lenses i skli**ri** fa**ki**
hardly me**ta** vi**as**
  hardly ever s-khe**thon** pot**eh**
hardware shop ta i**thi**
  kingale**ri**as
hat to ka**pe**lo
hate mi**so**
have* **e**kho
  can I have a ...? bo**ro** na **e**kho
  ena ...?
  do you have ...? e**khe**teh ...?
  what'll you have? ti тнa
  piiteh?
  I have to leave now **pre**pi na
  pi**ye**no **to**ra
  do I have to ...? **pre**pi na ...?
  can we have some ...?
  bo**roo**meh na e**khoo**meh
  me**ri**ka ...?
hayfever aler-**yi**a sti **yi**ri
hazelnuts to foon**doo**ki
he* af**tos**
  is he here? i**neh** e**tho**?
head to ke**fa**li
headache o pono**ke**falos
headlights i provo**lis**
headphones ta akoosti**ka**
health food shop ka**ta**stima
  iyi-i**non** tro**fon**
healthy iyi-**is**
hear a**koo**-o

dialogue

can you hear me? meh akoos?
I can't hear you, could you repeat that? then seh akoo-o, boris na to epanalavis?

hearing aid ta akoostika
heart i karthia
heart attack i karthiaki prosvoli
heat i zesti
heater i THermansi
(radiator) to kalorifer
heating i THermansi
heavy varis
heel (of foot) i fterna
(of shoe) to takooni
could you heel these? boriteh na moo valeteh kenooryia takoonia safta?
heelbar o tsagaris
height to ipsos
helicopter to elikoptero
hello ya sas
(familiar) ya soo
(answer on phone) ebros
helmet (for motorcycle) to kranos
help i vo-iTHia
(verb) vo-iTHo
help! vo-iTHia!
can you help me? boriteh na meh vo-iTHiseteh?
thank you very much for your help efkharisto ya ti vo-iTHia sas
helpful exipiretikos
hepatitis i ipatititha

her*: I haven't seen her then tin ekho thi
to her saftin
with her mazi tis
for her yaftin
that's her afti ineh
that's her towel afti ineh i petseta tis
herbal tea tsa-i too voonoo
herbs ta votana
here etho
here is/are ... na ...
here you are (offering) oristeh
hers* thiko tis
that's hers afto ineh thiko tis
hey! eh!
hi! (hello) ya soo
hide (something) krivo
(oneself) krivomeh
high psilos
highchair to kareklaki moroo
highway i eTHniki othos
hill o lofos
him*: I haven't seen him then ton ekho thi
to him safton
with him mazi too
for him yafton
that's him aftos ineh
hip o gofos
hire niki-azo
for hire eniki-azonteh
where can I hire a bike? poo boro na niki-aso ena pothilato?
his*: it's his car ineh to aftokinito too
that's his ineh thiko too

hit khtipao
hitch-hike kano otostop
hobby to khobi
hold kratao
hole i tripa
holiday i thiakopes
  on holiday seh thiakopes
Holy Week i Megali
  Evthomatha
home to spiti
  at home (in my house etc) sto
  spiti
  (in my country) stin patritha
  moo
  we go home tomorrow
  piyeno stin patritha moo
  avrio
honest timios
honey to meli
honeymoon o minas too
  melitos
hood (US) to kapo
hope elpizo
  I hope so etsi elpizo
  I hope not elpizo pos okhi
hopefully meh kali tikhi
horn (of car) to klaxon
horrible friktos
horse to alogo
horse riding i ipasia
hospital to nosokomio
hospitality i filoxenia
  thank you for your hospitality
  sas efkharisto ya ti filoxenia sas
hot zestos
  (spicy) kafteros, kaftos
  I'm hot zestenomeh
  it's hot today kani poli zesti
  simera

hotel to xenothokhio
hotel room: in my hotel
  room sto thomatio too
  xenothokhioo
hour i ora
house to spiti
house wine to krasi too
  magazioo
hovercraft to hovercraft, o
  a-erolistнitiras
how pos
  how many? posi?
  how do you do? khero poli

dialogues

how are you? pos iseh?
fine, thanks, and you? poli
kala, efkharisto; ki esi?

how much is it? poso kani
afto?
5000 drachmas pendeh
khiliathes thrakhmes
I'll take it тнa to paro

humid igros
humour to khioomor
hungry pinasmenos
  are you hungry? pinas?
hurry (verb) viazomeh
  I'm in a hurry viazomeh
  there's no hurry then iparkhi
  via
  hurry up! viasoo!
hurt travmatizomeh
  it really hurts pona-i poli
husband o sizigos
hydrofoil to iptameno thelfini

I

I ego
ice o pagos
  with ice meh pago
  no ice, thanks khoris pago, efkharisto
ice cream to pagoto
ice-cream cone to pagoto khonaki
iced coffee to frapeh
ice lolly to pagoto xilaki
idea i ithea
idiot o vlakas
if an
ignition i miza
ill arostos
  I feel ill imeh arostos
illness i arostia
imitation (leather etc) i apomimisi
immediately amesos
important spootheos
  it's very important ineh poli simandiko
  it's not important then ineh spootheo
impossible athinaton
impressive endiposiakos
improve veltiono
  I want to improve my Greek THelo na kaliterepso ta Elinika moo
in: it's in the centre ineh sto kendro
  in my car mesa sto aftokinito moo
  in Athens stin ATHina

in two days from now seh thio meres apo tora
in May sto Ma-io
in English sta Anglika
in Greek sta Elinika
is he in? ineh eki?
in five minutes seh pendeh lepta
inch* i intsa
include perilamvano
  does that include meals? afto perilamvani keh fayito?
  is that included in the price? perilamvaneteh stin timi?
inconvenient akatalilos, avolos
incredible apithanos
Indian (adj) Inthikos
indicator to flas, o thiktis
indigestion i thispepsia
indoor pool i esoteriki pisina
indoors mesa
inexpensive ftinos
  see cheap
inner tube (for tyre) i sabrela
infection i molinsi
infectious kolitikos
inflammation i anaflexi
informal anepisimos
information i plirofori-es
  do you have any information about ...? ekheteh tipoteh plirofori-es skhetika meh ...?
information desk i plirofori-es
injection i enesi
injured travmatismenos
  she's been injured khtipiseh
in-laws ta peTHerika
innocent aTHo-os

insect to endomo

insect bite to tsibima endomoo

do you have anything for insect bites? ekheteh tipoteh ya tsibimata apo endoma?

insect repellent to AUTAN®

inside mesa

inside the hotel mesa sto xenothokhio

let's sit inside as katsoomeh mesa

insist epimeno

I insist epimeno

insomnia i a-ipnia

instant coffee to neskafeh

instead andi

give me that one instead thosteh moo afto sti THesi too aloo

instead of ... sti THesi too ...

insulin i insoolini

insurance i asfalia

intelligent exipnos

interested: I'm interested in ... enthiaferomeh poli ya ...

interesting enthiaferon

that's very interesting ineh poli enthiaferon

international thi-ethnis

internet to Internet

interpret thi-erminevo

interpreter o/i thi-ermineas

intersection to stavrothromi

interval (at theatre) to thi-alima

into mesa

I'm not into ... then moo aresi ...

introduce sistino

may I introduce ...? boro na sas sistiso ton ...?

invitation i prosklisi

invite proskalo

Ionian Sea to I-onio pelagos

Ireland i Irlanthia

Irish Irlanthos

I'm Irish (man/woman) imeh Irlanthos/Irlantheza

iron (for ironing) to ilektriko sithero

can you iron these for me? boriteh na moo ta sitheroseteh?

is* ineh

island to nisi

it afto

it is ... ineh ...

is it ...? ineh ...?

where is it? poo ineh?

it's him ineh aftos

it was ... itan ...

Italian (adj) Italos

(language) ta Italika

Italy i Italia

itch: it itches meh tro-i

J

jack (for car) o grilos

jacket to sakaki

jar to vazaki

jam i marmelatha

jammed: it's jammed ineh frakarismeno

January o I-anooarios

jaw to sagoni

jazz i tzaz

jealous ziliaris
jeans ta tzins
jellyfish i tsookhtra
jersey to fanelaki
jetty o molos
Jewish Evra-ikos
jeweller's to khrisokho-io
jewellery ta kosmimata
job i thoolia
jogging to jogging
 to go jogging pao ya jogging
joke to astio
journey to taxithi
 have a good journey! kalo
 taxithi!
jug i kanata
 a jug of water mia kanata
 nero
juice o khimos
July o I-oolios
jump pithao
jumper to poolover
jump leads ta kalothia batarias
junction i thiastavrosi
June o I-oonios
just (only) monon
 just two mono thio
 just for me mono ya mena
 just here akrivos etho
 not just now okhi tora
 we've just arrived molis
 ftasameh

K

keep krato
 keep the change krata ta
 resta

can I keep it? boro na to
 kratiso?
 please keep it kratisteh to, sas
 parakalo
ketchup to ketsap
kettle i booyota, o vrastiras
key to klithi
 the key for room 201, please
 to klithi ya to 201 (thiakosia
 ena), parakalo
key ring to brelok
kidneys ta nefra
kill skotono
kilo* ena kilo
kilometre* ena khiliometro
 how many kilometres is it
 to ...? posa khiliomctra ineh
 mekhri to ...?
kind (generous) evyenikos
 that's very kind ineh poli
 evyeniko

dialogue

 which kind do you want? ti
 ithos THeleteh?
 I want this/that kind THelo
 afto/ekino to ithos

king o vasilias
kiosk to periptero
kiss to fili
 (verb) filao
kitchen i koozina
kitchenette i koozinoola
Kleenex® ta khartomandila
knee to gonato
knickers i kilota
knife to makheri

knitwear plekta rookha
knock khtipo
knock down khtipo
he's been knocked down
  khtipiтнikeh
knock over (object) anapotho-
  yirizo
  (pedestrian) khtipo
know (somebody) gnorizo
  (something, a place) xero
  I don't know then xero
  I didn't know that then to
  ixera
  do you know where I can
  find ...? mipos xereteh poo
  boro na vro ...?

L

label i etiketa
ladies' (toilets) i too-aleta ton
  yinekon
ladies' wear yinekia ithi
lady i kiria
lager i bira
lake i limni
lamb (meat) to arni
lamp i lamba
lane (on motorway) i loritha
  (small road) i parothos
language i glosa
language course maтнimata
  xenis glosas
large megalos
last telefteos
  last week i perasmeni
  evthomatha
  last Friday tin perasmeni

Paraskevi
  last night kh-тнes vrathi
  what time is the last train
  to Salonika? ti ora ineh
  to telefteo treno ya tin
  тнesaloniki?
late arga
  sorry I'm late meh
  sinkhoriteh poo aryisa
  the train was late to treno
  ikheh katнisterisi
  we must go – we'll be late
  prepi na piyenoomeh – тнa
  aryisoomeh
  it's getting late nikhtoni
later argotera
  I'll come back later тнa yiriso
  argotera
  see you later adio, тнa ta
  xanapoomeh
later on argotera
latest o pi-o prosfatos
  by Wednesday at the latest
  tin Tetarti to argotero
laugh yelo
launderette to plindirio
  rookhon
laundromat to plindirio
  rookhon
laundry (clothes) i boogatha,
  ta aplita
  (place) to katнaristirio
lavatory i too-aleta
law o nomos
lawn to grasithi
lawyer o/i thikigoros
laxative to katнartiko
lazy tebelis
lead (electrical) o agogos

(verb) othigo
where does this lead to? poo othiyi afto?
leaf to filo
leaflet to thiafimistiko
leak i thiaro-i
(verb) stazo
the roof leaks i steyi stazi
learn matheno
least: not in the least katholoo
at least toolakhiston
leather to therma
leave (bag etc) afino
(go away) fevgo
(forget) xekhnao
I am leaving tomorrow fevgo avrio
he left yesterday efiyeh kh-thes
may I leave this here? boro nafiso afto etho?
I left my coat in the bar afisa tin tsanda moo sto bar
when does the bus for Athens leave? poteh fevyi to leoforio ya tin Athina?
leeks ta prasa
left aristera
on the left pros ta aristera
to the left pros ta aristera
turn left stripseh aristera
there's none left then emineh tipoteh
left-handed aristerokhiras
left luggage (office) o khoros filaxis aposkevon
leg to pothi
lemon to lemoni
lemonade i lemonatha

lemon tea tsai meh lemoni
lend thanizo
will you lend me your ... ? tha moo thanisis to thiko soo ...?
lens (of camera) o fakos
lesbian i lesvia
less ligotero
less than ligotero apo
less expensive ligotero akrivo
lesson to mathima
let (allow) epitrepo
will you let me know? tha moo to pis?
I'll let you know tha soo po
let's go for something to eat pameh na fameh kati
let off katevazo
will you let me off at ...? tha meh katevaseteh sto ...?
letter to grama
do you have any letters for me? ekho kanena grama?
letterbox to gramatokivotio
lettuce to marooli
lever o levi-es
library i vivliothiki
licence i athi-a
lid to kapaki
lie (tell untruth) leo psemata
lie down xaplono
life i zo-i
lifebelt i zoni asfalias
lifeguard o navagosostis
life jacket to sosivio
lift (in building) to asanser
could you give me a lift? boriteh na meh pateh?

would you like a lift? THeleteh na sas pao?
light to fos
(not heavy) elafros
do you have a light? (for cigarette) ekhis fotia?
light green anikhto prasino
light bulb i lamba, o glombos
I need a new light bulb khriazomeh mia kenoorya lamba
lighter (cigarette) o anaptiras
lightning i astrapi
like (verb) moo aresi
I like it moo aresi afto
I like going for walks moo aresi na piyeno peripato
I like you moo aresis
I don't like it then moo aresi afto
do you like it? soo aresi afto?
I'd like to go swimming THa iTHela na pao ya kolimbi
I'd like a beer THa iTHela mia bira
would you like a drink? THa iTHeles ena poto?
would you like to go for a walk? THa iTHeles na pameh mia volta?
what's it like? meh ti miazi?
I want one like this THelo ena san ki afto
lime to moskholemono
lime cordial to lime
line (on paper) i grami
(phone) i tilefoniki grami
could you give me an outside line? THa moo thoseteh grami?

lips ta khilia
lip salve to vootiro kakao
lipstick to krayon
liqueur to liker
listen akoo-o
litre* ena litro
a litre of white wine ena litro aspro krasi
little mikros
just a little, thanks ligo mono, efkharisto
a little milk ligo gala
a little bit more ligo akomi
live zo
we live together sizoomeh

dialogue

> **where do you live?** poo menis?
> **I live in London** meno sto Lonthino

lively thrastirios
liver to sikoti
loaf i fradzola
lobby (in hotel) to saloni
lobster o astakos
local dopios
can you recommend a local wine/restaurant? boriteh na mas sistiseteh ena dopio krasi/ estiatorio?
lock i klitharia
(verb) klithono
it's locked ineh klithomeno
lock in klithono mesa
lock out klithono apo exo
I've locked myself out

klithoтнika apexo
locker (for luggage etc) i тнiritha
lollipop to glifidzoori
London to Lonтнino
long makris
  how long will it take to fix it?
  poso kero тна pari ya na to
  ftiaxeteh?
  how long does it take? posi
  ora kani?
  a long time polis keros, poli
  ora
  one day/two days longer mia
  mera/thio meres parapano
long-distance call to iperastiko
  tilefonima
look: I'm just looking, thanks
  efkharisto, vlepo mono
  you don't look well then
  feneseh kala
  look out! prosexe!
  can I have a look? boro na
  tho?
look after prosekho, frondizo
look at kitazo
look for psakhno
  I'm looking for ... psakhno
  ya ...
look forward to perimeno meh
  khara
  I'm looking forward to it to
  perimeno pos keh pos
loose (handle etc) khalaros
lorry to fortigo
lose khano
  I've lost my way ekho khaтнi
  I'm lost, I want to get to ...
  ekho khaтнi, тнelo na pao
  sto ...

I've lost my (hand)bag ekhasa
  tin tsanda moo
lost property (office) to grafio
  apolesтнendon
lot: a lot, lots pola
  not a lot okhi pola
  a lot of people poli anтнropi
  a lot bigger poli megalitero
  I like it a lot moo aresi poli
lotion i losion
loud thinatos
lounge to saloni
love i agapi
  (verb) agapo
  I love Greece latrevo tin
  Elatha
lovely oreos
low khamilos
luck i tikhi
  good luck! kali tikhi!
luggage i aposkeves
luggage trolley to karotsaki ya
  tis aposkeves
lump (on body) to priximo
lunch to yevma
lungs o pnevmonas
luxurious (hotel, furnishings)
  politelis
luxury politelias

M

Macedonia i Makethonia
machine i mikhani
mad (insane) trelos
  (angry) trelos apo тнimo
magazine to periothiko
maid (in hotel) i servitora

maiden name to patronimo
mail ta gramata, to
   takhithromio
   (verb) takhithromo
   is there any mail for me?
   ekho kanena grama?
mailbox to gramatokivotio
main kirios
main course to kirio piato
Mainland Greece i Ipirotiki
   Elatha
main post office kendriko
   takhithromio
main road (in town) o kendrikos
   thromos
   (in country) o aftokinito-
   thromos
main switch o kendrikos
   thiakoptis
make (brand name) i marka
   (verb) kano
   I make it 500 drachmas
   ipoloyizo oti kani pedakosi-es
   thrakhmes
   what is it made of? apo ti
   ineh ftiagmeno?
make-up to make-up
man o andras
manager o thi-efrhindis, o
   manager
   can I see the manager? boro
   na tho ton thi-efrhindi?
manageress i thi-efrhindria
manual to aftokinito meh
   kanonikes takhitites
many pola
   not many liga, okhi pola
map o khartis
March o Martios

margarine i margarini
market i agora
marmalade i marmelatha
married: I'm married (said
   by a man/woman) imeh
   pandremenos/pandremeni
   are you married? (said to a man/
   woman) isteh pandremenos/
   pandremeni?
mascara i maskara
match (football etc) to mats, o
   agonas
matches ta spirta
material (fabric) to ifasma
matter: it doesn't matter then
   pirazi
   what's the matter? ti simveni?
mattress to stroma
May o Ma-ios
may: may I have another one?
   тна iтнela ki alo ena?
   may I come in? boro na bo?
   may I see it? boro na to tho?
   may I sit here? boro na
   катнiso etho?
maybe isos
mayonnaise i ma-yoneza
me* emena
   that's for me afto ineh ya
   mena
   send it to me stilteh to seh
   mena
   me too ki ego episis
meal to fa-yito

dialogue

did you enjoy your meal?
sas areseh to fayito?

it was excellent, thank you itan poli nostimo, efkharisto

mean: what do you mean? ti eno-iteh?

dialogue

what does this word mean? ti simeni afti i lexi?
it means ... in English simeni ... sta Anglika

measles i ilara
meat to kreas
mechanic o mikhanikos
medicine to farmako
Mediterranean i Meso-yios
medium (adj: size) metrios
medium-dry imixiro krasi
medium-rare misopsimeno
medium-sized metrio meyeтнos
meet sinandao
 nice to meet you kharika poo sas gnorisa
 where shall I meet you? poo тна sas sinandiso?
meeting i sinandisi
meeting place to meros sinandisis
melon to peponi
men i anthres
mend thiorтнono
 could you mend this for me? boriteh na moo to ftiaxeteh?
menswear ta anthrika ithi
mention anafero

don't mention it parakalo
menu to menoo
 may I see the menu, please? boro na tho to menoo, parakalo?
 see Menu Reader page 174
message to minima
 are there any messages for me? iparkhi kanena minima ya mena?
 I want to leave a message for ... thelo nafiso ena minima ya ...
metal to metalo
metre* to metro
microwave (oven) o foornos mikrokimaton, to microwave
midday to mesimeri
 at midday to mesimeri
middle: in the middle sti mesi
 in the middle of the night arga ti nikhta
 the middle one to meseo
midnight ta mesanikhta
 at midnight ta mesanikhta
might: I might тна boroosa
 I might not тна boroosa
 I might want to stay another day bori na тнelo na mino akomi mia mera
migraine i imikrania
mild (weather) eтнrios
 (taste) elafros
mile* ena mili
milk to gala
milkshake to milkshake
millimetre* ena khiliosto
minced meat o kimas
mind: never mind then pirazi

I've changed my mind alaxa gnomi

dialogue

do you mind if I open the window? seh pirazi an anixo to parathiro?
no, I don't mind okhi, then meh pirazi

mine*: it's mine ineh thiko moo
mineral water to emfialomeno nero
mint (sweet) i menda
minute to lepto
in a minute seh ena lepto
just a minute ena lepto
mirror o kathreftis
Miss thespinis
miss khano
I missed the bus ekhasa to leoforio
missing lipi
one of my ... is missing lipi ena ...
there's a suitcase missing lipi mia valitsa
mist i katakhnia
mistake to lathos
I think there's a mistake nomizo oti iparkhi ena lathos etho
sorry, I've made a mistake meh sinkhoriteh, ekana lathos
misunderstanding i parexiyisi
mix-up: sorry, there's been

a mix-up meh sinkhoriteh, iparkhi ena berthema
modern modernos
modern art gallery i galeri modernas tekhnis
Modern Greek ta Nea Elinika
moisturizer i ithatiki krema
moment: I won't be a moment mia stigmi parakalo
monastery to monastiri
Monday i theftera
money ta lefta
month o minas
monument to mnimio
moon to fengari
moped to mikhanaki
more* perisoteros
can I have some more water, please? akomi ligo nero, parakalo
more expensive/interesting pio akrivo/enthiaferon
more than 50 perisotero apo peninda
more than that pio poli ap afto
a lot more poli perisotero

dialogue

would you like some more? tha thelateh ligo akomi?
no, no more for me, thanks okhi, okhi alo ya mena, efkharisto
how about you? ki esis?
I don't want any more, thanks then thelo alo, efkharisto

morning to pro-i
 this morning simera to pro-i
 in the morning to pro-i
mosquito to koon**oo**pi
mosquito repellent to fith**a**ki
 ya ta koon**oo**pia
most: I like this one most of all
 af**to** moo ar**e**si p**io** poli ap**o o**la
 most of the time sin**i**тнos
 most tourists i peris**o**teri
 toor**i**stes
mostly k**i**rios
mother i mit**e**ra
motorbike i motosikl**e**ta
motorboat i v**a**rka meh
 mikh**a**ni
motorway i eтнnik**i** oth**o**s
mountain to voon**o**
 in the mountains p**a**no sta
 voon**a**
mountaineering i oriv**a**sia
mouse to pond**i**ki
moustache to moost**a**ki
mouth to st**o**ma
mouth ulcer pliy**i** sto st**o**ma
move metakin**o**
 he's moved to another room
 piyeh seh **a**lo thom**a**tio
 could you move your car?
 bor**i**teh na metakin**i**seteh to
 aftok**i**nito sas?
 could you move up a little?
 bor**i**teh na metakin**i**тнiteh
 l**i**go?
 where has it moved to? poo
 metaf**e**rтнikeh?
movie to film
movie theater o kinimato-
 gr**a**fos, to sinem**a**

Mr k**i**ri-eh
Mrs kir**i**a
Ms thespin**i**s
much pol**i**
 much better/worse pol**i**
 kal**i**tera/khir**o**tera
 much hotter pol**i** p**io** zest**a**
 not much **o**khi pol**i**
 not very much **o**khi para pol**i**
 I don't want very much then
 тн**e**lo para pol**i**
mud i l**a**spi
mug (for drinking) i k**oo**pa
 I've been mugged meh
 l**i**stepsan
mum i mam**a**
mumps i parotit**i**tha
museum to moos**i**o
mushrooms ta manit**a**ria
music i moosik**i**
musician o/i moosik**o**s
Muslim (adj) Moosoolmanik**o**s
mussels ta m**i**thia
must: I must ... pr**e**pi na ...
 I mustn't drink alcohol then
 pr**e**pi na p**io** alko-**o**l
mustard i moost**a**rtha
my* o/i/to ... moo
myself: I'll do it myself тна to
 k**a**no o **i**thios
 by myself ap**o** m**o**nos moo

N

nail (finger) to n**i**khi
 (metal) to karf**i**
nailbrush i v**oo**rtsa ya
 ta n**i**khia

nail varnish to mano
name to onoma
  my name's John meh leneh
  John
  what's your name? pos seh
  leneh?
  what is the name of this
  street? pos leneh afto to
  thromo?
napkin i petseta
nappy i pana
narrow (street) stenos
nasty (person) apesios
  (weather, accident) askhimos
national ethnikos
nationality i ethnikotita
natural fisikos
nausea i naftia
navy (blue) ble maren
near konda
  is it near the city centre? ineh
  konda sto kendro tis polis?
  do you go near the
  Acropolis? pernateh apo tin
  Akropoli?
  where is the nearest ...? poo
  ineh to plisi-estero ...?
nearby etho konda
nearly skhethon
necessary aparetitos, anangeos
neck o lemos
necklace to koli-e
necktie i gravata
need: I need ...
  khriazomeh ...
  do I need to pay? khriazeteh
  na pliroso?
needle i velona
negative (film) to arnitiko

neither: neither (one) of them
  kanenas apo aftoos
  neither ... nor ... ooteh ...
  ooteh ...
nephew o anipsios
net (in sport) to thikhti
network map o khartis othikoo
  thiktioo
never poteh

dialogue

  have you ever been to
  Athens? ekheteh pa-i
  poteh stin Athina?
  no, never, I've never been
  there okhi, poteh, then
  ekho pa-i poteh eki

new neos, kenooryos
news (radio, TV etc) ta nea
newsagent's to praktorio
  efimerithon
newspaper i efimeritha
newspaper kiosk to periptero
  meh efimerithes
New Year to neo etos
  Happy New Year!
  eftikhismenos o kenooryos
  khronos!
New Year's Eve i protokhronia
New Zealand i Nea Zilanthia
New Zealander: I'm a New
  Zealander (man/woman) imeh
  Neozilanthos/Neozilantheza
next epomenos
  the next turning on the left i
  epomeni strofi sta aristera
  the next street on the left

o epomenos thromos sta aristera

at the next stop stin epomeni stasi

next week tin ali evthomatha

next to thipla apo

nice (food) nostimos

(looks, view etc) oreos

(person) kalos

niece i anipsia

night i nikhta

at night to vrathi

good night kalinikhta

dialogue

> **do you have a single room for one night?** ekheteh ena mono thomatio ya mia nikhta?
> **yes, madam** malista, kiria moo
> **how much is it per night?** poso kani ti mia nikhta?
> **it's 5000 drachmas for one night** ineh pendeh khiliathes thrakhmes ya mia nikhta
> **thank you, I'll take it** efkharisto, тна to kliso

nightclub to nait-klab

nightdress to nikhtiko

night porter o nikhterinos тнiroros

no okhi

I've no change then ekho psila

there's no ... left then emineh катноloo ...

no way! apokli-eteh!

oh no! (upset) okh!, o okhi!

nobody kanenas

there's nobody there then ineh kanis eki

noise i fasaria

noisy: it's too noisy ekhi poli fasaria

non-alcoholic khoris alko-ol

none kanis

non-smoking compartment o khoros ya mi kapnizondes

noon to mesimeri

no-one kanenas

nor: nor do I ooteh kego

normal fisiolo-yikos

north o voras

in the north sta vori-a

north of Athens vori-a tis Aтнinas

northeast o vorio-anatolikos

northwest o vorio-thitikos

northern vorios

Northern Ireland i Vorios Irlanthia

Norway i Norviyia

Norwegian (adj) Norviyikos

nose i miti

nosebleed i emorayia sti miti

not* then

no, I'm not hungry okhi, then pina-o

I don't want any, thank you efkharisto, then тнelo

it's not necessary then ineh aparetito

I didn't know that then to ixera
not that one – this one okhi
afto – to alo
note (banknote) to khartonomisma
notebook to blokaki, to
simiomatario
notepaper (for letters) to kharti
alilografias
nothing tipoteh
nothing for me, thanks
tipoteh ya mena, efkharisto
nothing else tipoteh alo
novel to miTHistorima
November o No-emvrios
now tora
number* o ariTHmos
I've got the wrong number
pira laTHos noomero
what is your phone number?
pio ineh to tilefono soo?
number plate i pinakitha
nurse (man/woman) o
nosokomos/i nosokoma
nursery slope i pista
ekmaTHisis
nut (for bolt) to paximathi
nuts to karithi

O
—

o'clock* i ora
occupied (toilet) katilimenos
October o Oktovrios
odd (strange) paraxenos
of* too
off (lights) klisto
it's just off Omonia Square

ligo pio eki apo tin Omoni-a
we're off tomorrow
fevgoomeh avrio
offensive (language, behaviour)
prosvlitikos
office (place of work) to grafio
officer (said to policeman)
astinomeh
often sikhna
not often okhi sikhna
how often are the buses?
kaTHeh poteh ekhi leoforia?
oil (for car) ta lathia
(for salad) to lathi
ointment i alifi
OK endaxi
are you OK? iseh kala?
is that OK with you? iseh
efkharistimenos etsi?
is it OK to ...? pirazi na ...?
that's OK thanks (it doesn't
matter) ineh endaxi, efkharisto
I'm OK (nothing for me) tipoteh
ya mena
(I feel OK) imeh mia khara
is this train OK for ...? afto
ineh to treno ya ...?
I said I'm sorry, OK? soo ipa
signomi, endaxi?
old (person) yeros
(thing) palios

dialogue

how old are you? poso
khronon iseh?
I'm twenty-five imeh ikosi-
pendeh khronon
and you? ki esi?

old-fashioned demodeh
old town (old part of town) i palia poli
 in the old town stin palia poli
olive oil to eleolatho
olives i eli-es
omelette i omeleta
on pano
 (lights) anikhto
 on the street/beach sto thromo/stin paralia
 is it on this road? ineh safto to thromo?
 on the plane mesa sto a-eroplano
 on Saturday to Savato
 on television stin tileorasi
 I haven't got it on me then to ekho mazi moo
 this one's on me (drink) ego kernao afti ti fora
 the light wasn't on to fos then itan anikhto
 what's on tonight? ti pezi simera?
once (one time) mia fora
 at once (immediately) amesos
one* enas, mia, ena
 the white one to aspro
one-way ticket: a one-way ticket to ... ena aplo ya ...
onion to kremithi
only mono
 only one mono ena
 it's only 6 o'clock ineh mono exi i ora
 I've only just got here molis eftasa
on/off switch o thiakoptis

open (adj) aniktos
 (verb: door, shop) anigo
 when do you open? poteh aniyeteh?
 I can't get it open then boro na to anixo
 in the open air stin ipeтнro
opening times ores litooryias
open ticket isitirio meh anikhti epistrofi
opera i opera
operation (medical) i enkhirisi
operator (telephone: man/woman) o tilefonitis/i tilefonitria
opposite: the opposite direction stin andiтнeti katefтнinsi
 the bar opposite to bar apenandi
 opposite my hotel apenandi apo to xenothokhio moo
optician o optikos
or i
orange (fruit) to portokali
 (colour) portokali
orange juice i portokalatha
orchestra i orkhistra
order: can we order now? (in restaurant) boroomeh na paragiloomeh tora?
 I've already ordered, thanks ekho ithi paragili, efkharisto
 I didn't order this then paragila afto
 out of order then litooryi
ordinary kanonikos
other alos, ali, alo
 the other one to alo
 the other day tis pro-ales

I'm waiting for the others
perimeno toos aloos
do you have any others?
ekheteh tipoteh ala?
otherwise thiaforetika
our* o/i/to ... mas
ours* thikos mas
out: he's out then ineh etho
three kilometres out of town
tria khiliometra exo apo tin
poli
outdoors exo
outside ... exo ...
can we sit outside?
borroomeh na katнisoomeh
exo?
oven o foornos
over: over here etho
over there eki, eki pera
over 500 pano apo pendakosia
it's over teliosa
overcharge: you've
overcharged me meh
khreosateh parapano
overcoat to palto
overlook: I'd like a room
overlooking the courtyard
тна iтнela ena thomatio meh
тнea stin avli
overnight (travel) oloniktio
overtake prosperno
owe: how much do I owe you?
poso sas khrostao?
own: my own ... thiko
moo ...
are you on your own? iseh
monos soo?
I'm on my own imeh monos
moo

owner (man/woman) o
ithioktitis/i ithioktitria

P

pack (verb) ftiakhno tis valitses
a pack of ... ena paketo ...
package (parcel) to paketo
package holiday i organomeni
ekthromi
packed lunch to etimo
mesimeriano
packet: a packet of cigarettes
ena paketo tsigara
padlock to looketo, i klitharia
page (of book) i selitha
could you page Mr ...?
boriteh na fonaxeteh ton
kirio ...?
pain o ponos
I have a pain here
esтнanomeh ena pono etho
painful othiniros
painkillers to pafsipono
paint i boya
painting o pinakas zografikis
pair: a pair of ... ena
zevgari ...
Pakistani (adj) Pakistanikos
palace to palati
pale khlomos
pale blue galazios
pan to tapsi
panties to slip, i kilotes
pants (underwear: men's) to
sovrako
(women's) to slip, i kilotes
(US: trousers) to pandaloni

pantyhose to kalson
paper to kharti
  (newspaper) i efimeriтнa
  a piece of paper ena komati
  kharti
paper handkerchiefs ta
  khartomandila
parcel to thema
pardon (me)? (didn't understand/
  hear) signomi?
parents: my parents i gonis
  moo
parents-in-law ta peтнerika
park to parko
  (verb) parkaro
  can I park here? boro na
  parkaro etho?
parking lot to parking
part to meros
partner (boyfriend, girlfriend) o
  filos, i fili
party (group) i omatha
  (celebration) to parti
pass (in mountains) to perasma
passenger o/i epivatis
passport to thiavatirio
past: in the past sto parelтнon
  just past the information
  office amesos meta to grafio
  pliroforion
path to monopati
pattern to s-khethio
pavement to pezothromio
  on the pavement sto
  pezothromio
pavement café kafenio sto
  thromo
pay plirono
  can I pay, please? boro na

pliroso, parakalo?
  it's already paid for ineh ithi
  pliromeno

dialogue

> who's paying? pios тнa
> plirosi?
> I'll pay ego тнa pliroso
> no, you paid last time,
> I'll pay okhi, esi pliroses
> tin teleftea fora, ego тнa
> pliroso

payphone to tilefono meh
  kermata
peaceful irinikos
peach to rothakino
peanuts fistikia arapika
pear to akhlathi
peas ta bizelia
peculiar (taste, custom)
  paraxenos
pedestrian crossing i thiavasi
  pezon
pedestrian precinct o pezo-
  thromos
peg (for washing) to mandalaki
  (for tent) to palooki
pen to stilo
pencil to molivi
penfriend (male/female) o filos
  thi' alilografias/i fili thi'
  alilografias
penicillin i penikilini
penknife o soo-yias
pensioner o/i sindaxiookhos
people i anтнropi
  the other people in the hotel

i ali anтhropi sto xeno-
thokhio
too many people ipervolika
poli anтhropi
pepper (spice) to piperi
(vegetable) i piperia
peppermint (sweet) i menda
per: per night tin vrathia
how much per day? poso tin
imera?
per cent tis ekato
perfect telios
perfume to aroma
perhaps isos
perhaps not isos okhi
period (time, menstruation) i
periothos
perm i permanand
permit i athia
person to atomo
personal stereo to walkman®
petrol i venzini
petrol can ena thokhio
venzinis
petrol station to venzinathiko
pharmacy to farmakio
phone to tilefono
(verb) perno tilefono, tilefono
phone book o tilefonikos
katalogos
phonecard i tilekarta
phone number o ariтнmos
tilefonoo
photo i fotografia
**excuse me, could you
take a photo of us?** meh
sinkhoriteh, тна boroosateh
na mas pareteh mia
fotografia?

phrase book to vivlio
thialogon
piano to piano
pickpocket o portofolas
**pick up: will you be there to
pick me up?** тна iseh eki na
meh paris?
picnic to piknik
picture i ikona
pie i pita
(meat) i kreatopita
(fruit) i frootopita
piece to komati
a piece of ... ena komati ...
pill to khapi
I'm on the pill perno
antisiliptika khapia
pillow to maxilari
pillow case i maxilaroтнiki
pin i karfitsa
pineapple o ananas
pineapple juice o khimos
anana
pink roz
pipe (for smoking) i pipa, to
tsibooki
(for water) o solinas
pipe cleaners katнaristis pipas
Piraeus o Pireas
pistachio nuts fistiki-a Eyinis
pity: it's a pity ineh krima
pizza i pitsa
place to meros
is this place taken? ineh
piasmeni afti i тнesi?
at your place sti тнesi soo
at his place sti тнesi too
plain (not patterned)
monokhromo

plane to a-eroplano
 by plane meh to
 a-eroplano
plant to fito
plaster cast o yipsos
plasters to lefkoplast
plastic plastikos
 (credit cards) i pistotiki karta
plastic bag i plastiki sakoola
plate to piato
plate-smashing spasimo
 pi-aton
platform i platforma
 which platform is for Patras,
 please? pia platforma ya tin
 Patra, parakalo?
play (in theatre) to THeatriko
 ergo
 (verb) pezo
playground to yipetho
pleasant efkharistos
please parakalo
 yes please neh, parakalo
 could you please ...? THa
 boroosateh, parakalo,
 na ...?
 please don't stamata, seh
 parakalo
 pleased to meet you kharika
 poli
pleasure: i efkharistisi
 my pleasure efkharistisi
 moo
plenty: plenty of ... poli/
 pola ...
 there's plenty of time iparkhi
 arketi ora
 that's plenty, thanks
 efkharisto, arki

pliers i pensa
plug (electrical) i briza
 (for car) to boozi
 (in sink) i tapa
plumber o ithravlikos
pm* meta mesimvrias
poached egg to avgo poseh
pocket i tsepi
point: two point five thio koma
 pendeh
 there's no point then iparkhi
 logos
points (in car) i platines
poisonous thilitiriothis
police i astinomia
 call the police! kalesteh tin
 astinomia!
policeman o astifilakas
police station to astinomiko
 tmima
policewoman i astinomikos
polish to verniki
polite evgenikos
polluted molismenos
pony to poni
pool (for swimming) i pisina
poor (not rich) ftokhos
 (quality) kakos
pop music i moosiki pop
pop singer o tragoothistis
 pop, i tragoothistria pop
population o pliTHismos
pork to khirino
port (for boats) to limani
 (drink) i mavrothafni
porter (in hotel) o akh-THoforos
portrait to portreto
posh (restaurant) akrivos
 (people) kiriles

possible thinat**o**s
is it possible to ...? ineh
  thinat**o**n na ...?
as ... as possible **o**so to
  thinat**o**n ...
post (mail) ta gr**a**mata
  (verb) takhithr**o**mo
could you post this for
  me? b**o**riteh na moo to
  takhithromiseteh?
postbox to gramatokiv**o**tio
postcard i kartpost**a**l
postcode o takhithromik**o**s
  kothik**o**s
poster (for room) to p**o**ster
  (in street) i af**i**sa
post office to takhithr**o**mio
poste restante post rest**a**nd
pots and pans (cooking
  implements) katsar**o**les keh
  tig**a**nia
potato i pat**a**ta
potato chips ta tsips
pottery ta keramik**a**
pound* (money) i l**i**ra
  (weight) i l**i**bra
power cut i thiak**o**pi r**e**vmatos
power point o revmatoth**o**tis
practise: I want to practise my
  Greek тн**e**lo na exask**i**so ta
  Elinik**a** moo
prawns i gar**i**thes
  (larger) i kar**a**vitha
prefer: I prefer ... protim**o** ...
pregnant **e**ngios
prescription (for chemist) i
  sind**a**yi
present (gift) to th**o**ro
president (of country) o pro-

ethros
pretty (beautiful) **o**morfos, or**e**os
  (quite) arket**a**
it's pretty expensive ineh
  arket**a** akriv**o**
price i tim**i**
priest o pap**a**s
prime minister o proтн**i**-
  poorg**o**s
printed matter ta **e**ndipa
priority (in driving) i protere**o**tita
prison i filak**i**
private ithiotik**o**s
private bathroom to ithiotik**o**
  b**a**nio
probably piтнan**o**n
problem to pr**o**vlima
no problem! kan**e**na
  pr**o**vlima!
program(me) to pr**o**grama
promise: I promise
  ip**o**skhomeh
pronounce: how is this
  pronounced? pos to prof**e**ris
  aft**o**?
properly (repaired, locked etc)
  opos pr**e**pi
protection factor (of suntan
  lotion) o vaтнm**o**s prostas**i**as
Protestant o
  thiamartir**o**menos
public convenience i
  kin**o**khristi too**a**leta
public holiday i thim**o**sia ary**i**a
pudding (dessert) to gl**i**kisma
pull trav**a**o
pullover to pool**o**ver
puncture to foo-**i**t
purple mov

purse (for money) to portofoli
(US: handbag) i tsanda
push sprokhno
pushchair to karotsaki
put vazo
  where can I put ...? poo boro
  na valo ...?
  could you put us up for
  the night? boriteh na mas
  filoxeniseteh ya ena vrathi?
pyjamas i pitzames

Q

quality i piotita
quarantine i karantina
quarter to tetarto
quayside: on the quayside stin
  provlita
question i erotisi
queue i oora
quick grigora
  that was quick afto itan
  grigoro
  what's the quickest way
  there? pios ineh o pio
  grigoros thromos?
  fancy a quick drink? ekhis
  orexi ya ena poto sta grigora?
quickly grigora
quiet (place, hotel) isikhos
  quiet! siopi!
quince to kithoni
quite (fairly) arketa
  (very) telios
  that's quite right poli sosta
  quite a lot arketa

R

rabbit o lagos
race (for runners, cars) i koorsa
racket i raketa
radiator (in room) to kalorifer
  (of car) to psiyio aftokinitoo
radio to rathiofono
  on the radio sto rathiofono
rail: by rail sithirothromikos
railway o sithirothromos
rain i vrokhi
  in the rain mes tin vrokhi
  it's raining vrekhi
raincoat i kabardina, to
  athiavrokho
rape o viasmos
rare (steak) okhi poli
  psimeno
rash (on skin) to exanthima
raspberry to vatomooro
rat o arooreos
rate (for changing money) i timi
  sinalagmatos
rather: it's rather good ineh
  malon kalo
  I'd rather ... тна protimoosa
  na ...
razor (dry) to xirafaki
  (electric) i xiristiki mikhani
razor blades to xirafaki
read thiavazo
ready etimos
  are you ready? (to man/woman)
  iseh etimos/etimi?
  I'm not ready yet then imeh
  etimos akomi

dialogue

when will it be ready?
poteh THa ineh etimo?
it should be ready in a
couple of days THa prepi
na ineh etimo seh mia-thio
meres

real pragmatikos
really pragmatika
 (very) poli
 really! (surprise, doubt) psemata!
 really? (interest) aliтнia?
rearview mirror o kaтнreftis
 aftokinitoo
reasonable (prices etc) loyikos
receipt i apothixi
recently prosfata
reception (in hotel) i resepsion
 (for guests) i thexiosi
 at reception stin paralavi
reception desk to grafio
 ipothokhis
receptionist i/o resepsionist
recognize anagnorizo
recommend: could you
 recommend ...? boriteh na
 moo sistiseteh ...?
record (music) o thiskos
red kokinos
red wine to kokino krasi
refund i epistrofi khrimaton
 can I have a refund? moo
 epistrefondeh khrimata?
region i periokhi
registered: by registered mail
 sistimeno
registration number o

ariтнmos kikloforias
relative o/i singenis
religion i тнriskia
remember: I don't remember
 then тнimameh
 I remember тнimameh
 do you remember?
 тнimaseh?
rent (for apartment etc) to enikio
 (verb) niki-azo
 to/for rent eniki-azonteh
rented car to enikiasmeno
 aftokinito
repair i episkevi
 can you repair it? boriteh na
 to episkevaseteh?
repeat epanalamvano
 could you repeat that?
 boriteh na to
 epanalaveteh?
reservation (train, bus) to
 klisimo тнesis

dialogue

I have a reservation ekho
kani mia kratisi
yes sir, what name please?
malista, kiri-eh; seh ti
onoma, parakalo?

reserve krato

dialogue

can I reserve a table for
tonight? boro na kliso ena
trapezi ya apopseh?
yes madam, for how many

people? malista, kiria
moo; ya posa atoma?
for two ya thio
and for what time? keh ya
ti ora?
for eight o'clock ya tis
okhto
**and could I have your
name please?** to onoma
sas, parakalo?
see **alphabet** page 209 for
spelling

rest: I need a rest khriazomeh
xekoorasi
the rest of the group to
ipolipo groop
restaurant to estiatorio
rest room i too-aleta
retired: I'm retired imeh seh
sindaxi
return: a return to ... ena
isitirio met epistrofis ya to ...
reverse charge call to
tilefonima kolekt
reverse gear i opisтнen
revolting apesios
Rhodes i Rothos
rib to plevro
rice to rizi
rich (person) ploosios
(food) varis
ridiculous yelios
right (correct) sostos
(not left) thexia
you were right ikhes thikio
that's right sosta
this can't be right afto then
bori na ineh sosto

right! endaxi!
is this the right road for ...?
ineh aftos o sostos thromos ya
...?
on the right sta thexia
turn right stripseh thexia
right-hand drive meh thexio
timoni
ring (on finger) to thaktilithi
I'll ring you тна soo tilefoniso
ring back тна seh paro piso
ripe (fruit) orimos
rip-off: it's a rip-off ineh listia
rip-off prices astronomikes
times
risky ripsokinthinos
river to potami
road (country) o thromos
(in town) i othos
is this the road for ...? ineh
aftos o thromos ya ...?
down the road parakato
road accident to
aftokinitistiko thistikhima
road map o othikos khartis
roadsign i pinakitha
rob: I've been robbed meh
listepsan
rock o vrakhos
(music) i rok moosiki
on the rocks (with ice) meh
pagakia
roll (bread) to psomaki
roof i orofi, i steyi
(flat) i taratsa
roof rack i s-khara
aftokinitoo
room to thomatio
(space) to meros

in my room sto thomatio moo

room service to servis thomatioo

rope to skhini

rosé (wine) to rozeh

roughly (approximately) pano-kato

round: it's my round ineh i sira moo

roundabout (for traffic) o kikloforiakos komvos, i platia

round trip ticket: a round trip ticket to ... ena isitirio met epistrofis ya to ...

route i poria

what's the best route for ...? pios ineh o kaliteros thromos ya ...?

rubber (material) lastikho (eraser) i svistra, i goma

rubber band to lastikhaki

rubbish (waste) ta skoopithia (poor quality goods) kaki piotita

rubbish! (nonsense) trikhes!

rucksack to sakithio

rude a-yenis

ruins ta eripia, i arkheotites

rum to roomi

rum and coke ena roomi meh koka kola

run (person) trekho

how often do the buses run? poso sikh-na pernoon ta leoforia?

I've run out of money moo teliosan ta khrimata

rush hour ora ekhmis

S

sad lipimenos

saddle i sela

safe (not in danger) asfalis (not dangerous) akinthinos, avlavis

safety pin i paramana

sail to pani

sailboard to windsurf

sailboarding to windsurf

salad i salata

salad dressing to lathoxitho

sale: for sale politeh

salmon o solomos

Salonika i THesaloniki

salt to alati

same: the same o ithios

the same as this to ithio opos afto

the same again, please to ithio xana, parakalo

it's all the same to me to ithio moo kani

sand i amos

sandals ta santhalia

sandwich to sandwich

sanitary napkins i servi-etes

sanitary towels i servi-etes

sardines i sartheles

Saturday to Savato

sauce i saltsa

saucepan i katsarola

saucer to piataki

sauna i sa-oona

sausage to lookaniko

say: how do you say ... in Greek? pos to leneh ... sta

Elinika?
what did he say? ti ipeh?
I said ... ipa ...
he said ... ipeh ...
could you say that again?
boriteh na to xanapiteh?,
boriteh na to epanalaveteh?
scarf (for neck) to kaskol
(for head) to mandili
scenery to topio
schedule (US) to programa
scheduled flight i
programatismeni ptisi
school to skholio
scissors: a pair of scissors to
psalithi
scotch to skots whisky
Scotch tape® to sellotape®
Scotland i Skotia
Scottish Skotsezikos
I'm Scottish (man/woman) imeh
Skotsezos/Skotseza
scrambled eggs ta khtipita
avga
scratch i gratzoonia
screw i vitha
screwdriver to katsavithi
scuba diving i anapnefstiki
siskevi katathiti
sea i THalasa
by the sea konda sti THalasa
seafood ta THalasina
seafood restaurant i psaro-
taverna
seafront i paralia
on the seafront stin paralia
seagull o glaros
search psakh-no
seashell i akhivaTHa

seasick: I feel seasick
esthanomeh naftia
I get seasick meh piani i
THalasa
seaside: by the seaside konda
stin paralia
seat i THesi
is this anyone's seat? ineh
kanenos afti i THesi?
seat belt i zoni asfalias
sea urchin o akhinos
seaweed ta fikia
secluded apomeros
second (of time) to theftero-
lepto
(adj) thefteros
just a second! mia stigmi!
second class (travel) thefteri
THesi
second floor o thefteros orofos
(US) o tritos orofos
second-hand apo theftero
kheri
see vlepo, kitazo
can I see? boro na tho?
have you seen ...? ekhis
thi ...?
see you! ta xanalemeh!
I see (I understand) katalava
I saw him this morning ton
itha simera to pro-i
self-catering apartment to
anexartito thiamerisma
self-service self-servis
sell poolo
do you sell ...? poolateh ...?
Sellotape® to sellotape®
send stelno
I want to send this to England

thelo na stilo afto stin Anglia
senior citizen o/i sindaxiookhos
separate (adj) khoristos
separated: I'm separated (man/
woman) imeh khorismenos/
khorismeni
separately (pay, travel)
xekhorista
September o Septemvrios
septic siptikos
serious sovaros
service charge (in restaurant) to
filothorima
service station to
venzinathiko
serviette i hartopetseta, i
petseta
set menu to tabl-dot
several arketi
sew ravo
  could you sew this back on?
  boriteh na to rapseteh pali sti
  THesi too?
sex to sex
shade: in the shade sti skia
shake: let's shake hands as
thosoomeh ta kheria
shallow (water) rikha nera
shame: what a shame! ti
krima!
shampoo to samboo-an
  a shampoo and set ena
  loosimo meh mizampli
share (verb: room, table etc)
mirazomeh
sharp (knife etc) kofteros
  (taste, pain) thinatos
shattered (very tired)

exandlimenos
shaver i xiristiki mikhani
shaving foam o afros
xirismatos
shaving point i priza xiristikis
mikhanis
she* afti
  is she here? ineh etho?
sheet (for bed) to sendoni
shelf to rafi
shellfish ta ostraka
sherry to seri
ship to plio
  by ship meh plio
shirt to pookamiso
shit! skata!
shock to sok
  **I got an electric shock from
  the ...** ilektristika meh ...
shock-absorber to amortiser
shocking (behaviour, prices)
exofrenikos
shoe to papootsi
  a pair of shoes ena zevgari
  papootsia
shoelaces ta korthonia
papootsion
shoe polish to verniki
papootsion
shoe repairer o tsangaris
shop to magazi
shopping: I'm going shopping
pao ya psonia
shopping centre to emboriko
kendro
shop window i vitrina
shore i akti
short (person) kondos
  (time) ligos

(journey) sindomos
shortcut o sindomos thromos
shorts to sorts
should: what should I do? ti prepi na kano?
he **shouldn't be long then** prepi na aryisi
you should have told me eprepeh na moo to ikhes pi
shoulder o omos
shout (verb) fonazo
show (in theatre) to ergo
could you show me? boriteh na moo thixeteh?
shower (in bathroom) to doos
(rain) i bora
with shower meh doos
shower gel to afrolootro
shut (verb) klino
when do you shut? poteh klineteh?
when do they shut? poteh klinoon?
they're shut ineh klista
I've shut myself out klistika apexo
shut up! skaseh!
shutter (on camera) to thiafragma
(on window) to exofilo, to pandzoori
shy dropalos
sick (ill) arostos
see **ill**
I'm going to be sick (vomit) ekho tasi pros emeto
side i plevra
the other side of town i ali akri tis polis

side lights ta khamila fota
side salad i salata ya garnitoora
side street to thromaki
sidewalk to pezothromio
sight: the sights of ... ta axiotheata too ...
sightseeing: we're going sightseeing pameh na thoomeh ta axiotheata
sightseeing tour i xenayisi sta axiotheata
sign (roadsign etc) to sima
signal: he didn't give a signal then ekaneh sima
signature i ipografi
signpost i pinakitha, i tabela
silence i siopi
silk to metaxi
silly ano-itos
silver to asimi
silver foil to aloominokharto
similar omios
simple (easy) aplos
since: since yesterday apo kh-thes
since I got here apo toteh poo irtha etho
sing tragootho
singer (man/woman) o tragoothistis/i tragoothistria
single (man/woman) monos
a single to ... ena aplo ya ...
I'm single imeh eleftheros/eleftheri
single bed to mono krevati
single room to mono thomatio
sink (in kitchen) o nerokhitis
sister i athelfi

sister-in-law (brother's wife) i nifi
(wife's sister) i kooniatha
sit: can I sit here? boro na
kaTHiso etho?
is anyone sitting here?
kaTHeteh kanis etho?
sit down kaTHomeh
sit down! katseh kato!
site to axioTHeato
(archaeological) arkheoloyikos
khoros
size to meh-yeTHos
skin to therma
skindiving i katathisis
skinny kokaliaris
skirt i foosta
sky o ooranos
sleep (verb) kimameh
did you sleep well? kimi-
THikes kala?
I need a good sleep
khriazomeh ena kalo ipno
sleeper (on train) i kooketa
sleeping bag to sleeping bag
sleeping car i klinamaxa, i
kooketa
sleeping pill to ipnotiko khapi
sleepy: I'm feeling sleepy
nistazo
sleeve to maniki
slide (photographic) to slide
slip (under dress) to misofori
slippery glisteros
slow argos
slow down! pio arga
slowly siga-siga
could you say it slowly?
boriteh na to piteh arga-arga?
very slowly poli arga

small mikros
smell: it smells (smells bad)
vroma-i
smile (verb) khamo-yelo
smoke o kapnos
do you mind if I smoke? sas
pirazi an kapniso?
I don't smoke then kapnizo
do you smoke? kapnizeteh?
snack: I'd just like a snack THa
iTHela na fao kati prokhiyo
snake to fithi
sneeze to ftarnisma
snorkel o anapnefstiras
snow to khioni
so: it's so good ineh poli kalo
not so fast okhi toso grigora
so am I keh ego to ithio
so do I keh ego episis
so-so etsi ki etsi
soaking solution (for contact
lenses) igro sindirisis fakon
epafis
soap to sapooni
soap powder to aporipandiko
sober xemeTHistos
socks i kaltses
socket (electrical) i priza
soda (water) i sotha
sofa o kanapes
soft (material etc) apalos
soft-boiled egg to melato avgo
soft drink to anapsiktiko
soft lenses i malaki faki
sole i sola
could you put new soles
on these? boriteh na moo
valeteh kenooryi-es soles
safta?

some: can I have some water/
  rolls? moo thineteh ligo
  nero?/liga psomakia?
  can I have some? boro na
  paro ligo?
somebody, someone kapios
something kati
something to drink kati na
  pi-iteh
sometimes merikes fores
somewhere kapoo
son o yos
song to tragoothi
son-in-law o gambros
soon sindoma
  I'll be back soon THa yiriso
  sindoma
  as soon as possible oso to
  thinaton grigorotera
sore: it's sore ineh
  ereTHismeno
sore throat pona-i o lemos
  moo
sorry: (I'm) sorry signomi
  sorry? (didn't understand/hear)
  pardon?, signomi?
sort: what sort of ...? ti
  ithos ...?
soup i soopa
sour (taste) xinos
south notos
  south of noti-a
  in the south sto noto
  to the south noti-a
South Africa i Noti-os Afriki
South African (adj) Notio-
  afrikanos
  I'm South African (man/woman)
  imeh Notio-afrikanos/

Notio-afrikana
southeast notio-anatolikos
southwest notio-thitikos
souvenir to enTHimio
Spain i Ispania
Spanish (adj) ispanikos
  (language) ta ispanika
spanner to klithi
spare part ta andalaktika
spare tyre i rezerva
spark plug to boozi
speak: do you speak English?
  milateh Anglika?
  I don't speak ... then milo ...

dialogue

can I speak to Costas?
boro na miliso ston Kosta,
parakalo?
who's calling? pios ton
zita-i?
it's Patricia i Patricia
I'm sorry, he's not in, can I
take a message? lipameh,
then ineh etho, boro na too
thoso kapio minima?
no thanks, I'll call back
later okhi, efkharisto, THa
xanaparo argotera
please tell him I called
parakalo, piteh too pos
tilefonisa

speciality i spesialiteh
spectacles ta yali-a
speed i takhitita
speed limit to orio takhititas
speedometer to konder

spell: how do you spell it? pos
to grafeteh?
see alphabet page 209
spend xothevo
spider i arakhni
spin-dryer to stegnotirio
splinter i agitha
spoke (in wheel) i aktina
spoon to kootali
sport to spor
sprain: I've sprained my ...
straboolixa to ...
spring (season) i anixi
(in seat etc) to elatirio
square (in town) i platia
stairs ta skalopatia, i skales
stale (bread, taste) bayatikos
stall: the engine keeps stalling
i mikhani sinekhos stamata
stamp to gramatosimo

dialogue

a stamp for England,
please ena gramatosimo ya
Anglia, parakalo
what are you sending? ti
тна stileteh?
this postcard afti tin karta

star to asteri
(in film) o/i star
start i arkhi, to xekinima
(verb) arkhizo
when does it start? poteh
arkhizi?
the car won't start to
aftokinito then xekina
starter (of car) i miza

(food) to proto piato
starters ta orektika
starving: I'm starving peтнeno
tis pinas
state (in country) i politia
the States (USA) i Inomenes
Politi-es
station o staтнmos
statue to agalma
stay: where are you staying?
poo meneteh?
I'm staying at ... meno sto ...
I'd like to stay another two
nights тна iтнela na mino ales
thio nikhtes
steak i brizola
steal klevo
my bag has been stolen
klepsaneh tin tsanda moo
steep (hill) apotomos
steering to timoni
step: on the steps sta
skalopati-a
stereo to stereofoniko
singrotima
sterling i lira sterlina
steward (on plane) o
a-erosinothos
stewardess i a-erosinothos
sticking plaster to lefkoplast
still: I'm still waiting akoma
perimeno
is he still there? ineh akoma
eki?
keep still! stasoo akinitos!
sting: I've been stung by ...
meh tsibiseh ...
stockings i na-ilon kaltses
stomach to stomakhi

stomach ache o ponos sto
  stomakhi, o stomakhoponos
stone (rock) i petra
stop stamatao
  please, stop here (to taxi driver
    etc) parakalo, stamatisteh etho
  do you stop near ...?
    stamatateh konda ...?
  stop doing that! stamata na to
    kanis afto!
stopover i stasi
storm i THi-ela
straight: it's straight ahead
  ineh olo efτHia
  a straight whisky ena sketo
    whisky
straightaway amesos
strange (odd) paraxenos
stranger (man/woman) o xenos/i
  xeni
  I'm a stranger here imeh
    xenos etho
strap to loori
strawberry i fraoola
stream to rema, to potamaki
street o thromos
  on the street sto thromo
streetmap o othikos khartis
string (cord) o spangos
  (guitar etc) i khorthi
strong thinatos
stuck frakarismenos
  the key's stuck koliseh to
    klithi
student o fititis, i fititria
stupid vlakas
suburb ta pro-astia
subway (US: railway) o ipo-yios
suddenly xafnika

suede to kastori
sugar i zakhari
suit (man's) to koostoomi
  (woman's) to ta-yer
  it doesn't suit me (jacket etc)
    then moo pa-i
  it suits you soo pa-i
suitcase i valitsa
summer to kalokeri
  in the summer to kalokeri
sun o ilios
  in the sun ston ilio
  out of the sun sti skia
sunbathe kano iliοτΗerapia
sunblock (cream) to andiliako
sunburn to kapsimo apo ton
  ilio
sunburnt kamenos apo ton ilio
Sunday i Kiriaki
sunglasses ta yalia ilioo
sun lounger i shez long
sunny: it's sunny ekhi liakatha
sun roof (in car) i tzamenia
  skepi
sunset i thisi too ilioo
sunshade i ombrela ilioo
sunshine i liakatha
sunstroke i ili-asi
suntan to mavrisma
suntan lotion to lathi
  mavrismatos
suntanned iliokamenos
suntan oil to lathi mavrismatos
super katapliktikos
supermarket to supermarket
supper to thipno
supplement (extra charge)
  epipleon, to prosτΗeto
sure: are you sure? iseh

sigooros?
sure! veveos!
surname to epiтнeto
swearword i vrisia
sweater to poolover
sweatshirt i fanela
Sweden i Soo-ithia
Swedish (adj) Soo-ithikos
sweet (taste) glikos
(dessert) to gliko
sweets i karameles
swelling to prixeno
swim kolimbao
I'm going for a swim pao ya
kolibi
let's go for a swim pameh ya
kolibi
swimming costume to ma-yo
swimming pool i pisina
swimming trunks to ma-yo
switch o thiakoptis
switch off (engine) svino
(TV, lights) klino
switch on (engine) anavo
(TV, lights) anigo
swollen prismenos

T

table to trapezi
a table for two ena trapezi ya
thio
tablecloth to trapezomandilo
table tennis to ping-pong
table wine to epitrapezio krasi
tailback (of traffic) i oora
tailor o raftis
take (lead) perno

(accept) thekhomeh
can you take me to the
airport? boriteh na meh
pateh sto a-erothromio?
do you take credit cards?
thekhesteh pistotikes kartes?
fine, I'll take it endaxi тнa to
paro
can I take this? (leaflet etc)
boro na paro afto?
how long does it take? posi
ora тнa pari?
it takes three hours perni tris
ores
is this seat taken? ineh
piasmeni i тнesi?
hamburger to take away
khamboorger ya to spiti
can you take a little off here?
(to hairdresser) boriteh na
pareteh ligo apo etho?
talcum powder i poothra talk
talk (verb) milo
tall psilos
tampons ta tampax®, ta tabon
tan to mavrisma
to get a tan mavrizo
tank (of car) to depozito
tap i vrisi
tape (cassette) i kaseta
(sticky) i tenia
tape measure to metro
tape recorder to magnitofono
taste i yefsi
can I taste it? boro na to
thokimaso?
taxi to taxi
will you get me a taxi? тнa
moo kaleseteh ena taxi?

where can I find a taxi? poo boro na vro ena taxi?

dialogue

to the airport/to the Hilton Hotel please
sto a-erothromio/sto xenothokhio Khilton, parakalo
how much will it be? poso THa stikhisi?
1,500 drachmas khili-es pendakosi-es thrakmes
that's fine, right here, thanks endaxi, etho pera ineh, efkharisto

taxi-driver o taxidzis
taxi rank o staTHmos taxi
tea to tsa-i
  tea for one/two please tsa-i ya enan/thio parakalo
teabags ta fakelakia tsa-i
teach: could you teach me? boris na meh maTHis?
teacher (man/woman) o thaskalos/i thaskala
team i omatha
teaspoon to kootalaki
tea towel i petseta koozinas
teenager o neos, i nea
telephone to tilefono
television i tileorasi
tell: could you tell him ...? boriteh na too piteh ...?
temperature (weather) i THermokrasia
  (fever) o piretos

temple (church) o na-os
tennis to tennis
tennis ball i bala too tennis
tennis court to yipetho tennis
tennis racket i raketa tennis
tent i skini
term (at university, school) i s-kholiki periothos
terminus (rail) to terma
terrible foveros
terrific exeretikos
text (message) to minima sto kinto
than* apo
  smaller than mikroteros apo
thanks, thank you efkharisto
  thank you very much efkharisto para poli
  thanks for the lift efkharisto poo meh pirateh
  no thanks okhi efkharisto

dialogue

thanks efkharisto
that's OK, don't mention it parakalo, then kani tipoteh

that ekinos, ekini, ekino
  that one ekino
  I hope that ... elpizo oti ...
  that's nice ti orea!
  is that ...? afto ineh ...?
  that's it (that's right) akrivos
the* o, i, to; (pl) i, i, ta
theatre to THeatro
their* o/i/to ... toos
theirs* thiki toos
them* toos, tis, ta

for them ya ekinoos
with them maftoos
I gave it to them to ethosa
saftoos
who? – them pi-i? – afti
then (at that time) toteh
(after that) katopin
there eki
over there eki pera
up there eki pano
is there ...? iparkhi ...?
are there ...? iparkhoon ...?
there is ... iparkhi ...
there are ... iparkhoon ...
there you are (giving something)
oristeh
thermometer to THermometro
Thermos flask® to THermos
these afti, aftes, afta
can I have these? boro na
ekho afta?
Thessaly i THesalia
they* afti, aftes, afta
thick pakhis
(stupid) khazos
thief (man/woman) o kleftis/i
kleftra
thigh to booti
thin leptos
(person) athinatos
thing to pragma
my things ta pragmata moo
think skeptomeh
(believe) nomizo
I think so etsi nomizo
I don't think so then nomizo
I'll think about it THa to skepto
third party insurance asfalia ya
khrisi apo tritoos

thirsty: I'm thirsty thipso
this aftos, afti, afto
this one afto etho
this is my wife apo etho i
yineka moo
is this ...? ineh ...?
those ekini, ekines, ekina
which ones? – those pi-a?
– afta
Thrace i THraki
thread i klosti
throat o lemos
throat pastilles pastili-es lemoo
through thiamesoo
does it go through ...? (train,
bus) perna-i apo to ...?
throw (verb) rikhno
throw away (verb) peto
thumb o andikhiras
thunderstorm i kateyitha
Thursday i Pempti
ticket to isitirio

dialogue

a return to Athens ena
isitirio epistrofis ya tin
ATHina
coming back when? poteh
ineh i epistrofi?
today/next Tuesday
simera/tin epomeni Triti
that will be 2,000
drachmas thio khiliathes
thrakhmes, parakalo

ticket office (bus, rail) i THiritha
tide i paliri-a
tie (necktie) i gravata

tight (clothes etc) stenos
 it's too tight ineh poli steno
tights to kalson
till mekhri
time* o khronos
 (occasion) i fora
 what's the time? ti ora ineh?
 this time afti ti fora
 last time tin perasmeni fora
 next time tin epomeni fora
 four times teseris fores
timetable to programa
tin (can) i konserva
tinfoil to asimokharto
tin-opener to anikhtiri
tiny mikroskopikos
tip (to waiter etc) to filothorima
tired koorasmenos
 I'm tired imeh koorasmenos
tissues ta khartomandila
to: to Salonica/London ya tin
 THesaloniki/to Lonthino
 to Greece/England ya tin
 Elatha/Anglia
 to the post office sto
 takhithromio
toast (bread) to tost
today simera
toe to thakhtilo too pothioo
together mazi
 we're together (in shop etc)
 imasteh mazi
 can we pay together?
 boroomeh na plirosoomeh
 mazi?
toilet i too-aleta
 where is the toilet? poo ineh i
 too-aleta?
 I have to go to the toilet prepi

na pao stin too-aleta
toilet paper kharti iyias
tomato i domata
tomato juice to domatozoomo,
 o domatokhimos
tomato ketchup to ketsap
tomorrow avrio
tomorrow morning avrio to
 pro-i
 the day after tomorrow
 methavrio
toner (cosmetic) to tonotiko
tongue i glosa
tonic (water) to tonik
tonight apopseh
tonsillitis i amigthalititha
too (excessively) poli
 (also) episis
 too hot poli kafto
 too much para poli
 me too kego episis
tooth to thondi
toothache o ponothondos
toothbrush i othondovoortsa
toothpaste i othondokrema
top: on top of ... pano apo ...
 at the top stin korifi
top floor to retire
topless yimnostitHi
torch o fakos
total to sinolo
tour i peri-iyisi, i xenayisi
 is there a tour of ...? iparkhi
 peri-iyisi ya ...?
tour guide o/i xenagos
tourist (man/woman) o tooristas/
 i tooristria
tourist information office
 Grafio Pliroforion E-OT

tour operator to taxithiotiko
    grafio
towards pros
towel i petseta
town i poli
  in town stin poli
  just out of town akrivos exo
    apo tin poli
town centre to kendro tis polis
town hall to thimarkhio
toy to pekh-nithi
track (US) i platforma
    see platform
tracksuit i aтнlitiki forma
traditional parathosiakos
traffic i kikloforia
traffic jam i kikloforiaki
    simforisi
traffic lights ta fanaria tis
    trokheas
trailer (for carrying tent etc) i
    rimoolka
    (US: caravan) to trokhospito
trailer park topoтнesia ya
    trokhospita
train to treno
  by train meh treno

dialogue

is this the train for ...? afto
ineh to treno ya ...?
sure neh
no, you want that platform
there okhi, тна pateh seh
ekini tin platforma eki

trainers (shoes) ta aтнlitika
    papootsia

train station o sithiro-
    thromikos staтнmos
tram to tram
translate metafrazo
  could you translate that?
    boriteh na metafraseteh afto?
translation i metafrasi
translator o/i metafrastis
trashcan o skoopithodenekes
travel taxithevo
  we're travelling around
    taxithevoomeh triyiro
travel agent's to taxithiotiko
    grafio
traveller's cheque i
    taxithiotiki epitayi
tray o thiskos
tree to thendro
tremendous tromeros
trendy modernos
trim: just a trim please (to
    hairdresser) ligo konditera,
    parakalo
trip (excursion) to taxithi
  I'd like to go on a trip to ...
    тна iтнela na pao ena taxithi
    stin ...
trolley to trolley, to karotsaki
trolleybus to trolley
trouble o belas
  I'm having trouble with ...
    ekho provlimata meh ...
  sorry to trouble you meh
    sinkhoriteh poo sas vazo seh
    mbela
trousers to pandaloni
true aliтнinos
  that's not true then ineh
    aliтнia

English → Greek

trunk (US: of car) to port-bagaz
trunks (swimming) to mayo
try prospatно, thokimazo
 can I have a try? boro na
 thokimaso?
try on provaro
 can I try it on? boro na to
 thokimaso pano moo?
T-shirt to bloozaki
Tuesday i Triti
tuna o tonos
tunnel i siraga
Turkey i Toorkia
Turkish (adj) Toorkikos
Turkish coffee Toorkikos
 kafes, Elinikos kafes
Turkish-Cypriot (adj) Toorkiko-
 Kipriakos
turn: turn left/right stripseh
 aristera/thexia
 where do I turn off? poo
 strivo?
turn off: can you turn the
 heating off? boris na klisis ti
 тнermansi/to kalorifer?
turn on: can you turn the
 heating on? boris na anixis ti
 тнermansi/to kalorifer?
turning (in road) 1 strofi
TV i tileorasi
tweezers to tsimbithaki
twice thio fores
 twice as much ta thipla
twin beds thio krevatia
twin room to thomatio meh
 thio krevatia
twist: I've twisted my ankle
 stramboolixa ton astragalo
 moo

type to ithos
 a different type of ... ena alo
 ithos apo ...
typical kharaktiristikos
tyre to lastikho

U

ugly askhimos
UK to Inomeno Vasili-o
ulcer to elkos
umbrella i ombrela
uncle o тhios
unconscious anesтhitos
under apo kato
 (less than) ligotero apo
underdone (meat) misop-
 simenos
underground (railway) o ipo-
 yios
underpants to sovrako, to slip
understand: I understand
 katalaveno
 I don't understand then
 katalaveno
 do you understand?
 katalavenis?
unemployed anergos
United States i Inomenes
 Politi-es
university to panepistimio
unleaded petrol i amolivthi
 venzini
unlimited mileage aperiorista
 khiliometra
unlock xeklithono
unpack anigo tis valitses
until mekhri

English → Greek

Un

99

unusual asiniTHistos

up pano

(upwards) pros ta pano

up there eki pano

he's not up yet (not out of bed) then sikoTHikeh akomi

what's up? (what's wrong?) ti yineteh?

upmarket (restaurant etc) akrivos

upset stomach o stomakhoponos

upside down ta pano kato

upstairs pano

urgent epigon

us* mas

with us meh mas

for us ya mas

use khrisimopi-o

may I use ...? boro na khrisimopi-iso ...?

useful khrisimos

usual siniTHismenos

the usual (drink etc) to siniTHismeno

V

vacancy: do you have any vacancies? (hotel) ekheteh elefTHera thomatia?

vacation i thiakopes

see holiday

vaccination o emvoliasmos

vacuum cleaner i ilektriki skoopa

valid (ticket etc) engiros

how long is it valid for? ya poso is-khi-i?

valley i kilatha

valuable (adj) politimos

can I leave my valuables here? boro na afiso ta timalfi moo etho?

value i axia

van to trokhospito

vanilla i vanilia

a vanilla ice cream ena pagoto vanilia

vary: it varies metavaleteh

vase to vazo

veal to moskhari

vegetables ta lakhanika

vegetarian o/i khortofagos

vending machine o aftomatos politis

very poli

very little for me poli ligo ya mena

I like it very much moo aresi para poli

vest (under shirt) to fanelaki

via thia mesoo

video (film) i video-tenia

(video recorder) to video

view i THea

villa i vila

village to khorio

vinegar to xithi

vineyard to ambeli

visa i viza

visit (verb) episkeptomeh

I'd like to visit ... THa iTHela na episkefto ...

vital: it's vital that ... ineh vasiko na ...

vodka i votka

voice i foni

volleyball to volley-ball, i khirosferisi
voltage i tasis
vomit (verb) kano emeto

W

waist i mesi
waistcoat to yileko
wait perimeno
  wait for me perimeneh meh!
  don't wait for me mi meh perimenis
  can I wait until my wife gets here? boro na paragilo otan elthi i yineka moo?
  can you do it while I wait? perimeno na to kaneteh?
  could you wait here for me? boriteh na meh perimeneteh na yiriso?
waiter o servitoros
  waiter! garson!
waitress i garsona, i servitora
  waitress! sas parakalo!
wake: can you wake me up at 5.30? boriteh na meh xipniseteh stis pendeh keh misi?
wake-up call tilefonima ya xipnima
Wales i Oo-alia
walk: is it a long walk? ineh poli perpatima?
  it's only a short walk ekhi ligo perpatima
  I'll walk tha perpatiso

I'm going for a walk pao ena peripato
Walkman® to walkman®
wall o tikhos
wallet to portofoli
wander: I like just wandering around moo aresi na khazevo triyiro
want: I want a ... thelo ena ...
  I don't want any ... then thelo ...
  I want to go home thelo na pao spiti moo
  I don't want to then thelo
  he wants to ... theli na ...
  what do you want? ti thelis?
ward (in hospital) o thalamos
warm zestos
  I'm so warm zestenomeh arketa
was*: I was ... imoon ...
  he/she/it was ... itan ...
wash (verb) pleno
  (oneself) plenomeh
  can you wash these? boriteh na plineteh afta?
washer (for bolt etc) i rothela
washhand basin o niptiras
washing (clothes) i boogatha
washing machine to plindirio
washing powder i skoni plindirioo, to aporipandiko
washing-up liquid to sapooni piaton
wasp i sfinga
watch (wristwatch) to rolo-i
  will you watch my things for me? boriteh na prosekheteh

ta pragmata moo?
watch out! prosekheh!
watch strap to looraki roloyioo
water to nero
may I have some water? moo thineteh ligo nero?
waterproof (adj) athiavrokhos
waterskiing to THalasio ski
wave (in sea) to kima
way: could you tell me the way to ...? boriteh na moo piteh pos THa pa-o sto ..?
it's this way apo etho ineh
it's that way apo eki ineh
is it a long way to ...? ineh makri-a ya to ...?
no way! apokli-eteh!

dialogue

could you tell me the way to ...? boriteh na moo thixeteh to thromo ya ...?
go straight on until you reach the traffic lights piyeneteh olo isia mekhri na ftaseteh sta fanaria
turn left stripsteh aristera
take the first on the right parteh ton proto thromo sta thexia
see where

we* emis
weak athinatos
weather o keros

dialogue

what's the weather forecast? ti ipeh to theltio keroo?
it's going to be fine THa ineh kalos keros
it's going to rain THa vrexi
it'll brighten up later THa anixi o keros argotera

wedding o gamos
wedding ring i vera
Wednesday i Tetarti
week i evthomatha
a week (from) today seh mia evthomatha apo simera
a week (from) tomorrow seh mia evthomatha apo avrio
weekend to Savatokiriako
at the weekend to Savatokiriako
weight to varos
weird paraxenos
weirdo o trelaras
welcome: welcome to ... kalos ilTHateh sto ...
you're welcome (don't mention it) parakalo
well: I don't feel well then esTHanomeh kala
she's not well ekini then ineh kala
you speak English very well milateh poli kala Anglika
well done! bravo
this one as well ki afto episis
well well! (surprise) ya thes!

dialogue

how are you? ti kanis?
very well, thanks poli kala,
efkharisto
and you? ki esi?

well-done (meat)
kalopsimenos
Welsh Oo-alos
I'm Welsh (man/woman) imeh
Oo-alos/Oo-ali
were*: we were imasteh
you were isasteh/isteh
they were itan
west thitikos
in the west sta thitika
West Indian (adj) apo tis
thitikes Inthi-es
wet vregmenos
what? ti?
what's that? ti ineh ekino?
what should I do? ti prepi na
kano?
what a view! ti THea!
what bus do I take? ti
leoforio prepi na paro?
wheel i rotha
wheelchair i anapiriki
poliTHrona
when? poteh?
when we get back otan
yirisoomeh
when's the train/ferry? poteh
fevyi to treno/to karavi?
where? poo?
I don't know where it is then
xero poo ineh

dialogue

where is the cathedral?
poo ineh o katнethrikos
naos?
it's over there ineh eki pera
could you show me where
it is on the map? boriteh
na moo thixeteh sto kharti
poo ineh?
it's just here ineh akrivos
etho

see way

which: which bus? pio
leoforio?

dialogue

which one? pio?
that one ekino
this one? afto?
no, that one okhi, ekino

while: while I'm here oso imeh
etho
whisky to whisky
white aspros
white wine to aspro krasi
who? pios?
who is it? pios ineh?
the man who ... o anthropos
poo ...
whole: the whole week oli tin
evthomatha
the whole lot ola
whose: whose is this? pianoo
ineh afto?
why? yati?

Wh

103

why not? yati okhi?

wide platis

wife: my wife i sizigos moo

will: will you do it for me? THa moo to kanis afto?

wind o anemos

window to paraTHiro

near the window konda sto paraTHiro

in the window (of shop) sti vitrina

window seat i THesi sto paraTHiro

windscreen to parbriz

windscreen wiper o ialokaTHaristiras

windsurfing to windsurfing

windy: it's so windy ekhi poli a-era

wine to krasi

can we have some more wine? boroomeh na ekhoomeh ligo krasi akoma?

wine list o katalogos ton krasion

winter o khimonas

in the winter ton khimona

winter holiday i khimerines thiakopes

wire to sirma

(electric) to ilektriko kalothio

wish: best wishes poles efkhes with meh

I'm staying with ... meno meh ...

without khoris

witness o/i martiras

will you be a witness for me? THa iseh martiras

moo?

woman i yineka

wonderful THavmasios

won't*: it won't start then THa xekinisi

wood (material) to xilo

woods (forest) to thasos

wool to mali

word i lexi

work i thoolia

it's not working then thoolevi

I work in ... ergazomeh seh ...

world o kosmos

worry: I'm worried stenokhori-emeh

worry beads to kombolo-i

worse: it's worse ineh khirotera

worst o khiroteros

worth: is it worth a visit? axizi mia episkepsi?

would: would you give this to ...? boriteh na thoseteh afto ston ...?

wrap: could you wrap it up? boriteh na to tilixeteh?

wrapping paper to kharti peritiligmatos

(for presents) kharti ya thora

wrist o karpos

write grafo

could you write it down? boriteh na moo to grapseteh?

how do you write it? pos to grafeteh?

writing paper to kharti alilografias

wrong: it's the wrong key afto

ineh laтноs klithi
the bill's wrong o logariasmos
ineh laтноs
sorry, wrong number signomi,
laтноs noomero
sorry, wrong room signomi,
laтноs thomatio
**there's something wrong
with ...** iparkhi kapio laтноs
meh ...
what's wrong? ti simveni?

X

X-ray i aktinografia

Y
—

yacht to yot
yard* i yartha
(courtyard, backyard) i avli
year o khronos
yellow kitrinos
yes neh
yesterday kh-тнes
yesterday morning kh-тнes
to pro-i
the day before yesterday
prokh-тнes
yet akomi

dialogue

has it arrived yet? akomi
then eftaseh?
no, not yet okhi, okhi
akomi

**you'll have to wait a little
longer yet** тна prepi na
perimeneteh akomi ligo

yoghurt to ya-oorti
you* (fam) esi
(pl or polite) esis
I'll see you later тна seh tho
argotera
this is for you afto ineh ya sas
with you mazi sas
young neos
your* (fam) o/i/to ... soo
(pl or polite) o/i/to ... sas
your camera i fotografiki
mikhani soo/sas
yours (fam) thiko soo
(pl or polite) thiko sas
youth hostel o xenonas neon

Z

zero mithen
zip to fermoo-ar
**could you put a new zip
in?** boriteh na valeteh ena
kenoor-yio fermoo-ar?
zip code o takhithromikos
kothikos
zoo o zo-oloyikos kipos

Greek

→

English

Colloquial Greek

The following are words or expressions you might well hear. You shouldn't be tempted to use any of the stronger ones unless you are sure of your audience.

άντε γαμήσου [andeh gamisoo] fuck off!

βλάκα [vlaka] idiot, blockhead

βρωμο... [vromo] bloody ...

γαμώ το! [gamo to] fuck!

γκόμενα [gomena] bird, chick

γουστάρω [goostaro] I feel like it

δεν πειράζει [den pirazi] it doesn't matter

είσαι; [iseh] do you want to?

έλα [ela] come on!, move!

θαυμάσια! [THavmasia] great!

in [in] fashionable

καμάκι [kamaki] stud, Don Juan

κερατάς [keratas] bastard

μαλάκα [malaka] wanker

μου τα'πρηξες [moo taprixes] you're getting on my tits, you're getting up my nose

μπάτσος [batsos] cop

Παναγία μου [Panayia moo] my God!

πούστης [poostis] faggot, poofter

πουτάνα [pootana] whore

πώ πώ! [po po] bloody hell!

ρε Κώστα [reh Kosta] Kostas, my old pal

ρε μαλάκα [reh malaka] you stupid wanker

σκάσε! [skaseh] shut up!

σκατά! [skata] shit!

στ'αρχίδια μου [starkhidia moo] I don't give a fuck

τζάμπα [tzamba] dirt cheap

τί γίνεται; [ti yineteh] how is it going?

τί νά κάνουμε; [ti na kanoomeh] what can you do?

τύφλα στο μεθύσι [tifla sto meTHisi] pissed (drunk)

A

αγάπη (η) [agapi (i)] love

αγαπημένος [agapimenos] favourite

αγαπώ [agapo] love (verb)

αγγίζω [angizo] touch (verb)

ΑΓΓΛΙΑ Αγγλία (η) [Anglia (i)] England

Αγγλίδα (η) [Anglitha (i)] Englishwoman

ΑΓΓΛΙΚΑ Αγγλικά (τα) [Anglika (ta)] English

ΑΓΓΛΙΚΟΣ Αγγλικός [Anglikos] English

άγγλος (ο) [Anglos (o)] Englishman

αγελάδα (η) [ayelatha (i)] cow

αγενής [ayenis] rude

άγκυρα (η) [angira (i)] anchor

αγκώνας (ο) [angonas (o)] elbow

ΑΓΝΟ ΠΑΡΘΕΝΟ ΜΑΛΛΙ αγνό παρθένο μαλλί pure new wool

ΑΓΟΡΑ αγορά (η) [agora (i)] market

αγοράζω [agorazo] buy (verb)

αγόρι (το) [agori (to)] boy

άγριος [agrios] wild, fierce

αγρόκτημα (το) [agroktima (to)] farm

αγρότης (ο) [agrotis (o)] farmer

αγώνας (ο) [agonas (o)] fight, struggle; game

άδεια (η) [athia (i)] licence; permission

άδεια οδηγήσεως (η) [athia othiyiseos (i)] driving licence

άδειος [athios] empty, vacant

αδελφή (η) [athelfi (i)] sister

ΑΔΕΛΦΟΙ αδελφοί brothers

αδελφός (ο) [athelfos (o)] brother

ΑΔΙΕΞΟΔΟ αδιέξοδο cul-de-sac, dead end

αδύνατος [athinatos] impossible; weak

Α.Ε. public limited company

ΑΕΡΑΝΤΛΙΑ αεραντλία (η) air pump

αέρας (ο) [aeras (o)] air; wind; choke

ΑΕΡΟΔΡΟΜΙΟ αεροδρόμιο (το) [aerothromio (to)] airport

ΑΕΡΟΛΙΜΗΝ αερολιμήν (ο) [aerolimin (o)] airport

αεροπλάνο (το) [aeroplano (to)] plane

αεροπορική εταιρεία (η) [aeroporiki eteria (i)] airline

ΑΕΡΟΠΟΡΙΚΩΣ αεροπορικώς [aeroporikos] by air; by air mail

ΑΕΡΟΣΥΝΟΔΟΣ αεροσυνοδός (ο/η) [aerosinothos (o/i)] steward, stewardess

ΑΘΗΝΑ Αθήνα (η) [ATHina (i)] Athens

αθλητής (ο) [aTHlitis (o)] athlete

ΑΘΛΗΤΙΚΑ αθλητικά (τα) [aTHlitika (ta)] sports shop

αθλητικά παπούτσια (τα) [aTHlitika papootsia (ta)] trainers

ΑΘΛΗΤΙΚΕΣ ΕΓΚΑΤΑΣΤΑΣΕΙΣ αθλητικές εγκαταστάσεις sporting facilities

αθλητική φόρμα (η) [aTHlitiki forma (i)] tracksuit

ΑΘΛΗΤΙΚΟ ΚΕΝΤΡΟ αθλητικό

κέντρο (το) [aTHlitiko kendro (to)] sports centre

αθώος [aTHoos] innocent

ΑΙΓΑΙΟ Αιγαίο (το) [E-yeo (to)] Aegean

ΑΙΘΟΥΣΑ ΤΡΑΝΖΙΤ αίθουσα τράνζιτ transit lounge

αίμα (το) [ema (to)] blood

αιμορραγώ [emorago] bleed

αισθάνομαι [esTHanomeh] feel (verb)

ΑΙΤΗΣΗ αίτηση (η) [etisi (i)] application form; application

αιτία (η) [etia (i)] cause; reason εξ αιτίας ... [exetias ...] because of ...

αιώνας (ο) [eonas (o)] century

ΑΚΑΤΑΛΛΗΛΟ ακατάλληλο adults only

Α΄ ΚΑΤΗΓΟΡΙΑΣ Α΄ κατηγορίας first class

ακολουθώ [akolooTHo] follow

ακόμα, ακόμη [akoma, akomi] still, yet; even; also

ακουστικά (τα) [akoostika (ta)] hearing aid; headphones

ΑΚΟΥΣΤΙΚΟ ακουστικό (το) [akoostiko (to)] receiver

ακούω [akoo-o] hear; listen

άκρη (η) [akri (i)] edge; end; tip

ΑΚΡΙΒΕΣ ΑΝΤΙΤΙΜΟ ΜΟΝΟ ακριβές αντίτιμο μόνο exact fare only

ακριβός [akrivos] expensive

ακροατήριο (το) [akroatirio (to)] audience

ΑΚΡΥΛΙΚΟ ακρυλικό [akriliko] acrylic

ΑΚΤΗ ακτή (η) [akti (i)] beach; coast, shore

ακυρώνω [akirono] cancel

ΑΛΒΑΝΙΑ Αλβανία (η) [Alvania (i)] Albania

αληθινός [aliTHinos] true; real

αλλά [alla] but

ΑΛΛΑΓΗ ΛΑΔΙΩΝ αλλαγή λαδιών oil change

αλλάζω [allazo] change (verb)

αλλάζω ρούχα [allazo rookha] change one's clothes

ΑΛΛΕΡΓΙΑ αλλεργία (η) [alleryia (i)] allergy

ΑΛΛΕΡΓΙΑ ΣΤΗ ΓΥΡΗ αλλεργία στη γύρη [alleryia sti yiri] hay fever

αλλεργικός σε [alleryikos seh] allergic to

άλλη [ali] other; else

άλλη μία [ali mia] another

άλλο [alo] other; else; another

όχι άλλο [okhi alo] no more

άλλο ένα [alo ena] another

άλλος [alos] other; else

άλλος ένας [alos enas] another

αλλού [aloo] elsewhere

αλμυρός [almiros] salty

άλογο (το) [alogo (to)] horse

ΑΛΟΙΦΗ αλοιφή (η) [alifi (i)] ointment

αλουμινόχαρτο (το) [aloominokharto (to)] aluminium foil

ΑΛΣΟΣ άλσος (το) [alsos (to)] wooded park, grove

αλτ! [alt!] stop!

αλυσίδα (η) [alisitha (i)] chain

ΑΜΑΞΑ άμαξα (η) [amaxa (i)] coach, car (on train)

ΑΜΑΞΙ αμάξι (το) [amaxi (to)] car (on train)

ΑΜΑΞΟΣΤΟΙΧΙΑ αμαξοστοιχία (η) [amaxostikhia (i)] train

Αμερικανίδα (η) [Amerikanitha (i)] American (woman)

Αμερικανικός [Amerikanikos] American (adj)

Αμερικανός (ο) [Amerikanos (o)] American (man)

ΑΜΕΡΙΚΗ Αμερική (η) [Ameriki (i)] America

ΑΜΕΣΟΣ ΔΡΑΣΙΣ άμεσος δράσις emergencies

αμέσως [amesos] immediately

αμμόλοφοι (οι) [amolofi (i)] sand dunes

άμμος (η) [amos (i)] sand

αμορτισέρ (το) [amortiser (to)] shock-absorber

αμπέλι (το) [ambeli (to)] vineyard

αμπέρ (το) [amper] amp

ΑΜΠΟΥΛΕΣ αμπούλες ampoules

αν [an] if

ΑΝΑΒΡΑΖΟΝΤΑ ΔΙΣΚΙΑ αναβράζοντα δισκία effervescent tablets

ανάβω [anavo] light (verb)

αναγκαίος [anangeos] necessary

ανάγκη [anangi] need

αναγνωρίζω [anagnorizo] recognize, acknowledge, admit

ανακατεύω [anakatevo] mix (verb)

ΑΝΑΚΟΙΝΩΣΗ ανακοίνωση (η) [anakinosi (i)] announcement

ΑΝΑΚΛΗΣΙΣ ανάκλησις (η)

[anaklisis (i)] withdrawal

ΑΝΑΛΗΨΗ ανάληψη withdrawal(s) (of money)

αναμείνατε στο ακουστικό [anaminateh sto akoostiko] hold the line please

ανάμεσα [anamesa] among; between

αναπαύομαι [anapavomeh] rest, relax

ανάπαυση (η) [anapafsi (i)] rest

αναπαυτικός [anapaftikos] comfortable

αναπηρική πολυθρόνα (η) [anapiriki polithrona (i)] wheelchair

ανάπηρος [anapiros] disabled

αναπνέω [anapneo] breathe

αναποδογυρίζω [anapothoyirizo] knock over

αναπτήρας (ο) [anaptiras (o)] lighter

αναπτύσσω [anaptiso] develop; explain

ανατολή (η) [anatoli (i)] east; dawn

ανατολή του ήλιου (η) [anatoli too ilioo (i)] sunrise

ΑΝΑΧΩΡΕΙ ΚΑΘΗΜΕΡΙΝΑ ΓΙΑ ... αναχωρεί καθημερινά γιά ... departs daily to ...

ΑΝΑΧΩΡΗΣΕΙΣ αναχωρήσεις departures

ΑΝΑΧΩΡΗΣΗ αναχώρηση (η) [anakhorisi (i)] departure

ΑΝΑΨΥΚΤΗΡΙΟ αναψυκτήριο refreshments

άνδρας (ο) [anthras (o)] man

ΑΝΔΡΙΚΑ ανδρικά (τα) [anthrika

(ta)] menswear

ΑΝΔΡΙΚΑ ΕΙΔΗ ΚΑΙ ΑΞΕΣΟΥΑΡ ανδρικά είδη και αξεσουάρ [anthrika ithi ke axesooar] men's fashions and accessories

ΑΝΔΡΙΚΑ ΕΝΔΥΜΑΤΑ ανδρικά ενδύματα [anthrika enthimata] menswear

ΑΝΔΡΙΚΑ ΕΣΩΡΟΥΧΑ ανδρικά εσώρουχα [anthrika esorookha] men's underwear

ΑΝΔΡΙΚΑΙ ΚΟΜΜΩΣΕΙΣ ανδρικαί κομμώσεις [anthrikeh komosis] men's hairdresser

ΑΝΔΡΙΚΑ ΥΠΟΔΗΜΑΤΑ ανδρικά υποδήματα [anthrika ipothimata] men's footwear

ΑΝΔΡΙΚΑ ΥΠΟΚΑΜΙΣΑ ανδρικά υποκάμισα [anthrika ipokamisa] men's shirts

ΑΝΔΡΩΝ ανδρών gents' (toilet), men's room

ανεβαίνω [aneveno] get in (car); get up; go up

ΑΝΕΛΚΥΣΤΗΡΑΣ ανελκυστήρας (ο) [anelkistiras (o)] lift, elevator

ΑΝΕΜΙΣΤΗΡΑΣ ανεμιστήρας (ο) [anemistiras (o)] fan

άνεμος (ο) [anemos (o)] wind

ΑΝΕΞΑΡΤΗΤΟ ΔΙΑΜΕΡΙΣΜΑ ανεξάρτητο διαμέρισμα (το) [anexartito thiamerisma (to)] self-catering apartment

ανεξάρτητος [anexartitos] independent

άνεργος [anergos] unemployed

ανήκω [aniko] belong

ανησυχώ [anisikho] be anxious, be worried

ανησυχώ για [anisikho ya] worry about

ανηψιά (η) [anipsia (i)] niece

ανηψιός (ο) [anipsios (o)] nephew

ΑΝΘΟΠΩΛΕΙΟ ανθοπωλείο (το) [anтнopolio (to)] florist's

άνθρωποι (οι) [anтнropi (i)] people

αν και [an keh] although

ΑΝΟΔΟΣ άνοδος (η) [anothos (i)] ascent, way up

ανοίγω [anigo] open (verb); switch on

ανοίγω τις βαλίτσες [anigo tis valitses] unpack

ΑΝΟΙΚΤΑ ανοικτά [anikta] open

ΑΝΟΙΚΤΟ ΑΠΟ ... ΩΣ ... ανοικτό από ... ως ... [anikto apo ... os ...] open from ... to ...

ΑΝΟΙΚΤΟΝ ανοικτόν [anikton] open (adj)

ανοικτός [aniktos] open (adj); on (light)

άνοιξη (η) [anixi (i)] spring (season)

ανοιχτήρι (το) [anikhtiri (to)] tin opener; corkscrew

ΑΝΟΙΧΤΟ ανοιχτό [anikhto] open; light (colour)

ΑΝΤΑΛΛΑΚΤΙΚΑ ανταλλακτικά (τα) spare parts

ΑΝΤΑΛΛΑΚΤΙΚΑ ΑΥΤΟΚΙΝΗΤΩΝ ανταλλακτικά αυτοκινήτων (τα) auto spares

ανταλλάσω [andalaso] exchange (verb)

άντε! [andeh!] come on!

αντέχω [andekho] endure, tolerate

αντί [andi] instead of

ΑΝΤΙΒΙΟΤΙΚΟ αντιβιοτικό (το) [andiviotiko (to)] antibiotic

ΑΝΤΙ-ΙΣΤΑΜΙΝΙΚΟ ΦΑΡΜΑΚΟ αντι-ισταμινικό φάρμακο (το) [andi-istaminiko farmako (to)] antihistamine

αντίκα (η) [andika (i)] antique

ΑΝΤΙΚΕΣ αντίκες [andikes] antiques

αντίο [andio] goodbye

αντιπαθητικός [andipaτHitikos] obnoxious

ΑΝΤΙΠΡΟΣΩΠΕΙΑ ΑΥΤΟΚΙΝΗΤΩΝ αντιπροσωπεία αυτοκινήτων (η) [andiprosopia aftokiniton (i)] car dealer

ΑΝΤΙΠΡΟΣΩΠΟΣ αντιπρόσωπος (ο) [andiprosopos (o)] agent

αντιπυρετικό [andipiretiko] anti-fever

ΑΝΤΙΣΗΠΤΙΚΟ αντισηπτικό (το) [andisiptiko (to)] antiseptic

ΑΝΤΙΣΥΛΛΗΠΤΙΚΟ αντισυλληπτικό (το) [andisiliptiko (to)] contraceptive

ΑΝΤΙΣΥΛΛΗΠΤΙΚΟ ΧΑΠΙ αντισυλληπτικό χάπι (το) [andisiliptiko khapi (to)] contraceptive pill

ΑΝΤΙΤΙΜΟ (ΔΙΑΔΡΟΜΗΣ) αντίτιμο (διαδρομής) (το) [anditimo (thiathromis) (to)] fare

ΑΝΤΙΦΛΕΓΜΩΔΕΣ

αντιφλεγμώδες anti-inflammation

αντλία (η) [andlia (i)] pump

ΑΝΤΛΙΑ ΒΕΝΖΙΝΗΣ αντλία βενζίνης petrol/gas pump

ΑΝΤΛΙΑ ΝΤΙΖΕΛ αντλία ντίζελ diesel pump

ΑΝΩ άνω [ano] up

ΑΞΕΣΟΥΑΡ ΑΥΤΟΚΙΝΗΤΩΝ αξεσουάρ αυτοκινήτων (τα) auto accessories

άξονας (ο) [axonas (o)] axle

ΑΠΑΓΟΡΕΥΕΤΑΙ απαγορεύεται it is prohibited

ΑΠΑΓΟΡΕΥΕΤΑΙ Η ΕΙΣΟΔΟΣ απαγορεύεται η είσοδος no entry, no admission

ΑΠΑΓΟΡΕΥΕΤΑΙ Η ΚΑΤΑΠΟΣΙΣ απαγορεύεται η κατάποσις do not swallow

ΑΠΑΓΟΡΕΥΕΤΑΙ Η ΚΑΤΑΣΚΗΝΩΣΗ απαγορεύεται η κατασκήνωση no camping

ΑΠΑΓΟΡΕΥΕΤΑΙ Η ΚΟΛΥΜΒΗΣΗ απαγορεύεται η κολύμβηση no swimming

ΑΠΑΓΟΡΕΥΕΤΑΙ Η ΛΗΨΙΣ ΔΙΑ ΤΟΥ ΣΤΟΜΑΤΟΣ απαγορεύεται η λήψις διά του στόματος not to be taken orally

ΑΠΑΓΟΡΕΥΕΤΑΙ Η ΣΤΑΘΜΕΥΣΗ απαγορεύεται η στάθμευση no parking

ΑΠΑΓΟΡΕΥΕΤΑΙ Η ΣΤΑΣΗ απαγορεύεται η στάση no waiting, no stopping

ΑΠΑΓΟΡΕΥΕΤΑΙ Η ΧΟΡΗΓΗΣΗ ΑΝΕΥ ΣΥΝΤΑΓΗΣ ΙΑΤΡΟΥ απαγορεύεται η χορήγηση άνευ συνταγής ιατρού available on prescription only

ΑΠΑΓΟΡΕΥΕΤΑΙ Ο ΓΥΜΝΙΣΜΟΣ απαγορεύεται ο γυμνισμός nudism prohibited

ΑΠΑΓΟΡΕΥΟΝΤΑΙ ΟΙ ΚΑΤΑΔΥΣΕΙΣ απαγορεύονται οι καταδύσεις no diving

ΑΠΑΓΟΡΕΥΕΤΑΙ ΤΟ ΚΑΜΠΙΝΓΚ απαγορεύεται το κάμπινγκ no camping

ΑΠΑΓΟΡΕΥΕΤΑΙ ΤΟ ΚΑΠΝΙΖΕΙΝ απαγορεύεται το καπνίζειν no smoking

ΑΠΑΓΟΡΕΥΕΤΑΙ ΤΟ ΚΑΠΝΙΣΜΑ απαγορεύεται το κάπνισμα no smoking

ΑΠΑΓΟΡΕΥΕΤΑΙ ΤΟ ΚΥΝΗΓΙ απαγορεύεται το κυνήγι no hunting

ΑΠΑΓΟΡΕΥΕΤΑΙ ΤΟ ΠΡΟΣΠΕΡΑΣΜΑ απαγορεύεται το προσπέρασμα no overtaking, no passing

ΑΠΑΓΟΡΕΥΕΤΑΙ ΤΟ ΨΑΡΕΜΑ απαγορεύεται το ψάρεμα no fishing

ΑΠΑΓΟΡΕΥΜΕΝΗ ΠΕΡΙΟΧΗ απαγορευμένη περιοχή restricted area

απαγορευμένος [apagorevmenos] forbidden

απαίσιος [apesios] appalling

απαιτώ [apeto] demand (verb)

απαλός [apalos] soft

απαντάω [apandao] answer (verb)

απάντηση (η) [apandisi (i)] answer

απέντανος [apendaros] broke

απίθανος [apiTHanos] incredible

ΑΠΛΗ ΒΕΝΖΙΝΗ απλή βενζίνη **(η)** [apli venzini (i)] two-star petrol/gas

ΑΠΛΗ ΔΙΑΔΡΟΜΗ απλή διαδρομή **(η)** [apli thiathromi (i)] single/one-way fare

ΑΠΛΟ ΕΙΣΙΤΗΡΙΟ απλό εισιτήριο **(το)** [aplo isitirio (to)] single/one-way ticket

απλός [aplos] simple

απλώνω [aplono] stretch (verb)

από [apo] from; since; than

από το ... στο ... [apo to ... sto ...] from ... to ...

από κάτω [apo kato] below, under

από πάνω [apo pano] over, above

αποβιβάζομαι [apovivazomeh] land (verb)

απογειώνομαι [apoyionomeh] take off (verb)

απόγευμα (το) [apoyevma (to)] afternoon

το απόγευμα [to apoyevma] in the afternoon

ΑΠΟΓΕΥΜΑΤΙΝΗ ΠΑΡΑΣΤΑΣΗ απογευματινή παράσταση **(η)** [apoyevmatini parastasi (i)] matinee

απογοητευμένος [apogo-itevmenos] disappointed

ΑΠΟΔΕΙΞΗ απόδειξη **(η)** [apoTHixi (i)] receipt, evidence

ΑΠΟ ΔΕΥΤΕΡΟ ΧΕΡΙ από δεύτερο χέρι [apo theftero kheri] second-hand

ΑΠΟΛΥΜΑΝΤΙΚΟ απολυμαντικό (το) [apolimandiko (to)] disinfectant

ΑΠΟΣΚΕΥΕΣ αποσκευές (οι) [aposkeves (i)] luggage, baggage

ΑΠΟΣΜΗΤΙΚΟ αποσμητικό (το) [aposmitiko (to)] deodorant

ΑΠΟΣΤΟΛΕΑΣ αποστολέας [apostoleas] sender

απότομος [apotomos] steep

απότομος βράχος (ο) [apotomos vrakhos (o)] cliff

αποφασίζω [apofasizo] decide

απόψε [apopseh] tonight

ΑΠΡΙΛΙΟΣ Απρίλιος (ο) [Aprilios (o)] April

Α΄ ΠΡΟΒΟΛΗΣ α΄ προβολής major cinema/movie theater

απρόσμενος [aprosmenos] surprising

ΑΠΩΛΕΣΘΕΝΤΑ ΑΝΤΙΚΕΙΜΕΝΑ απωλεσθέντα αντικείμενα [apolesτHenda adikimena] lost property

αράχνη (η) [arakhni (i)] spider

αργά [arga] late; slowly

αργίες (οι) [aryies (i)] public holidays

αργός [argos] slow

αργότερα [argotera] later

αργώ [argo] arrive late; go slowly

ΑΡΙΘΜΟΣ αριθμός (ο) [ariΤHmos (o)] number

ΑΡΙΘΜΟΣ ΘΕΣΕΩΣ αριθμός θέσεως [ariΤHmos ΤHeseos] seat number

αριστερά [aristera] left

αριστερόχειρας [aristerokhiras] left-handed

αρκετά [arketa] enough; quite

αρκετοί [arketi] several

αρνητικό (το) [arnitiko (to)] negative

αρουραίος (ο) [aroureos (o)] rat

αρραβωνιασμένος [aravoniasmenos] engaged (to be married)

αρραβωνιαστικιά (η) [aravoniastikia (i)] fiancée

αρραβωνιαστικός (ο) [aravoniastikos (o)] fiancé

αρρενωπός [arenopos] manly; macho

αρρώστια (η) [arostia (i)] disease

άρρωστος [arostos] ill, sick

ΑΡΤΟΠΟΙΕΙΟ αρτοποιείο (το) [artopi-io (to)] bakery

αρχαιολογία (η) [arkheoloyia (i)] archaeology

αρχαίος [arkheos] ancient

αρχαιότητες (οι) [arkhcotites (i)] ruins

αρχάρια (η) [arkharia (i)] beginner

αρχάριος (ο) [arkharios (o)] beginner

αρχή (η) [arkhi (i)] beginning

αρχίζω [arkhizo] begin

αρχιτέκτων (ο/η) [arkhitekton (o/i)] architect

άρωμα (το) [aroma (to)] perfume

ΑΣΑΝΣΕΡ ασανσέρ (το) [asanser

(to)] lift, elevator

ασετόν (το) [aseton (to)] nail varnish remover

ΑΣΗΜΕΝΙΟΣ ασημένιος [asimenios] silver

ΑΣΗΜΙΚΑ ασημικά (τα) [asimika (ta)] silver(ware)

ΑΣΘΕΝΟΦΟΡΟ ασθενοφόρο (το) [asTHenoforo (to)] ambulance

ΑΣΘΜΑ άσθμα (το) [asTHma (to)] asthma

ΑΣΠΙΡΙΝΗ ασπιρίνη (η) [aspirini (i)] aspirin

άσπρος [aspros] white

άστατος [astatos] changeable

αστείο (το) [astio (to)] joke

αστείος [astios] funny, amusing

αστέρι (το) [asteri (to)] star

αστράγαλος (ο) [astragalos (o)] ankle

ΑΣΤΥΝΟΜΙΑ αστυνομία (η) [astinomia (i)] police

ΑΣΤΥΝΟΜΙΚΟ ΤΜΗΜΑ αστυνομικό τμήμα (το) [astinomiko tmima (to)] police station

αστυφύλακας (ο) [astifilakas (o)] policeman

αστυνομικός (η) [astinomikos (i)] policewoman

ΑΣΦΑΛΕΙΑ ασφάλεια (η) [asfalia (i)] fuse; insurance

ΑΣΦΑΛΕΙΑΙ ασφάλειαι [asfali-eh] insurance

ασφαλής [asfalis] safe

άσχημα [askhima] badly

άσχημος [askhimos] ugly

ατζέντα (η) [atzenda (i)] address

book

ατμόπλοιο (το) [atmoplio (to)] steamer

άτομο (το) [atomo (to)] person

ΑΥΓΟΥΣΤΟΣ Αύγουστος (ο) [Avgoostos (o)] August

αυθεντικός [afтнendikos] genuine

αύριο [avrio] tomorrow

Αυστραλέζα (η) [Afstraleza (i)] Australian (woman)

Αυστραλέζικος [Afstralezikos] Australian (adj)

ΑΥΣΤΡΑΛΙΑ Αυστραλία (η) [Afstralia (i)] Australia

Αυστραλός (ο) [Afstralos (o)] Australian (man)

αυτά, αυτές [afta, aftes] these; they; them

αυτή [afti] she; this (one)

αυτής [aftis] of her

αυτί (το) [afti (to)] ear

αυτό [afto] it; this

αυτό εδώ [afto etho] this one

αυτοί [afti] these; they

ΑΥΤΟΚΙΝΗΤΟ αυτοκίνητο (το) [aftokinito (to)] car

αυτόματος [aftomatos] automatic (adj)

αυτό που [afto poo] what

αυτός [aftos] he; this (one)

αυτός ο ίδιος [aftos o ithios] himself

αυτού [aftoo] of him, of it

αυτούς [aftoos] them

ΑΥΤ/ΤΟ αυτ/το car

αυτών [afton] of them

αφεντικό (το) [afendiko (to)] boss

ΑΦΕΤΗΡΙΑ αφετηρία (η) [afetiria (i)] terminus

αφήνω [afino] leave (verb)
ΑΦΙΞΕΙΣ αφίξεις arrivals
ΑΦΙΞΗ άφιξη (η) [afixi (i)] arrival
αφίσα (η) [afisa (i)] poster
ΑΦΟΙ. αφοί. bros.
ΑΦΟΡΟΛΟΓΗΤΑ αφορολόγητα (τα) [aforoloyita (ta)] duty-free
αφροδίσιο νόσημα (το) [afrothisio nosima (to)] VD
ΑΦΡΟΣ ΞΥΡΙΣΜΑΤΟΣ αφρός ξυρίσματος (ο) [afros xirismatos (o)] shaving foam
αφρός (ο) [afros (o)] surf
αχθοφόρος (ο) [akhтнoforos (o)] doorman
αχινός (ο) [akhinos (o)] sea urchin

B
■

ΒΑΓΟΝΙ βαγόνι (το) [vagoni (to)] coach, car (train)
ΒΑΓΚΟΝ-ΛΙ βαγκόν-λι [vagon-li] sleeper, sleeping car
βάζο (το) [vazo (to)] vase
βάζω [vazo] put
ΒΑΘΙΑ ΝΕΡΑ βαθιά νερά deep water
βάθος: στο βάθος [sto vaтнos] in the background; at the bottom
βαθύς [vaтнis] deep
βαλβίδα (η) [valvitha (i)] valve
βαλίτσα (η) [valitsa (i)] bag, suitcase
ΒΑΜΒΑΚΕΡΟ βαμβακερό (το) [vamvakero (to)] cotton
βαρετός [varetos] boring

ΒΑΡΚΑ βάρκα (η) [varka (i)] small boat; dinghy
βάρκα με κουπιά [varka meh koopia] rowing boat
βάρκα με μηχανή [varka meh mikhani] motorboat
ΒΑΡΟΣ βάρος (το) [varos (to)] weight
βαρύς [varis] heavy; rich (food)
βασιλιάς (ο) [vasilias (o)] king
βασίλισσα (η) [vasilisa (i)] queen
ΒΑΦΗ βαφή (η) [vafi (i)] hair dye
βάφω [vafo] paint; tint (verb)
βγάζω φωτογραφία [vgazo fotografia] photograph (verb)
βγαίνω [vgeno] go out
ΒΓΑΛΤΕ ΤΗΝ ΚΑΡΤΑ βγάλτε την κάρτα remove the card
βέβαια [veveh-a] of course
βελόνα (η) [velona (i)] needle
βελτιώνω [veltiono] improve
ΒΕΝΖΙΝΑΔΙΚΟ βενζινάδικο (το) [venzinathiko (to)] petrol station, gas station
ΒΕΝΖΙΝΗ βενζίνη (η) [venzini (i)] petrol, gas(oline)
βεντιλατέρ (το) [vendllater (to)] fan belt
ΒΕΡΝΙΚΙ ΠΑΠΟΥΤΣΙΩΝ βερνίκι παπουτσιών (το) [verniki papootsion (to)] shoe polish
ΒΗΧΑΣ βήχας (ο) [vikhas (o)] cough
βήχω [vikho] cough (verb)
βιάζομαι [viazomeh] hurry (verb)
βιάσου! [viasoo!] hurry up!
βιασμός (ο) [viasmos (o)] rape
βιβλίο (το) [vivlio (to)] book

βιβλίο διαλόγων [vivlio thialogon] phrase book

ΒΙΒΛΙΟΘΗΚΗ βιβλιοθήκη (η) [vivlioτHiki (i)] library

ΒΙΒΛΙΟΠΩΛΕΙΟ βιβλιοπωλείο (το) [vivliopolio (to)] bookshop, bookstore

ΒΙΔΑ βίδα (η) [vitha (i)] screw

ΒΙΖΑ βίζα (η) [viza (i)] visa

βίλλα (η) [vila (i)] villa

βίντεο (το) [video (to)] video

ΒΙΤΑΜΙΝΕΣ βιταμίνες (οι) [vitamines (i)] vitamins

Β΄ ΚΑΤΗΓΟΡΙΑΣ Β΄ κατηγορίας second class

βλάβη (η) [vlavi (i)] breakdown (car)

βλάκας (ο) [vlakas (o)] idiot; stupid

βλέπω [vlepo] see

βοήθεια (η) [voiTHia (i)] help

βοηθώ [vo-iTHo] help (verb)

βόμβα (η) [vomva (i)] bomb

Βόρειος Ιρλανδία (η) [vorios Irlanthia (i)] Northern Ireland

ΒΟΥΛΓΑΡΙΑ Βουλγαρία (η) [voolgaria (i)] Bulgaria

Βουλγαρικός [voolgarikos] Bulgarian (adj)

βουλιάζω [vooliazo] sink (verb)

ΒΟΥΛΚΑΝΙΖΑΤΕΡ βουλκανιζατέρ [voolkanizater] tyre repairs

βουνό (το) [voono (to)] mountain

βούρτσα (η) [voortsa (i)] brush

βουτάω [vootao] dive (verb)

Β΄ ΠΡΟΒΟΛΗΣ β΄ προβολής local cinema/movie theater

βράδυ (το) [vrathi (to)] evening

το βράδυ [to vrathi] in the evening

βραδυά (η) [vrathia (i)] evening

ΒΡΑΔΥΝΗ ΠΑΡΑΣΤΑΣΗ βραδυνή παράσταση evening performance

βράζω [vrazo] boil (verb)

βράχια (τα) [vrakhia (ta)] rocks; cliffs

βραχιόλι (το) [vrakhioli (to)] bracelet

βράχος (ο) [vrakhos (o)] rock

ΒΡΕΤΑΝΝΙΑ Βρεταννία (η) [vretania (i)] Britain

Βρεταννίδα (η) [vretanitha (i)] Briton (woman)

Βρεταννικός [vretanikos] British

Βρεταννός (ο) [vretanos (o)] Briton (man)

βρέχει [vrekhi] it's raining

βρίσκω [vrisko] find (verb)

βροντή (η) [vrondi (i)] thunder

βροχή (η) [vrokhi (i)] rain

βρύση (η) [vrisi (i)] tap, faucet

βρώμικος [vromikos] dirty

βυζαίνω [vizeno] breastfeed

βυθός (ο) [viτHos (o)] bottom (of sea)

Γ

γάιδαρος (ο) [gaitharos (o)] donkey

ΓΑΛΑΚΤΟΠΩΛΕΙΟ γαλακτοπωλείο (το) [galaktopolio (to)] shop/take-away café selling dairy products

ΓΑΛΑΚΤΩΜΑ ΚΑΘΑΡΙΣΜΟΥ

γαλάκτωμα καθαρισμού (το)
[galaktoma kaтHarismoo (to)]
cleansing lotion

ΓΑΛΛΙΑ Γαλλία (η) [galia (i)]
France

Γαλλικός [galikos] French (adj)

γάμος (ο) [gamos (o)] wedding

γαμπρός (ο) [gambros (o)]
bridegroom; son-in-law;
brother-in-law

γάντια (τα) [gandia (ta)] gloves

γάτα (η) [gata (i)] cat

γειά σου! [yia soo!] hello!; bless
you!; cheers!

γείτονας (ο) [yitonas (o)]
neighbour

γελοίο [yelio] ridiculous

γελώ [yelo] laugh (verb)

γεμάτος [yematos] full

γεμίζω [yemizo] fill (verb)

γενέθλια (τα) [yeneтHlia (ta)]
birthday

γένια (τα) [yenia (ta)] beard

γενναίος [yeneos] brave

ΓΕΡΜΑΝΙΑ Γερμανία (η)
[Yermania (i)] Germany

Γερμανικός [Yermanikos]
German (adj)

γέρος [yeros] old (person)

ΓΕΥΜΑ γεύμα (το) [yevma (to)]
meal

γεύση (η) [yefsi (i)] flavour; taste

ΓΕΦΥΡΑ γέφυρα (η) [yefira (i)]
bridge

ΓΗΠΕΔΟ γήπεδο (το) [yipetho
(to)] football pitch

ΓΗΠΕΔΟ ΤΕΝΝΙΣ γήπεδο
τέννις [yipetho tenis] tennis
court

για [ya] for

για μένα [ya mena] for me

γιαγιά (η) [yaya (i)] grandmother

ΓΙΑ ΕΞΩΤΕΡΙΚΗ ΧΡΗΣΗ
ΜΟΝΟΝ για εξωτερική χρήση
μόνον for external use only

ΓΙΑ ΕΣΩΤΕΡΙΚΗ ΧΡΗΣΗ
ΜΟΝΟΝ για εσωτερική χρήση
μόνον for internal use only

ΓΙΑ ΤΟ ΣΠΙΤΙ για το σπίτι [ya to
spiti] to take away, to go (food)

ΓΙΑΤΡΟΣ γιατρός (ο/η) [yatros
(o/i)] doctor

γίνομαι [yinomeh] become;
happen

τι γίνεται; [ti yineteh?] what's
happening?

ΓΙΟΡΤΗ ΚΡΑΣΙΟΥ γιορτή
κρασιού (η) [yorti krasioo (i)]
wine festival

γιός (ο) [yos (o)] son

γιώτ (το) [yot (to)] yacht

γκάζι (το) [gazi (to)] gas;
accelerator

ΓΚΑΛΕΡΙ γκαλερί (η) [galeri (i)]
art gallery

ΓΚΑΡΑΖ γκαράζ (το) [garaz (to)]
garage (for parking/repairs)

ΓΚΑΡΝΤΑΡΟΜΠΑ
γκαρνταρόμπα (η) [gardaroba (i)]
cloakroom (for coats)

Γ΄ ΚΑΤΗΓΟΡΙΑΣ
Γ΄ κατηγορίας third class

γκολφ (το) [golf (to)] golf

γκρίζος [grizos] grey

γκρουπ (το) [groop (to)] group

γλάρος (ο) [glaros (o)] seagull

ΓΛΙΦΙΤΖΟΥΡΙ γλιφιτζούρι (το)
[glifidzoori (to)] lollipop

ΓΛΥΚΟ γλυκό (το) [gliko (to)]
sweet, candy

γλυκός [glikos] sweet (adj)

γλυστερός [glisteros] slippery

γλυστράω [glistrao] skid (verb)

γλώσσα (η) [glosa (i)] language;
tongue

γνωρίζω [gnorizo] know
δεν γνωρίζω [then gnorizo] I
don't know

γόνατο (το) [gonato (to)] knee

γονείς (οι) [gonis (i)] parents

γουίντσερφ (το) [gooindserf (to)]
sailboard

ΓΟΥΝΑΡΙΚΑ γουναρικά (τα)
[goonarika (ta)] furrier

ΓΟΥΝΕΣ γούνες [goones] furs

γουόκμαν (το) [goo-okman (to)]
personal stereo

γουρούνι (το) [goorooni (to)] pig

γοφός (ο) [gofos (o)] hip

γραβάτα (η) [gravata (i)] tie,
necktie

γράμμα (το) [grama (to)] letter

γράμματα (τα) [gramata (ta)]
post, mail

γραμματική (η) [gramatiki (i)]
grammar

ΓΡΑΜΜΑΤΟΚΙΒΩΤΙΟ
γραμματοκιβώτιο (το)
[gramatokivotio (to)] letterbox,
mailbox

γραμματόσημο (το) [gramatosimo
(to)] stamp

ΓΡΑΜΜΕΣ ΤΡΑΙΝΟΥ γραμμές
τραίνου railway crosses road

ΓΡΑΜΜΗ γραμμή (η) [grami (i)]

route, line

γρασίδι (το) [grasithi (to)] lawn

γραφείο (το) [grafio (to)] office

ΓΡΑΦΕΙΟ ΤΑΞΙΔΙΩΝ γραφείο
ταξιδίων [grafio taxithion] travel
agency

γραφομηχανή (η) [grafomikhani (i)]
typewriter

γράφω [grafo] write

γρήγορα [grigora] quick;
quickly

γρήγορος [grigoros] fast

ΓΡΙΠΠΗ γρίππη (η) [gripi (i)] flu

γρύλλος (ο) [grilos (o)] jack

γυαλί (το) [yali (to)] glass (material)

ΓΥΑΛΙΑ γυαλιά (τα) [yalia (ta)]
glasses, eyeglasses

ΓΥΑΛΙΑ ΗΛΙΟΥ γυαλιά ηλίου
[yalia ilioo] sunglasses

ΓΥΜΝΑΣΙΟ γυμνάσιο (το)
[yimnasio (to)] secondary school

γυμνασμένος [yimnasmenos] fit
(healthy)

ΓΥΜΝΑΣΤΗΡΙΟ γυμναστήριο
(το) [yimnastirio (to)] gym

γυμνός [yimnos] naked

γυναίκα (η) [yineka (i)] woman;
wife

ΓΥΝΑΙΚΕΙΑ γυναικεία (τα)
[yinekia (ta)] ladies' wear

ΓΥΝΑΙΚΕΙΑΙ ΚΟΜΜΩΣΕΙΣ
γυναικείαι κομμώσεις (οι)
[yinekieh komosis (i)] ladies'
salon

ΓΥΝΑΙΚΕΙΑ ΦΟΡΕΜΑΤΑ
γυναικεία φορέματα [yinekia
foremata] ladies' dresses

**ΓΥΝΑΙΚΕΙΕΣ ΚΑΛΤΣΕΣ -
ΚΑΛΣΟΝ** γυναικείες κάλτσες -

καλσόν [yinekies kaltses - kalson] ladies' socks - stockings

ΓΥΝΑΙΚΩΝ γυναικών ladies' (toilet), ladies' room

γυρνώ [yirno] turn (verb)

γυρνώ πίσω [yirno piso] arrive back, return; take back

γυρνώ σπίτι [yirno spiti] return home

Δ
—

δακτυλίδι (το) [thaktilithi (to)] ring (on finger)

δανείζομαι [thanizomeh] borrow

δανείζω [thanizo] lend

δασκάλα (η) [thaskala (i)] instructor; teacher

δάσκαλος (ο) [thaskalos (o)] instructor; teacher

δάσος (το) [thasos (to)] forest

δάχτυλο (το) [thakhtilo (to)] finger

δάχτυλο του ποδιού [thakhtilo too pothioo] toe

δε [theh] ξου

Δ.Ε.Η. public electricity company

δείκτης (ο) [thiktis (o)] gauge; index finger

ΔΕΙΠΝΟ δείπνο (το) [thipno (to)] evening meal

δείχνω [thikhno] show (verb)

δέκα [theka] ten

δεκαεννιά [theka-enia] nineteen

δεκαέξι [theka-exi] sixteen

δεκαεπτά [theka-epta] seventeen

δεκαοχτώ [theka-okhto] eighteen

δεκαπενθήμερο [thekapenTHimero] fortnight

δεκαπέντε [thekapendeh] fifteen

ΔΕΚΑΡΙΚΟ δεκάρικο (το) [thekariko (to)] 10-drachma coin

δεκατέσσερα [thekatesera] fourteen

δέκατος [thekatos] tenth

δεκατρία [thekatria] thirteen

ΔΕΚΕΜΒΡΙΟΣ Δεκέμβριος (ο) [thekemvrios (o)] December

δέμα (το) [thema (to)] parcel

ΔΕΜΑΤΑ δέματα parcels, packages

δεν [then] not

δένδρο (το) [thenthro (to)] tree

ΔΕΝ ΛΕΙΤΟΥΡΓΕΙ δεν λειτουργεί [then litooryi] out of order

ΔΕΝ ΣΙΔΕΡΩΝΕΤΑΙ δεν σιδερώνεται do not iron

δεξιός, δεξιά [thexios, thexia] right (side)

δεξίωση (η) [thexiosi (i)] reception (party)

ΔΕΡΜΑ δέρμα (το) [therma (to)] skin; leather

ΔΕΡΜΑΙΑ δέρματα (τα) [thermata (ta)] leather goods

ΔΕΣΠΟΙΝΙΔΑ δεσποινίδα (η) [thespinitha (i)] young woman; Miss; Ms

ΔΕΣΠΟΙΝΙΣ δεσποινίς [thespinis] Miss; Ms

ΔΕΥΤΕΡΑ Δευτέρα (η) [theftera (i)] Monday

ΔΕΥΤΕΡΗ ΘΕΣΗ δεύτερη θέση second class

δευτερόλεπτο (το) [thefterolepto]

(to)] second

δεύτερος [thefteros] second (adj)

ΔΕΥΤΕΡΟ ΧΕΡΙ δεύτερο χέρι [theftero kheri] second-hand

δέχομαι [thekhomeh] accept; receive

δηλητηρίαση (η) [thilitiriasi (i)] poisoning

δηλητήριο (το) [thilitirio (to)] poison

ΔΗΜΑΡΧΕΙΟ δημαρχείο (το) [thimarkhio (to)] town hall

ΔΗΜΟΣΙΑ ΛΟΥΤΡΑ δημόσια λουτρά (τα) [thimosia lootra (ta)] public baths

δημόσιος [thimosios] public

δημοσιογράφος (ο/η) [thimosiografos (o/i)] reporter

δημοτική μουσική (η) [thimotiki moosiki (i)] folk music

διαβάζω [thiavazo] read

ΔΙΑΒΑΣΗ ΠΕΖΩΝ διάβαση πεζών (η) pedestrian crossing

ΔΙΑΒΑΤΗΡΙΟ διαβατήριο (το) [thiavatirio (to)] passport

διαβητικός (ο) [thiavitikos (o)] diabetic

διαβητική (η) [thiavitiki (i)] diabetic

ΔΙΑΔΡΟΜΗ ΜΕΤ' ΕΠΙΣΤΡΟΦΗΣ διαδρομή μετ' επιστροφής (η) [thiathromi met' epistrofis (i)] return/round trip fare

διάδρομος (ο) [thiathromos (o)] corridor

διάθεση (η) [thiaTHesi (i)] mood

δίαιτα (η) [thieta (i)] diet

διακοπές (οι) [thiakopes (i)] holiday, vacation

διακοπή (η) [thiakopi (i)] interruption; power cut

διακόπτης (ο) [thiakoptis (o)] switch

διακόπτω [thiakopto] interrupt

διακόσια [thiakosia] two hundred

διαλέγω [thialego] choose

ΔΙΑΛΕΙΜΜΑ διάλειμμα (το) [thialima (to)] interval, intermission

διάλεκτος (η) [thialektos (i)] dialect

ΔΙΑΛΥΜΑ διάλυμα (το) [thialima (to)] solution

διαμάντι (το) [thiamandi (to)] diamond

Διαμαρτυρόμενος (ο) [thiamartiromenos (o)] Protestant

ΔΙΑΜΕΡΙΣΜΑ διαμέρισμα (το) [thiamerisma (to)] apartment, flat

διά μέσου [thia mesoo] through

διαμονή (η) [thiamoni (i)] accommodation; stay

ΔΙΑΝΥΚΤΕΡΕΥΟΝ διανυκτερεύον open all night

διάρκεια (η) [thiarkia (i)] duration

ΔΙΑΡΚΕΙΑ ΠΤΗΣΕΩΣ διάρκεια πτήσεως [thiarkia ptiseos] flight time

διαρροή (η) [thiaroi (i)] leak

ΔΙΑΡΡΟΙΑ διάρροια (η) [thiaria (i)] diarrhoea

διάσημος [thiasimos] famous

ΔΙΑΣΤΑΥΡΩΣΗ διασταύρωση (η) [thiastavrosi (i)] junction,

crossroads, intersection
διασχίζω [thiaskhizo] go through
ΔΙΑΤΗΡΕΙΤΑΙ ΣΕ ΨΥΓΕΙΟ
διατηρείται σε ψυγείο keep
refrigerated
διαφημιστικό (το) [thiafimistiko
(to)] leaflet; advertisements (on
TV); trailer (cinema)
διαφορετικά [thiaforetika]
otherwise
διαφορετικός [thiaforetikos]
different
διάφραγμα (το) [thiafragma (to)]
shutter (in camera)
διαχειριστής (ο) [thiakhiristis (o)]
manager
διαχειρίστρια (η) [thiakhiristria (i)]
manageress
διδάσκω [thithasko] teach
δίδυμοι (οι) [thithimi (i)] twins
ΔΙΕΥΘΥΝΣΗ διεύθυνση (η)
[thiefτHinsi (i)] address
δίκαιος [thikeos] fair, just
δικά μας [thika mas] ours
δικά μου [thika moo] mine
δικά σας, δικά σου [thika sas, thika
soo] yours
ΔΙΚΑΣΤΗΡΙΟ δικαστήριο (το)
[thikastirio (to)] law court
δικά της [thika tis] hers
δικά του [thika too] his, its
δικά τους [thika toos] theirs
δικηγόρος (ο/η) [thikigoros (o/i)]
lawyer
δική μας [thiki mas] ours
δική μου [thiki moo] mine
δική σας, δική σου [thiki sas, thiki
soo] yours
δική του [thiki too] his

δική τους [thiki toos] theirs
ΔΙΚΛΙΝΟ ΔΩΜΑΤΙΟ δίκλινο
δωμάτιο (το) [thiklino thomatio
(to)] double room
δικό μας [thiko mas] ours
δικό μου [thiko moo] mine
δικό σας, δικό σου [thiko sas, thiko
soo] yours
δικό τους [thiko toos] theirs
δικό της [thiko tis] hers
δικό του [thiko too] his; its
δικός μας [thikos mas] ours
δικός μου [thikos moo] mine
δικός σας, δικός σου [thikos sas,
thikos soo] yours
δικός του [thikos too] his
δικός τους [thikos toos] theirs
δίνω [thino] give
ΔΙΟΔΙΑ διόδια (τα) [thiothia
(ta)] toll
διορθώνω [thiorτHono] mend,
correct
ΔΙΠΛΗ ΤΑΡΙΦΑ διπλή ταρίφα
(η) double tariff
διπλό [thiplo] double
ΔΙΠΛΟ ΔΩΜΑΤΙΟ διπλό
δωμάτιο (το) [thiplo thomatio (to)]
double room
διπλό κρεβάτι (το) [thiplo krevati
(to)] double bed
ΔΙΣ. δις. Miss
ΔΙΣΚΑΔΙΚΟ δισκάδικο (το)
[thiskathiko (to)] record shop
ΔΙΣΚΟΙ - ΚΑΣΕΤΕΣ δίσκοι -
κασέτες [thiski - kasetes] records
- cassettes
δίσκος (ο) [thiskos (o)] record;
tray
Δ΄ ΚΑΤΗΓΟΡΙΑΣ

Δ΄ κατηγορίας fourth class

δοκιμάζω [thokimazo] taste (verb);
try (on)

ΔΟΛΛΑΡΙΟ δολλάριο (το)
[tholario (to)] dollar

δόντι (το) [thondi (to)] tooth

ΔΟΣΟΛΟΓΙΑ ΕΝΗΛΙΚΩΝ
δοσολογία ενηλίκων adult
dosage

ΔΟΣΟΛΟΓΙΑ ΠΑΙΔΩΝ
δοσολογία παίδων children's
dosage

δουλειά (η) [thoolia (i)] job; work

δουλειές (οι) [thoolies (i)] business

δουλεύω [thoolevo] work (verb)
δεν δουλεύει [then thoolevi] it's
not working

ΔΡΑΧΜΗ δραχμή (η) [thrakhmi
(i)] drachma

ΔΡΟΜΟΛΟΓΙΑ δρομολόγια (τα)
[thromoloyia (ta)] timetable, (US)
schedule

δρόμος (ο) [thromos (ο)] road;
street

δροσερός [throseros] cool

ΔΡΧ. δρχ. drachma

δυνατός [thinatos] loud;
possible; strong

δύο [thio] two

ΔΥΟ ΠΑΡΑΣΤΑΣΕΙΣ δύο
παραστάσεις two shows

δυσάρεστος [thisarestos]
unpleasant

δύση του ήλιου (η) [thisi too ilioo
(i)] sunset

ΔΥΣΚΟΙΛΙΑ δυσκοιλια (η)
[thiskilia (i)] constipation

δύσκολος [thiskolos] difficult

ΔΥΣΠΕΨΙΑ δυσπεψία (η)

[thispepsia (i)] indigestion

δυστύχημα (το) [thistikhima (to)]
accident

δυστυχώς [thistikhos]
unfortunately

δώδεκα [thotheka] twelve

ΔΩΔΕΚΑΔΑ δωδεκάδα (η)
[thothekatha (i)] dozen

ΔΩΜΑΤΙΟ δωμάτιο (το)
[thomatio (to)] room

ΔΩΡΑ δώρα gifts

ΔΩΡΕΑΝ δωρεάν [thorean] free
(of charge)

δώρο (το) [thoro (to)] gift

ΔΩΡΟ ΠΑΣΧΑ Δώρο
Πάσχα [thoro Paskha] Easter
supplement paid to taxi
drivers

ΔΩΡΟ ΧΡΙΣΤΟΥΓΕΝΝΩΝ
Δώρο Χριστουγέννων [thoro
khristooyenon] Christmas
supplement paid to taxi
drivers

Ε

Ε.Α.Σ. Athens Public
Transport Corporation

εβδομάδα (η) [evthomatha (i)]
week

εβδομήντα [evthominda] seventy

έβδομος [evthomos] seventh

Εβραίος [Evreos] Jewish

έγγραφο (το) [engrafo (to)]
document

εγγύηση (η) [egi-isi (i)] guarantee

έγινε! [eyineh!] OK, coming up!

εγκαίρως [engeros] on time

έγκαυμα από τον ήλιο (το)
[engavma apo ton ilio (to)]
sunburn

έγκυος [engios] pregnant

έγκυρος [engiros] valid

έγχρωμο φιλμ (το) [enkhromo film
(to)] colour film

εγώ [ego] I

εγώ ο ίδιος [ego o ithios] myself

εδώ [etho] here

έθιμο (το) [eThimo (to)] custom

ΕΘΝΙΚΗ ΟΔΟΣ εθνική οδός (η)
[eThniki othos (i)] motorway,
highway, freeway

ΕΘΝΙΚΗ ΠΙΝΑΚΟΘΗΚΗ
Εθνική Πινακοθήκη [EThniki
PinakoTHiki] National Art
Gallery

ΕΘΝΙΚΟΤΗΤΑ εθνικότητα (η)
[eThnikotita (i)] nationality

ΕΙΔΗ είδη (τα) [ithi (ta)] goods

ΕΙΔΗ ΑΥΤΟΚΙΝΗΤΟΥ είδη
αυτοκινήτου auto accessories

ΕΙΔΗ ΔΩΡΩΝ είδη δώρων gifts

ΕΙΔΗ ΜΠΕΜΠΕ είδη μπεμπέ
[ithi bebeh] babywear

ΕΙΔΗ ΡΟΥΧΙΣΜΟΥ είδη
ρουχισμού [ithi roukhismoo]
clothes

ΕΙΔΗ ΣΠΟΡ είδη σπορ [ithi spor]
sports equipment, sportswear

ΕΙΔΗ ΧΑΡΤΟΠΩΛΕΙΟΥ είδη
χαρτοπωλείου [ithi khartopolioo]
stationery

ΕΙΔΙΚΗ ΠΡΟΣΦΟΡΑ ειδική
προσφορά special price, special
offer

ειδικώς [ithikos] especially

είχες [ikhes] you had

ΕΙΚΟΣΑΡΙΚΟ εικοσάρικο
[ikosariko] 20-drachma coin

είκοσι [ikosi] twenty

ειλικρινής [ilikrinis] sincere

είμαι [imeh] I am

είμαστε [imasteh] we are

είναι [ineh] he/she/it is; they
are

είστε [isteh] you are

ΕΙΣΑΓΩΓΗΣ εισαγωγής
imported

είσαι [iseh] you are

ΕΙΣΙΤΗΡΙΟ εισιτήριο (το)
[isitirio (to)] ticket

ΕΙΣΙΤΗΡΙΟ ΜΕ ΕΠΙΣΤΡΟΦΗ
εισιτήριο με επιστροφή [isitirio
meh epistrofi] return/round
trip ticket

ΕΙΣΟΔΟΣ είσοδος (η) [isothos (i)]
entrance, way in

ΕΙΣΟΔΟΣ ΕΛΕΥΘΕΡΑ είσοδος
ελευθέρα admission free

ΕΙΣΟΔΟΣ ΠΡΑΤΗΡΙΟΥ είσοδος
πρατηρίου entrance to petrol/
gas station

ΕΙΣΠΡΑΚΤΩΡ εισπράκτωρ (ο)
ticket collector

είχα [ikha] I had

είχαμε [ikhameh] we had

είχαν [ikhan] they had

είχατε [ikhateh] you had

είχε [ikheh] he/she/it had

είχες [ikhes] you had

Ε΄ ΚΑΤΗΓΟΡΙΑΣ
Ε΄ κατηγορίας fifth class

εκατό [ekato] hundred

εκατομμύριο: ένα εκατομμύριο
[ena ekatomirio] one million

ΕΚΔΟΣΗ ΕΙΣΙΤΗΡΙΩΝ έκδοση

εισιτηρίων [ekthosi isitirion] ticket office

εκεί [eki] there, over there

εκεί κάτω [eki kato] down there

εκείνα, εκείνες [ekina, ekines] those

εκείνη, εκείνο [ekini, ekino] that

εκείνοι [ekini] those

εκείνος [ekinos] that

ΕΚΘΕΣΗ έκθεση (η) [ekтHesi (i)] exhibition, showroom

ΕΚΚΛΗΣΙΑ εκκλησία (η) [eklisia (i)] church

E.K.O. Greek state petrol company

εκπληκτικός [ekpliktikos] surprising

έκπληξη (η) [ekplixi (i)] surprise

ΕΚΠΤΩΣΕΙΣ εκπτώσεις (οι) sales

ΕΚΤΑΚΤΗ ΑΝΑΓΚΗ έκτακτη ανάγκη (η) [ektakti anangi (i)] emergency

εκτός [ektos] except

έκτος [ektos] sixth

έλα! [ela!] you don't say!; come on!, hurry up!

ΕΛ.ΑΣ. Greek police

ΕΛΑΣΤΙΚΑ ελαστικά tyres

ελαστικός [elastikos] elastic

ελατήριο (το) [elatirio (to)] spring (in seat etc)

ελαττωματικός [elatomatikos] faulty

ΕΛΑΤΤΩΣΑΤΕ ΤΑΧΥΤΗΤΑ ελαττώσατε ταχύτητα reduce speed

ελαφρός [elafros] light (not heavy)

ελάχιστος [elakhistos] smallest; few

ελεγκτής (ο) [elenktis (o)] inspector (bus)

ΕΛΕΓΧΟΣ έλεγχος (ο) [elenkhos (o)] check, inspection

ΕΛΕΓΧΟΣ ΑΠΟΣΚΕΥΩΝ έλεγχος αποσκευών baggage control

ΕΛΕΓΧΟΣ ΔΙΑΒΑΤΗΡΙΩΝ έλεγχος διαβατηρίων passport control

ΕΛΕΓΧΟΣ ΕΙΣΙΤΗΡΙΩΝ έλεγχος εισιτηρίων ticket inspection

ΕΛΕΓΧΟΣ ΕΠΙΒΑΤΩΝ έλεγχος επιβατών passenger control

ΕΛΕΥΘΕΡΑ ΕΙΣΟΔΟΣ ελευθέρα είσοδος [elefтHera isothos] admission free

ΕΛΕΥΘΕΡΟΝ ελεύθερον [elefтHeron] free; for hire (taxi)

ελεύθερος [elefтHeros] free; single (unmarried)

ελιά (η) [elia (i)] olive; spot (blemish)

ελικόπτερο (το) [elikoptero (to)] helicopter

ελκυστικός [elkistikos] attractive

ΕΛΛΑΔΑ Ελλάδα (η) [Elatha (i)] Greece

Έλληνας (ο) [Elinas (o)] Greek (man)

Ελληνίδα (η) [Elinitha (i)] Greek (woman)

ΕΛΛΗΝΙΚΑ Ελληνικά (τα) [Elinika (ta)] Greek (language)

ΕΛΛΗΝΙΚΗ ΑΣΤΥΝΟΜΙΑ Ελληνική Αστυνομία (η) Greek

police
ΕΛΛΗΝΙΚΗ ΡΑΔΙΟΦΩΝΙΑ
Ελληνική Ραδιοφωνία Greek
radio
ΕΛΛΗΝΙΚΗ ΤΗΛΕΟΡΑΣΗ
Ελληνική Τηλεόραση Greek
television
ΕΛΛΗΝΙΚΗΣ ΚΑΤΑΣΚΕΥΗΣ
Ελληνικής κατασκευής made
in Greece
ΕΛΛΗΝΙΚΟ ΠΡΟΙΟΝ Ελληνικό
προιόν produce of Greece
ΕΛΛΗΝΙΚΟΣ Ελληνικός
[Elinikos] Greek (adj)
Ε.Λ.Π.Α. [E.L.P.A.] Greek
motoring organization
ελπίζω [elpizo] hope (verb)
ΕΛ.ΤΑ. Greek Post Office
εμάς [emas] us
εμβολιασμός (ο) [emvoliasmos (o)]
vaccination
εμβόλιο (το) [emvolio (to)] vaccine
εμείς [emis] we
εμένα [emena] me
ΕΜΠΟΡΙΚΟ ΚΕΝΤΡΟ
εμπορικό κέντρο (το) [emboriko
kendro (to)] shopping centre
εμπρός [ebros] come in; hello
(response on phone)
ένα(ν) [ena(n)] a; one
εναντίον [enandion] against
ένας [enas] a; one
ένατος [enatos] ninth
ενδιαφέρον [enthiaferon]
interesting
ενενήντα [eneninda] ninety
ένεση (η) [enesi (i)] injection
ενήλικη (η) [eniliki (i)] adult
ΕΝΗΛΙΚΟΣ ενήλικος (ο)

[enilikos (o)] adult
ΕΝΘΥΜΙΟ ενθύμιο (το)
[enTHimio (to)] souvenir
εννιά [enia] nine
εννοώ [enoo] mean (verb)
ΕΝΟΙΚΙΑΖΟΝΤΑΙ
ενοικιάζονται [enikiazondeh] for
hire, to rent
ΕΝΟΙΚΙΑΖΟΝΤΑΙ
ΑΥΤΟΚΙΝΗΤΑ ενοικιάζονται
αυτοκίνητα car rental
ΕΝΟΙΚΙΑΖΟΝΤΑΙ ΒΑΡΚΕΣ
ενοικιάζονται βάρκες boats
for hire
ΕΝΟΙΚΙΑΖΟΝΤΑΙ ΔΩΜΑΤΙΑ
ενοικιάζονται δωμάτια rooms
to let
ΕΝΟΙΚΙΑΣΗ ΑΥΤΟΚΙΝΗΤΩΝ
ενοικίαση αυτοκινήτων car
rental
ενοίκιο (το) [enikio (to)] rent
ενός [enos] of a
ενοχλητικός [enokhlitikos]
annoying
ενοχλώ [enokhlo] disturb
εντάξει [endaxi] that's all right;
OK
έντεκα [endeka] eleven
έντομο (το) [endomo (to)]
insect
ΕΝΤΥΠΑ έντυπα printed
matter
ενώ [eno] while
εξαιρετικός [exeretikos] terrific
εξ αιτίας [ex etias] because of
εξαρτάται [exartateh] it depends
ΕΞΑΤΜΙΣΗ εξάτμιση (η)
[exatmisi (i)] exhaust
εξαφανίζομαι [exafanizomeh]

disappear

ΕΞΕΤΑΣΕΙΣ εξετάσεις (οι)
[exetasis (i)] check-up; exams

εξηγώ [exigo] explain

εξήντα [exinda] sixty

έξι [exi] six

ΕΞΟΔΟΣ έξοδος (η)
[exothos (i)] exit; gate (at airport); door

ΕΞΟΔΟΣ ΑΥΤ/ΤΩΝ έξοδος αυτ/των vehicle exit

ΕΞΟΔΟΣ ΚΙΝΔΥΝΟΥ έξοδος κινδύνου emergency exit

εξοχή (η) [exokhi (i)] countryside

έξοχος [exokhos] excellent

ΕΞΠΡΕΣ εξπρές [expres] special delivery; express

εξυπηρετώ [exipireto] serve (verb), assist

έξυπνος [exipnos] clever, intelligent

έξω! [exo!] get out!

ΕΞΩΣΤΗΣ εξώστης [exostis] circle (in cinema etc)

εξωτερικός [exoterikos] external
στο εξωτερικό [sto exoteriko] abroad

ΕΞΩΤΕΡΙΚΟΥ εξωτερικού postage abroad

εξωφρενικός [exofrenikos] shocking

Ε.Ο.Κ. [Ε.Ο.Κ.] EEC, EU

Ε.Ο.Τ. [Ε.Ο.Τ.] National Tourist Agency

επαληθεύω [epaliτHevo] check (verb), verify

επαναλαμβάνω [epanalamvano] repeat

επαφή: έρχομαι σε επαφή

[erkhomeh seh epafi] contact (verb)

Ε.Π.Ε. Ltd

επείγον [epigon] urgent

επειδή [epithi] because

επέκταση (η) [epektasi (i)] extension lead

επέτειος (η) [epetios (i)] anniversary

ΕΠΙΒΑΤΗΣ επιβάτης (ο/η)
[epivatis (o/i)] passenger

επιβεβαιώνω [epiveveono] confirm

επίδεσμος (ο) [epithesmos (o)] bandage

επίθεση (η) [epiτHesi (i)] attack (noun)

επιθετικός [epiτHetikos] aggressive

ΕΠΙΘΕΤΟ επίθετο (το) [epiτHeto (to)] surname

επικίνδυνος [epikinthinos] dangerous

ΕΠΙΛΕΞΑΤΕ ΤΟΝ ΑΡΙΘΜΟ επιλέξατε τον αριθμό dial the number

επίπεδος [epipethos] flat (even)

έπιπλα (τα) [epipla (ta)] furniture

ΕΠΙΠΛΩΜΕΝΑ ΔΩΜΑΤΙΑ επιπλωμένα δωμάτια furnished rooms

επίσης [episis] too, also

επισκέπτομαι [episkeptomeh] visit (verb)

ΕΠΙΣΚΕΥΑΖΟΝΤΑΙ ΥΠΟΔΗΜΑΤΑ επισκευάζονται υποδήματα shoe repairs

επισκευή (η) [episkevi (i)] repair

επίσκεψη (η) [episkepsi (i)] visit

επιστήμη (η) [epistimi (i)] science
ΕΠΙΣΤΟΛΕΣ επιστολές letters
επιστρέφω [epistrefo] give back; arrive back
ΕΠΙΣΤΡΕΦΩ ΣΕ 5΄ επιστρέφω σε 5΄ back in 5 minutes
ΕΠΙΤΑΓΗ επιταγή (η) [epitayi (i)] cheque, (US) check
επιτέλους [epiteloos] at last
επίτηδες [epitithes] deliberately
επιτρέπω [epitrepo] let (allow)
επιτρέπεται [epitrepeteh] it is permitted
επιτυχία (η) [epitikhia (i)] success
επόμενος (ο) [epomenos (o)] next
εποχή (η) [epokhi (i)] season
επτά [epta] seven
E.P.A. Greek radio
ΕΡΓΑ έργα roadworks
ΕΡΓΑ ΕΠΙ ΤΗΣ ΟΔΟΥ ΣΕ ΜΗΚΟΣ ... ΧΙΛ. έργα επί της οδού σε μήκος ... χιλ. roadworks for ... kms
εργάζομαι [ergazomeh] work (verb)
ΕΡΓΑΛΕΙΑ ΠΥΡΑΣΦΑΛΕΙΑΣ εργαλεία πυρασφάλειας fire-fighting equipment
εργαλείο (το) [ergalio (to)] tool
ΕΡΓΑΣΤΗΡΙΟ ΗΛΕΚΤΡΟΝΙΚΩΝ εργαστήριο ηλεκτρονικών electronics
εργένης (ο) [eryenis (o)] bachelor
εργοστάσιο (το) [ergostasio (to)] factory
ερυθρά (η) [eriTHra (i)] German measles
έρχομαι [erkhomeh] come
έρωτας (ο) [erotas (o)] love

κάνω έρωτα [kano erota] make love
ερώτηση (η) [erotisi (i)] question
εσάς, εσείς, εσένα [esas, esis, esena] you
ΕΣΤΙΑΤΟΡΙΟ εστιατόριο (το) [estiatorio (to)] restaurant
εσύ [esi] you
Ε.Σ.Υ. National Health Service
εσώρουχα (τα) [esorookha (ta)] underwear
ΕΣΩΡΟΥΧΑ ΓΥΝΑΙΚΕΙΑ εσώρουχα γυναικεία [esorookha yinekia] ladies' underwear
ΕΣΩΤΕΡΙΚΟΥ εσωτερικού inland postage
E.T. Greek television
εταιρεία (η) [eteria (i)] company
ετικέτα (η) [etiketa (i)] label
ΕΤΟΙΜΑ ΓΥΝΑΙΚΕΙΑ έτοιμα γυναικεία ladies' clothing
ετοιμάζω [etimazo] prepare
ΕΤΟΙΜΑ ΠΑΙΔΙΚΑ έτοιμα παιδικά children's clothing
έτοιμος [etimos] ready
έτσι [etsi] so; like this
έτσι κι έτσι [etsi ki etsi] so-so
ευαίσθητος [evesTHitos] sensitive
ευγενικός [evyenikos] kind; polite
ευγνώμων [evgnomon] grateful
ΕΥΚΑΙΡΙΑ ευκαιρία (η) [efkeria (i)] bargain
ΕΥΚΑΙΡΙΕΣ ευκαιρίες bargains
εύκολος [efkolos] easy
ΕΥΡΩΠΑΪΚΟΣ Ευρωπαϊκός [Evropa-ikos] European
ΕΥΡΩΠΗ Ευρώπη (η) [Evropi (i)] Europe

ευτυχισμένος [eftikhismenos] happy

ευτυχώς [eftikhos] fortunately

ευχαριστημένος [efkharistimenos] glad; pleased

ευχάριστος [efkharistos] pleasant

ευχαριστώ [efkharisto] thank you

ΕΦΗΜΕΡΙΔΑ εφημερίδα (η) [efimeritha (i)] newspaper

εφημεριδοπώλης (ο) [efimerithopolis (o)] newsagent

ΕΦΟΡΙΑ εφορία (η) [eforia (i)] tax office

έχει [ekhi] he/she/it has

έχεις [ekhis] you have

έχεις ...; [ekhis ...?] do you have ...?

έχετε [ekheteh] you have

έχετε ...; [ekheteh ...?] do you have ...?

έχουμε [ekhoomeh] we have

έχουν [ekhoon] they have

έχω [ekho] I have

Z

ζακέτα (η) [zaketa (i)] cardigan

ΖΑΧΑΡΟΠΛΑΣΤΕΙΟ ζαχαροπλαστείο (το) [zakharoplastio (to)] cake shop or café selling cakes and soft drinks

ζέστη (η) [zesti (i)] heat

κάνει ζέστη [kani zesti] it's warm

ΖΕΣΤΟ ζεστό [zesto] hot

ΖΕΣΤΟ ΝΕΡΟ ζεστό νερό [zesto nero] hot water

ζεστός [zestos] hot; warm

ζευγάρι (το) [zevgari (to)] pair

ζηλιάρης [ziliaris] jealous

ζημιά (η) [zimia (i)] damage

ζημιές: κάνω ζημιές [kano zimies] break (verb)

ζητάω συγγνώμη [zitao signomi] apologize

ζω [zo] live (verb)

ζωγραφίζω [zografizo] paint (verb: pictures)

ζωγραφική (η) [zografiki (i)] painting

ζωή (η) [zoi (i)] life

ζώνη (η) [zoni (i)] belt

ζώνη ασφαλείας (η) [zoni asfalias (i)] seat belt

ζωντανός [zondanos] alive

ζώο (το) [zo-o (to)] animal

ΖΩΟΛΟΓΙΚΟΣ ΚΗΠΟΣ ζωολογικός κήπος (ο) [zo-oloyikos kipos (o)] zoo

H

η [i] the

ή [i] or

ή ... ή ... [i ... i ...] either ... or ...

ήδη [ithi] already

ήθελα: θα ήθελα [THa iTHela] I would like

ηθοποιός (ο/η) [iTHopios (o/i)] actor, actress

ΗΛ/ΓΕΙΟ ηλ/γειο electrical goods

ΗΛΕΚΤΡΙΚΑ ΕΙΔΗ ηλεκτρικά

είδη [ilektrik**a** ithi] electrical goods

ηλεκτρική σκούπα (η) [ilektriki sk**oo**pa (i)] vacuum cleaner

ηλεκτρικό ρεύμα (το) [ilektrik**o** revma (to)] electricity

ΗΛΕΚΤΡΙΚΟΣ ηλεκτρικός (ο) [ilektrik**os** (o)] underground, (US) subway

ηλεκτρικό σίδερο (το) [ilektrik**o** sithero (to)] iron (for ironing)

ηλεκτρικός [ilektrik**os**] electric

ΗΛΕΚΤΡΟΛΟΓΟΣ ηλεκτρολόγος (ο) [ilektrol**o**gos (o)] electrician

ηλίαση (η) [il**i**asi (i)] sunstroke

ηλικία (η) [ilik**i**a (i)] age

ηλιοθεραπεία: κάνω ηλιοθεραπεία [kano ilioTHerap**i**a] sunbathe

ηλιόλουστος [ili**o**loostos] sunny

ήλιος (ο) [**i**lios (o)] sun

ήμαστε [**i**masteh] we were

ημέρα (η) [**i**mera (i)] day

ημερολόγιο (το) [imerol**o**yio (to)] calendar, diary

ημερομηνία (η) [imerominia (i)] date (time)

ΗΜΕΡΟΜΗΝΙΑ ΛΗΞΗΣ ημερομηνία λήξης best before

ΗΜΕΡΟΜΗΝΙΑ ΠΑΡΑΣΚΕΥΗΣ ημερομηνία παρασκευής date of manufacture

ΗΜΙΔΙΑΤΡΟΦΗ ημιδιατροφή (η) [imithiatrof**i** (i)] half board

ΗΜΙΣΚΛΗΡΟΙ ΦΑΚΟΙ ΕΠΑΦΗΣ ημίσκληροι φακοί επαφής (οι) [imiskliri faki epafis (i)] gas permeable lenses

ήμουν [**i**moon] I was

ΗΝΩΜΕΝΕΣ ΠΟΛΙΤΕΙΕΣ ΑΜΕΡΙΚΗΣ Ηνωμένες Πολιτείες Αμερικής (οι) [Inomenes Polities Amerikis (i)] United States of America

Η.Π.Α. (οι) [I.P.A. (i)] USA

ηρεμώ [**i**rem**o**] calm down

ΗΡΩΩΝ ηρώων (το) [ir**o**-on (to)] war memorial

ήσουν, ήστε [**i**soon, isteh] you were

ΗΣΥΧΙΑ ησυχία [isikhia] quiet

ήσυχος [**i**sikhos] quiet

ήταν [**i**tan] he/she/it was; they were

Θ

θάλασσα (η) [TH**a**lasa (i)] sea

ΘΑΛΑΣΣΙΑ ΣΠΟΡ θαλάσσια σπορ water sports

ΘΑΛΑΣΣΙΟ ΣΚΙ θαλάσσιο σκι (το) [TH**a**lasio ski (to)] waterskiing

θάνατος (ο) [TH**a**natos (o)] death

θα σε δω! [TH**a** seh tho!] see you!

θαυμάσιος [TH**a**vm**a**sios] wonderful

θεά (η) [TH**e**a (i)] goddess

θέα (η) [TH**e**a (i)] view

ΘΕΑΤΡΙΚΟ ΕΡΓΟ θεατρικό έργο (το) [TH**e**h-atrik**o** **e**rgo (to)] play (theatre)

ΘΕΑΤΡΟ θέατρο (το) [TH**e**atro (to)] theatre

θεία (η) [THía (i)] aunt

θείος (ο) [THíos (o)] uncle

θέλετε ...; [THeleteh ...?] do you want ...?

θέλω [THelo] want (verb)

θεός (ο) [THeos (o)] God

ΘΕΡΙΝΟΣ θερινός (ο) open-air cinema/movie theater

θέρμανση (η) [THermansi (i)] heating

θερμοκρασία (η) [THermokrasia (i)] temperature

θερμόμετρο (το) [THermometro (to)] thermometer

θερμός (το) [THermos (to)] Thermos® flask

ΘΕΣΕΙΣ θέσεις seats

ΘΕΣΕΙΣ ΚΑΘΗΜΕΝΩΝ θέσεις καθημένων seats

ΘΕΣΕΙΣ ΟΡΘΙΩΝ θέσεις ορθίων standing room

θέση (η) [THesi (i)] seat

κλείνω θέση [klino THesi] book a seat

ΘΕΩΡΕΙΑ θεωρεία [THeoria] boxes (in theatre)

θλιμμένος [THlimenos] depressed; sad

θορυβώδης [THorivothis] noisy

θρησκεία (η) [THriskia (i)] religion

θύελλα (η) [THiela (i)] storm; thunderstorm

θυμάμαι [THimameh] remember

θυμωμένος [THimomenos] angry

θυρωρός (ο) [THiroros (o)] doorman; caretaker

I
∎

ΙΑΜΑΤΙΚΕΣ ΠΗΓΕΣ ιαματικές πηγές [iamatikes piyes] spa

ΙΑΝΟΥΑΡΙΟΣ Ιανουάριος (ο) [Ianooarios (o)] January

ιδέα (η) [ithea (i)] idea

ιδιοκτήτης (ο) [ithioktitis (o)] owner

ιδιοκτήτρια (η) [ithioktitria (i)] owner

ΙΔΙΟΚΤΗΤΟ ΠΑΡΚΙΝΓΚ ιδιόκτητο πάρκινγκ private parking

ίδιος [ithios] same

ΙΔΙΩΤΙΚΗ/ΚΡΑΤΙΚΗ ΙΔΙΟΚΤΗΣΙΑ ιδιωτική/κρατική ιδιοκτησία private/state property

ΙΔΙΩΤΙΚΗ ΠΙΝΑΚΟΘΗΚΗ ιδιωτική πινακοθήκη private art gallery

ΙΔΙΩΤΙΚΟΣ ιδιωτικός [ithiotikos] private

ΙΔΙΩΤΙΚΟΣ ΔΡΟΜΟΣ ιδιωτικός δρόμος private road

ιδρώνω [ithrono] sweat (verb)

ιλαρά (η) [ilara (i)] measles

ΙΝΣΤΙΤΟΥΤΟ ΑΙΣΘΗΤΙΚΗΣ ινστιτούτο αισθητικής (το) [institooto esTHitikis (to)] beauty salon

ΙΟΥΛΙΟΣ Ιούλιος (ο) [Ioolios (o)] July

ΙΟΥΝΙΟΣ Ιούνιος (ο) [Ioonios (o)] June

ιππασία (η) [ipasia (i)] horse-riding

ΙΠΠΟΔΡΟΜΟΣ ιππόδρομος (ο)
[ipothromos (o)] race course (for horses)

Ιρλανδέζα (η) [Irlantheza (i)] Irishwoman

ΙΡΛΑΝΔΙΑ Ιρλανδία (η) [Irlanthia (i)] Ireland

Ιρλανδικός [Irlanthikos] Irish

Ιρλανδός (ο) [Irlanthos (o)] Irishman

ίσια [isia] straight

ΙΣΟΓΕΙΟ ισόγειο (το) [isoyio (to)] ground floor, (US) first floor

ΙΣΟΠΕΔΟΣ ΔΙΑΒΑΣΙΣ ισόπεδος διάβασις level crossing

ΙΣΠΑΝΙΑ Ισπανία (η) [Ispania (i)] Spain

Ισπανικός [Ispanikos] Spanish (adj)

ιστιοπλοΐα (η) [istioploia (i)] sailing

ιστιοπλοϊκό σκάφος (το) [istioploiko skafos (to)] sailing boat

ΙΣΤΙΟΦΟΡΟ ιστιοφόρο (το) [istioforo (to)] sailing boat

ιστορία (η) [istoria (i)] story; history

ίσως [isos] maybe, perhaps

ΙΤΑΛΙΑ Ιταλία (η) [Italia (i)] Italy

Ιταλικός [Italikos] Italian (adj)

ΙΧΘΥΟΠΩΛΕΙΟ ιχθυοπωλείο (το) [ikhThiopolio (to)] fishmonger's

Κ

Κ. κ. Mr

ΚΑ. κα. Mrs

ΚΑΖΙΝΟ καζίνο (το) [kazino (to)] casino

καθαρίζω [katharizo] clean

ΚΑΘΑΡΙΣΤΗΡΙΟ καθαριστήριο (το) [katharistirio (to)] laundry and dry cleaner's

ΚΑΘΑΡΙΣΤΙΚΟ ΔΕΡΜΑΤΟΣ καθαριστικό δέρματος (το) [katharistiko thermatos (to)] skin cleanser

ΚΑΘΑΡΟ ΒΑΡΟΣ καθαρό βάρος net weight

καθαρός [katharos] clean (adj)

ΚΑΘΑΡΤΙΚΟ καθαρτικό (το) [kathartiko (to)] laxative

κάθε [katheh] every

καθεμία, καθένα, καθένας [kathemia, kathena, kathenas] each

κάθε τι [katheh ti] everything

καθηγητής (ο) [kathiyitis (o)] teacher, professor

καθηγήτρια (η) [kathiyitria (i)] teacher, professor

ΚΑΘΗΜΕΡΙΝΑ καθημερινά [kathimerina] daily

καθήστε [kathisteh] please sit down

ΚΑΘΟΔΟΣ κάθοδος [kathothos] way down, descent

καθολικός [katholikos] Catholic (adj)

καθόλου [katholoo] not at all; none; any

κάθομαι [kaTHomeh] sit down

καθρέφτης (ο) [kaTHreftis (o)] mirror

καθρέφτης αυτοκινήτου (ο) [kaTHreftis aftokinitoo (o)] rearview mirror

ΚΑΘΥΣΤΕΡΗΣΗ καθυστέρηση (η) [kaTHisterisi (i)] delay

καθυστερώ [kaTHistero] delay (verb); be late

και [keh] and

και εγώ επίσης [k ego episis] me too

και οι δύο [k i thio] both of them

ΚΑΙ ΛΟΙΠΑ και λοιπά etc

καινούργιο [kenooryio] brand-new

ευτυχισμένος ο καινούργιος χρόνος! [eftikhismenos o kenooryios khronos!] happy New Year!

καιρός (ο) [keros (o)] weather

καίω [keo] burn (verb)

κακός [kakos] bad

καλά [kala] well

καλά! [kala!] good!

καλάθι (το) [kalaTHi (to)] basket

καλεί [kali] it's ringing

ΚΑΛΕΣΑΤΕ καλέσατε dial

ΚΑΛΕΣΤΕ ΤΟΝ ΑΡΙΘΜΟ καλέστε τον αριθμό dial number

καλή διασκέδαση [kali thiaskethasi] have fun

καλημέρα [kalimera] good morning

καληνύχτα [kalinikhta] good night

καλησπέρα [kalispera] good afternoon; good evening

καλλιτέχνιδα (η) [kalitekhnitha (i)] artist

καλλιτέχνης (ο) [kalitekhnis (o)] artist

ΚΑΛΛΥΝΤΙΚΑ καλλυντικά (τα) [kalindika (ta)] perfume and cosmetics

ΚΑΛΟΚΑΙΡΙ καλοκαίρι (το) [kalokeri (to)] summer

καλοκαιρινές διακοπές (οι) [kalokerines thiakopes (i)] summer holidays/vacation

καλοριφέρ (το) [kalorifer (to)] radiator (heater)

καλός [kalos] good; kind

καλοψημένος [kalopsimenos] well-done (meat)

καλσόν (το) [kalson (to)] tights, pantyhose

κάλτσες (οι) [kaltses (i)] socks

καλύτερος (ο) [kaliteros (o)] the best

καλύτερος [kaliteros] better

καλύτερος από [kaliteros apo] better than

καλώς ήλθατε! [kalos ilThateh!] welcome!

ΚΑΛΩΣ ΩΡΙΣΑΤΕ ΣΤΗΝ ... καλώς ωρίσατε στην ... welcome to ...

καμαριέρα (η) [kamariera (i)] chambermaid

καμμία [kamia] no-one

καμμιά φορά [kamia fora] sometimes

καμπάνα (η) [kabana (i)] bell

ΚΑΜΠΙΝΑ καμπίνα (η) [kabina

(i)] cabin (on ship)

ΚΑΜΠΙΝΓΚ κάμπινγκ (το)
[camping (to)] campsite, caravan
site, trailer park

ΚΑΜΠΙΝΕΣ καμπίνες [kabines]
changing rooms

ΚΑΝΑΔΑΣ Καναδάς (ο)
[Kanathas (o)] Canada

Καναδή (η) [Kanathi (i)]
Canadian (woman)

Καναδικός [Kanathikos]
Canadian (adj)

Καναδός (ο) [Kanathos (o)]
Canadian (man)

κανάτα (η) [kanata (i)] jug

κάνει ... [kani ...] it is ..., it
costs ...

κάνεις [kanis] you do

τι κάνεις; [ti kanis?] how are
you?, how do you do?

κανένα [kanena] nothing

κανένας [kanenas] no-one,
nobody

κάνετε [kaneteh] you do

τι κάνετε; [ti kaneteh?] how are
you?, how do you do?

κανό (το) [kano (to)] canoe

κάνω [kano] do; make

καπάκι (το) [kapaki (to)] lid, cap
(of bottle)

καπαρντίνα (η) [kapardina (i)]
raincoat

καπέλο (το) [kapelo (to)] hat, cap

ΚΑΠΕΤΑΝΙΟΣ καπετάνιος (ο)
[kapetanios (o)] captain (of ship)

ΚΑΠΝΙΖΟΝΤΕΣ καπνίζοντες
[kapnizondes] smoking

καπνίζω [kapnizo] smoke (verb)

ΚΑΠΝΙΣΤΕΣ καπνιστές

[kapnistes] smokers

**ΚΑΠΝΙΣΤΗΡΙΟ καπνιστήριο
(το)** [kapnistirio (to)] smoking
room

**ΚΑΠΝΟΠΩΛΕΙΟ καπνοπωλείο
(το)** [kapnopolio (to)]
tobacconist's

ΚΑΠΝΟΣ καπνός (ο) [kapnos (o)]
smoke; tobacco

καπό (το) [kapo (to)] bonnet (car),
(US) hood

κάποιος [kapios] somebody

κάπου [kapoo] somewhere

ΚΑΡΑΜΕΛΑ καραμέλα (η)
[karamela (i)] caramel

καρδιά (η) [karthia (i)] heart

καρδιακή προσβολή (η) [karthiaki
prosvoli (i)] heart attack

καρέκλα (η) [karekla (i)] chair

καρμπιρατέρ (το) [karbirater (to)]
carburettor

καρνέ επιταγών (το) [karneh
epitagon (to)] cheque book, (US)
check book

καροτσάκι (το) [karotsaki (to)]
pram; pushchair, buggy

καρπός (ο) [karpos (o)] wrist

ΚΑΡΤΑ κάρτα (η) [karta (i)]
postcard; business card

κάρτα επιβιβάσεως (η) [karta
epivivaseos (i)] boarding pass

κάρτα επιταγών (η) [karta
epitagon (i)] cheque card, (US)
check card

ΚΑΡΤΠΟΣΤΑΛ καρτποστάλ (η)
[kartpostal (i)] postcard

καρφί (το) [karfi (to)] nail (in wall)

καρφίτσα (η) [karfitsa (i)] pin;
brooch

A
B
Γ
Δ
E
Z
H
Θ
I
K
Λ
M
N
Ξ
O
Π
P
Σ
T
Y
Φ
X
Ψ
Ω

κασκόλ (το) [kaskol (to)] scarf (for neck)

ΚΑΣΣΕΤΑ κασσέτα (η) [kaseta (i)] cassette, tape

κασσεττόφωνο (το) [kasetofono (to)] cassette player

καστόρι (το) [kastori (to)] suede

κάστρο (το) [kastro (to)] castle

κατά [kata] against; about

κάταγμα (το) [katagma (to)] fracture

καταδύσεις (οι) [katathisis (i)] skin-diving

ΚΑΤΑΘΕΣΗ κατάθεση (η) [kataTHesi (i)] deposit

καταλαβαίνω [katalaveno] understand

δεν καταλαβαίνω [then katalaveno] I don't understand

ΚΑΤΑΛΛΗΛΟ κατάλληλο suitable for all ages

κατάλογος (ο) [katalogos (o)] list; menu

ΚΑΤΑΝΑΛΩΣΗ ΠΡΙΝ ... κατανάλωση πριν ... consume before ...

καταπίνω [katapino] swallow (verb)

καταρράκτης (ο) [kataraktis (o)] waterfall

ΚΑΤΑΣΚΕΥΑΖΟΝΤΑΙ ΚΛΕΙΔΙΑ κατασκευάζονται κλειδιά keys cut here

κατασκήνωση (η) [kataskinosi (i)] camping

ΚΑΤΑΣΤΗΜΑ ΑΦΟΡΟΛΟΓΗΤΩΝ κατάστημα αφορολογήτων (το) [katastima aforoloyiton (to)] duty-free shop

καταστροφή (η) [katastrofi (i)] disaster

ΚΑΤΑΣΤΡΩΜΑ κατάστρωμα (το) [katastroma (to)] deck

κατά τη διάρκεια [kata ti thiarkia] while, during

καταψύκτης (ο) [katapsiktis (o)] freezer

κατάψυξη (η) [katapsixi (i)] freezer compartment

κατεβαίνω [kateveno] get off; go down

ΚΑΤΕΙΛΗΜΜΕΝΟΣ κατειλημμένος [katilimenos] engaged, occupied

ΚΑΤΕΠΕΙΓΟΝ κατεπείγον [katepigon] express

κατευθείαν [katefTHian] direct

ΚΑΤΕΨΥΓΜΕΝΑ κατεψυγμένα (τα) [katepsigmena (ta)] frozen food

ΚΑΤΕΨΥΓΜΕΝΟ κατεψυγμένο [katepsigmeno] frozen (food)

κάτι [kati] something

κάτι άλλο [kati alo] something else

ΚΑΤΟΛΙΣΘΗΣΕΙΣ κατολισθήσεις falling rocks

ΚΑΤΟΣΤΑΡΙΚΟ κατοστάρικο (το) [katostariko (to)] 100-drachma note/bill

κατσαβίδι (το) [katsavithi (to)] screwdriver

κατσαρόλα (η) [katsarola (i)] saucepan

κατσίκα (η) [katsika (i)] goat

ΚΑΤΩ κάτω [kato] down; downstairs

κάτω από [kato apo] under

καυτερός [kafteros] spicy, hot
καυτός [kaftos] hot (to taste)
καφέ [kafe] brown
**ΚΑΦΕΚΟΠΤΕΙΟ καφεκοπτείο
(το)** [kafekoptio (to)] coffee shop
ΚΑΦΕΝΕΙΟ καφενείο (το)
[kafenio (to)] coffee house,
where Greek coffee is served
with traditional sweets
ΚΑΦΕΤΕΡΙΑ καφετέρια (η)
[kafeteria (i)] café, coffee shop
κάψιμο (το) [kapsimo (to)] burn
ΚΕΛΣΙΟΥ Κελσίου [Kelsioo]
centigrade
κέλυφος (το) [kelifos (to)] shell
ΚΕΝΤΗΜΑΤΑ κεντήματα (τα)
[kendimata (ta)] embroidery
κεντρική θέρμανση (η) [kendriki
THermansi (i)] central heating
ΚΕΝΤΡΟ κέντρο (το) [kendro
(to)] centre
κέντρο της πόλης [kendro tis
polis] city centre
ΚΕΡΑΜΙΚΑ κεραμικά (τα)
[keramika (ta)] ceramics
κερδίζω [kerthizo] earn; win
(verb)
κερί (το) [keri (to)] candle
ΚΕΡΚΥΡΑ Κέρκυρα (η) [Kerkira
(i)] Corfu
ΚΕΡΜΑ κέρμα (το) [kerma (to)]
coin
ΚΕΡΜΑΤΑ κέρματα [kermata]
coins
ΚΕΣ. κες. Mrs
κεφάλι (το) [kefali (to)] head
κηδεία (η) [kithia (i)] funeral
**ΚΗΠΟΘΕΑΤΡΟ κηποθέατρο
(το)** open-air theatre

ΚΗΠΟΣ κήπος (ο) [kipos (o)]
garden, park
κιβώτιο ταχυτήτων (το) [kivotio
takhititon (to)] gearbox
κιθάρα (η) [kitHara (i)] guitar
ΚΙΛΟ κιλό (το) [kilo (to)] kilo
ΚΙΝΔΥΝΟΣ κίνδυνος (ο)
[kinthinos (o)] danger; caution
**ΚΙΝΔΥΝΟΣ ΠΥΡΚΑΓΙΑΣ
κίνδυνος πυρκαγιάς** fire risk
κινηματογραφική μηχανή (η)
[kinimatografiki mikhani (i)]
camcorder
**ΚΙΝΗΜΑΤΟΓΡΑΦΟΣ
κινηματογράφος (ο)**
[kinimatografos (o)] cinema,
movie theater
κίτρινος [kitrinos] yellow
ΚΚ. κκ. Messrs
κλαίω [kleo] cry (verb)
κλάξον (το) [klaxon (to)] horn
(in car)
κλέβω [klevo] steal
κλειδαριά (η) [klitharia (i)] lock
κλειδί (το) [klithi (to)] key;
spanner, wrench
ΚΛΕΙΔΙΑ κλειδιά keys cut here
κλειδώνω [klithono] lock (verb)
**ΚΛΕΙΝΕΤΕ ΤΗΝ ΠΟΡΤΑ
κλείνετε την πόρτα** close the
door
κλείνω [klino] close (verb);
switch off
ΚΛΕΙΣΤΑ κλειστά [klista]
closed
**ΚΛΕΙΣΤΟ ΑΠΟ ... ΩΣ ...
κλειστό από ... ως ...** [klisto apo ...
os ...] closed from ...
to ...

ΚΛΕΙΣΤΟΝ κλειστόν [klist**o**n] closed

κλειστός [kl**i**st**o**s] closed; off (lights)

κλέφτης (ο) [kl**e**ftis (o)] thief

κλέφτρα (η) [kl**e**ftra (i)] thief

κλίμα (το) [kl**i**ma (to)] climate

ΚΛΙΜΑΤΙΖΟΜΕΝΟΣ κλιματιζόμενος [klimatiz**o**menos] air-conditioned

ΚΛΙΜΑΤΙΣΜΟΣ κλιματισμός (ο) [klimatism**o**s (o)] air-conditioning

κλοπή (η) [klop**i** (i)] theft

Κ.Λ.Π. κλπ etc

ΚΛΩΣΤΗ κλωστή (η) [klost**i** (i)] thread

κόβω [k**o**vo] cut (verb)

κοιλάδα (η) [kil**a**tha (i)] valley

κοιμάμαι [kim**a**meh] sleep (verb); be asleep

ΚΟΙΜΗΤΗΡΙΟ κοιμητήριο (το) [kimit**i**rio (to)] cemetery

ΚΟΙΝΟΤΙΚΟ ΓΡΑΦΕΙΟ κοινοτικό γραφείο (το) local government office

κοκκαλιάρης [kokali**a**ris] skinny

κόκκαλο (το) [k**o**kalo (to)] bone

κόκκινος [k**o**kinos] red

κόλλα (η) [k**o**la (i)] glue

κολλιέ (το) [koli**e** (to)] necklace

κόλπος (ο) [k**o**lpos (o)] vagina; gulf

ΚΟΛΥΜΒΗΤΗΡΙΟ κολυμβητήριο (το) [kolimvit**i**rio (to)] swimming pool

κολυμπάω [kolimb**a**o] swim (verb)

κολύμπι (το) [kol**i**bi (to)] swimming

κολυμπώ [kolimb**o**] swim (verb)

κολώνια (η) [kol**o**nia (i)] eau de toilette

κολώνια μετά το ξύρισμα [kol**o**nia meta to xirisma] aftershave

κομμάτι (το) [kom**a**ti (to)] piece

ΚΟΜΜΩΣΕΙΣ κομμώσεις (οι) [kom**o**sis (i)] hairdresser's

ΚΟΜΜΩΤΗΡΙΟ κομμωτήριο (το) [komot**i**rio (to)] hairdresser's

κομμώτρια (η) [kom**o**tria (i)] hairdresser

κομπιουτεράκι (το) [kombiooter**a**ki (to)] calculator

κομπολόι (το) [kombol**o**i (to)] worry beads

κοντά [kond**a**] near, close by

κοντέρ (το) [kond**e**r (to)] speedometer

ΚΟΝΤΙΣΙΟΝΕΡ κοντίσιονερ (το) [kond**i**sioner (to)] conditioner

κοντός [kond**o**s] short (person)

ΚΟΡΔΟΝΙΑ ΠΑΠΟΥΤΣΙΩΝ κορδόνια παπουτσιών (τα) [korth**o**nia papootsi**o**n (ta)] shoelaces

κόρη (η) [k**o**ri (i)] daughter

κορίτσι (το) [kor**i**tsi (to)] girl

κόρνα (η) [k**o**rna (i)] horn (in car)

κορυφή (η) [korif**i** (i)] top

ΚΟΣΜΗΜΑΤΑ κοσμήματα (τα) [kosm**i**mata (ta)] jewellery

ΚΟΣΜΗΜΑΤΟΠΩΛΕΙΟ κοσμηματοπωλείο (το) [kosmimatop**o**lio (to)] jeweller's

κόσμος (ο) [k**o**smos (o)] world; people, crowd

κοστίζει (το) [kost**i**zi] it costs

κόστος (το) [k**o**stos (to)] cost

κουβάς (ο) [koovas (o)] bucket

κουβέρτα (η) [kooverta (i)] blanket

κουδούνι (το) [koothooni (to)] bell (for door)

ΚΟΥΖΙΝΑ κουζίνα (η) [koozina (i)] cooker; kitchen

ΚΟΥΚΕΤΑ κουκέτα (η) [kooketa (i)] couchette

κουκέτες (οι) [kooketes (i)] bunk beds

κούκλα (η) [kookla (i)] doll

κουμπί (το) [koobi (to)] button

κουνέλι (το) [kooneli (to)] rabbit

κούνια (η) [koonia (i)] cot

κουνούπι (το) [koonoopi (to)] mosquito

κουπέ (το) [koopeh (to)] compartment

κουρασμένος [koorasmenos] tired

ΚΟΥΡΕΑΣ κουρέας (ο) [kooreas (o)] barber

ΚΟΥΡΕΙΟ κουρείο (το) [koorio (to)] barber's shop

κούρεμα (το) [koorema (to)] haircut

κουρτίνα (η) [koortina (i)] curtain

κουστούμι (το) [koostoomi (to)] suit

κουτάλι (το) [kootali (to)] spoon

ΚΟΥΤΑΛΙΕΣ ΓΛΥΚΟΥ κουταλιές γλυκού teaspoonfuls

ΚΟΥΤΑΛΙΕΣ ΣΟΥΠΑΣ κουταλιές σούπας tablespoonfuls

κουτί (το) [kooti (to)] box; can

κουφός [koofos] deaf

ΚΡΑΓΙΟΝ κραγιόν (το) [krayon (to)] lipstick

κράμπα (η) [kramba (i)] cramp

κρανίο (το) [kranio (to)] skull

κρατάω [kratao] hold; keep

ΚΡΑΤΗΣΕΙΣ ΘΕΣΕΩΝ κρατήσεις θέσεων reservations; seat reservations

κράτηση θέσης (η) [kratisi THesis (i)] reservation

κρεβάτι (το) [krevati (to)] bed

ΚΡΕΜΑ ΠΡΟΣΩΠΟΥ κρέμα προσώπου (η) [krema prosopoo (i)] moisturizer

κρεμάστρα (η) [kremastra (i)] coathanger; peg

ΚΡΕΟΠΩΛΕΙΟ κρεοπωλείο (το) [kreopolio (to)] butcher's

κρίμα: είναι κρίμα [ineh krima] it's a pity

κρουαζιέρα (η) [kroo-aziera (i)] cruise

κρύβομαι [krivomeh] hide (oneself)

κρύβω [krivo] hide (something)

κρύο (το) [krio (to)] cold
κάνει κρύο [kani krio] it's cold

ΚΡΥΟ ΝΕΡΟ κρύο νερό [krio nero] cold water

κρύος [krios] cold (adj)

κρύωμα (το) [krioma (to)] cold (illness)

Κ.Τ.Ε.Λ. long-distance bus station

κτηνίατρος (ο/η) [ktiniatros (o/i)] vet

κτίριο (το) [ktirio (to)] building

κυβέρνηση (η) [kivernisi (i)] government

κυκλοφορία (η) [kikloforia (i)] traffic

κυκλοφοριακή συμφόρηση (η)
[kikloforiaki simforisi (i)] traffic
jam

ΚΥΛΙΚΕΙΟ κυλικείο (το) [kilikio
(to)] snackbar

ΚΥΛΟΤΕΣ κυλότες (οι) [kilotes
(i)] panties; underpants

κύμα (το) [kima (to)] wave

κυνηγώ [kinigo] hunt (verb),
chase

ΚΥΠΡΟΣ Κύπρος (η) [Kipros (i)]
Cyprus

Κυρία (η) [Kiria (i)] Mrs; Ms

κυρία (η) [kiria (i)] lady; madam

ΚΥΡΙΑΚΕΣ ΚΑΙ ΕΟΡΤΕΣ
Κυριακές και Εορτές Sundays
and holidays

ΚΥΡΙΑΚΗ Κυριακή (η) [Kiriaki
(i)] Sunday

ΚΥΡΙΑΚΗ ΤΟΥ ΠΑΣΧΑ
Κυριακή του Πάσχα (η) [Kiriaki
too Paskha (i)] Easter Sunday

κύριε [kiri-eh] sir

ΚΥΡΙΕΣ κυρίες [kiries] Mrs

ΚΥΡΙΟΙ κύριοι Messrs

ΚΥΡΙΟΣ Κύριος (ο) [Kirios] Mr

κύριος (ο) [kirios (o)] gentleman

κύριος [kirios] main

κύστη (η) [kisti (i)] bladder

κυττάζω [kitazo] look (verb)

ΚΩΔΙΚΟΣ κωδικός (ο) [kothikos
(o)] code

ΚΩΔΙΚΟΣ ΑΡΙΘΜΟΣ κωδικός
αριθμός [kothikos ariTHmos]
dialling code

Λ

ΛΑΔΙ λάδι (το) [lathi (to)] oil

ΛΑΔΙΑ λάδια (τα) [lathia (ta)]
engine oil

ΛΑΔΙ ΜΑΥΡΙΣΜΑΤΟΣ λάδι
μαυρίσματος [lathi mavrismatos]
suntan oil

λάθος (το) [laTHos (to)] mistake

λάθος [laTHos] wrong

λάθος νούμερο [laTHos noomero]
wrong number

λαιμός (ο) [lemos (o)] neck;
throat

λακ (η) [lak (i)] hairspray

λάμπα (η) [lamba (i)] light bulb;
lamp

λαστιχάκι (το) [lastikhaki (to)]
rubber band

λάστιχο (το) [lastikho (to)] rubber
(material); tyre

λεβιές ταχυτήτων (ο) [levies
takhititon (o)] gear lever

λείπω [lipo] be missing; be out;
be away

λειτουργία (η) [litooryia (i)] mass
(church)

λεκές (ο) [lekes (o)] stain

ΛΕΜΒΟΣ λέμβος (η) [lemvos (i)]
lifeboat

λένε: λένε ότι [leneh oti] they
say that

με λένε ... [meh leneh ...] my
name is ...

πως σε λένε; [pos seh leneh?]
what's your name?

λέξη (η) [lexi (i)] word

λεξικό (το) [lexiko (to)] dictionary

λεπτό (το) [lepto (to)] minute

λεπτός [leptos] slim

λέσχη (η) [leskhi (i)] club

λευκοπλάστ (το) [lefkoplast (to)] (sticking) plaster, Bandaid®

ΛΕΦΤΑ λεφτά (τα) [lefta (ta)] money

λέω [leo] say

ΛΕΩΦΟΡΕΙΟ λεωφορείο (το) [leoforio (to)] bus

ΛΕΩΦΟΡΕΙΟ ΥΠ᾽ ΑΡΙΘΜ ... λεωφορείο υπ᾽ αριθμ ... bus number ...

ΛΕΩΦΟΡΟΣ λεωφόρος (η) [leoforos (i)] avenue

ΛΗΓΕΙ ΤΗΝ ... λήγει την ... expires on ...

λιακάδα (η) [liakatha (i)] sunshine

λίγα [liga] a few

λίγο [ligo] a little bit

ΣΕ ΛΙΓΟ σε λίγο [seh ligo] in a little while

λίγος [ligos] little, short

λιγότερος [ligoteros] fewer

λιγότερο [ligotero] less

ΛΙΜΑΝΙ λιμάνι (το) [limani (to)] harbour

λίμα νυχιών (η) [lima nikhion (i)] nailfile

ΛΙΜΕΝΑΡΧΕΙΟ λιμεναρχείο (το) port authorities

ΛΙΜΕΝΑΡΧΗΣ λιμενάρχης (ο) harbour master

ΛΙΜΕΝΙΚΗ ΑΣΤΥΝΟΜΙΑ Λιμενική Αστυνομία (η) [limeniki Astinomia (i)] harbour police

ΛΙΜΗΝ λιμήν (ο) [limin (o)] port

λίμνη (η) [limni (i)] lake

λιμνούλα (η) [limnoola (i)] pond

λίμπρα (η) [libra (i)] pound (weight)

λιπαρός [liparos] greasy

λιποθυμώ [lipoTHimo] faint (verb)

ΛΙΡΑ ΑΓΓΛΙΑΣ λίρα Αγγλίας (η) [lira Anglias (i)] pound sterling

ΛΙΤΑΝΕΙΑ λιτανεία (η) litany

ΛΙΤΡΟ λίτρο (το) [litro (to)] litre

ΛΟΓΑΡΙΑΣΜΟΣ λογαριασμός (ο) [logariasmos (o)] bill, (US) check

λογικός [loyikos] sensible

ΛΟΓΙΣΤΗΡΙΟ λογιστήριο (το) [loyistirio (to)] purser's office

ΛΟΝΔΙΝΟ Λονδίνο (το) [Lonthino (to)] London

λόξυγγας (ο) [loxingas (o)] hiccups

λουλούδι (το) [looloothi (to)] flower

λούσιμο (το) [loosimo (to)] wash

ΛΟΥΤΡΟ λουτρό (το) [lootro (to)] bathroom

λόφος (ο) [lofos (o)] hill

λυπάμαι [lipameh] I'm sorry

λυπημένος [lipimenos] sad

ΛΥΡΙΚΗ ΣΚΗΝΗ λυρική σκηνή (η) [liriki skini (i)] opera house

M

μαγαζί (το) [magazi (to)] shop

μαγειρεύω [mayirevo] cook (verb)

μαγειρικά σκεύη (τα) [mayirika skevi (ta)] cooking utensils

μαγείρισσα (η) [mayirisa (i)] cook

μάγειρος (ο) [mayiros (o)] cook

μάγκας (ο) [mangas (o)]

streetwise/smart person

μαγιό (το) [mayo (to)] swimming trunks

μάγουλο (το) [magoolo (to)] chin

μαζί [mazi] together

μαζί με [mazi meh] with, together with

μαθαίνω [maтнeno] learn

μάθημα (το) [maтнima (to)] lesson

κάνω μάθημα [kano maтнima] teach; take a lesson

ΜΑΘΗΜΑΤΑ ΣΚΙ μαθήματα σκι [maтнimata ski] skiing lessons

ΜΑΙΟΣ Μάιος (ο) [Maios (o)] May

μακριά [makria] far, at a distance

μαλάκας (ο) [malakas (o)] arsehole, wanker

μακρύς [makris] long

ΜΑΛΑΚΟΙ ΦΑΚΟΙ μαλακοί φακοί (οι) [malaki faki (i)] soft lenses

μάλιστα [malista] yes, certainly

μάλιστα! [malista!] well!

ΜΑΛΛΙ μαλλί (το) [mali (to)] wool

μαλλιά (τα) [malia (ta)] hair

ΜΑΛΛΙΝΟ μάλλινο [malino] wool

μάλλον [malon] rather; probably

μαλώνω [malono] fight (verb)

μαμά (η) [mama (i)] mum

ΜΑΝΑΒΗΣ μανάβης (ο) [manavis (o)] greengrocer's

ΜΑΝΟ μανό (το) [mano (to)] nail polish

μανταλάκι (το) [mandalaki (to)]

clothes peg

μαντήλι (το) [mandili (to)] handkerchief; headscarf

μαξιλάρι (το) [maxilari (to)] pillow

μαραγκός (ο) [marangos (o)] carpenter

ΜΑΡΙΝΑ μαρίνα (η) [marina (i)] marina

μαρκαδόρος (ο) [markathoros (o)] felt-tip pen

ΜΑΡΤΙΟΣ Μάρτιος (ο) [Martios (o)] March

μάρτυρας (ο) [martiras (o)] witness

μασέλα (η) [masela (i)] dentures

μας [mas] us; our

μάτι (το) [mati (to)] eye; ring (on cooker)

ματς (το) [mats (to)] match (sport)

μαυρίζω [mavrizo] tan (verb)

μαύρισμα (το) [mavrisma (to)] tan (colour)

μαύρισμα από τον ήλιο [mavrisma apo ton ilio] suntan

μαύρος [mavros] black

μαχαίρι (το) [makheri (to)] knife

μαχαιροπήρουνα (τα) [makheropiroona (ta)] cutlery

με [meh] with; by; me

με αυτοκίνητο [meh aftokinito] by car

ΜΕΓΑΛΗ ΒΡΕΤΑΝΝΙΑ Μεγάλη Βρεταννία (η) [Megali Vretania (i)] Great Britain

Μεγάλη Παρασκευή (η) [Megali Paraskevi (i)] Good Friday

μεγάλος [megalos] big

μεγαλύτερος [megaliteros] bigger

ΜΕΓΕΘΟΣ μέγεθος (το)
[meyeTHos (to)] size

μεγέθυνση (η) [meyeTHinsi (i)]
enlargement

ΜΕΓΙΣΤΟ ΒΑΡΟΣ μέγιστο
βάρος maximum permitted
weight

μέγιστος (ο) [meyistos (o)] biggest

μεζ (η) [mez (i)] highlights (in
hair)

μεθαύριο [meTHavrio] the day
after tomorrow

μεθυσμένος [meTHismenos] drunk

μέικ απ (το) [meik ap (to)] make-
up

μελανιά (η) [melania (i)] bruise

μέλλον (το) [melon (to)] future

ΜΕ ΜΠΑΝΙΟ με μπάνιο [meh
banio] with bathroom

ΜΕ ΝΤΟΥΣ με ντους [meh doos]
with shower

μένω [meno] live (in town etc);
stay (in hotel etc)

μέρα (η) [mera (i)] day

μερίδα (η) [meritha (i)] portion

μερικά, μερικές, μερικοί [merika,
merikes, meriki] some

μέρος (το) [meros (to)] part,
place; WC

μέσα [mesa] in; inside

μεσάνυχτα (τα) [mesanikhta (ta)]
midnight

μέση (η) [mesi (i)] middle; waist

μεσημέρι (το) [mesimeri (to)]
midday

Μεσόγειος (η) [Mesoyios (i)]
Mediterranean

μετά [meta] after; afterwards

μετά από σας [meta apo sas]
after you

μετά μεσημβρίας [meta
mesimvrias] pm

μετακινούμαι [metakinoomeh]
move (verb)

μέταλλο (το) [metalo (to)] metal

ΜΕΤΑΞΙ μετάξι (το) [metaxi
(to)] silk

μεταξύ [metaxi] between

μεταφέρω [metafero] carry

μεταφράζω [metafrazo] translate

μετεωρολογικό δελτίο (το)
[meteoroloyiko theltio (to)]
weather forecast

ΜΕΤΡΗΤΑ μετρητά [metrita]
cash

ΤΟΙΣ ΜΕΤΡΗΤΟΙΣ τοις
μετρητοίς [tis metritis] in cash

μετρητής βενζίνης (ο) [metritis
venzinis (o)] fuel gauge

μέτριο μέγεθος [metrio meyeTHos]
medium-sized

ΜΕΤΡΙΟΣ μέτριος [metrios]
medium; average

ΜΕΤΡΟ μέτρο (το) [metro (to)]
metre

μέτωπο (το) [metopo (to)]
forehead

μέχρι [mekhri] until

ΜΗ μη do not

ΜΗ ΒΓΑΖΕΤΕ ΤΗΝ ΚΑΡΤΑ
μη βγάζετε την κάρτα do not
remove the card yet

μηδέν [mithen] zero

ΜΗΝ ΚΑΠΝΙΖΕΤΕ μην
καπνίζετε no smoking

ΜΗ ΚΑΠΝΙΖΟΝΤΕΣ μη
καπνίζοντες [mi kapnizondes]
non-smoking

ΜΗ ΚΑΠΝΙΣΤΕΣ μη καπνιστές [mi kapnistes] non-smokers

μήκος (το) [mikos (to)] length

μήνας (ο) [minas (o)] month

μήνας του μέλιτος [minas too melitos] honeymoon

ΜΗΝ ΕΝΟΧΛΕΙΤΕ μην ενοχλείτε do not disturb

ΜΗΝ ΟΜΙΛΕΙΤΕ ΣΤΟΝ ΟΔΗΓΟ μην ομιλείτε στον οδηγό do not speak to the driver

ΜΗΝ ΠΑΤΑΤΕ ΤΟ ΧΟΡΤΟ μην πατάτε το χόρτο keep off the grass

ΜΗ ΠΟΣΙΜΟ (ΝΕΡΟ) μη πόσιμο (νερό) not for drinking (water)

μητέρα (η) [mitera (i)] mother

ΜΗ ΤΟΞΙΚΟ μη τοξικό non-toxic

μητρόπολη (η) [mitropoli (i)] cathedral

μηχανάκι (το) [mikhanaki (to)] moped

μηχανή (η) [mikhani (i)] engine

μηχανικός (ο) [mikhanikos (o)] mechanic; engineer

μία [mia] a; one

μία φορά [mia fora] once

μιάς [mias] of a

μίζα (η) [miza (i)] ignition

ΜΙΚΡΟ ΟΝΟΜΑ μικρό όνομα (το) [mikro onoma (to)] Christian name

ΜΙΚΡΟΣ μικρός [mikros] little, small

ΜΙΚΤΟ ΒΑΡΟΣ μικτό βάρος gross weight

μικρότερος [mikroteros] smaller

ΜΙΛΑΕΙ μιλάει [milai] engaged, occupied

μιλάω [milao] speak

μιλάτε ...; [milateh ...?] do you speak ...?

μισός [misos] half

ΜΙΣΟΤΙΜΗΣ μισοτιμής half-price

μισώ [miso] hate (verb)

μ.μ. [m.m.] pm

μνημείο (το) [mnimio (to)] monument

μόδα (η) [motha (i)] fashion

της μόδας [tis mothas] fashionable

ΜΟΔΕΣ μόδες fashions

μοιάζει [miazi] it looks/seems

μοιράζομαι [mirazomeh] share (verb)

μοκέτα (η) [moketa (i)] carpet

μολύβι (το) [molivi (to)] pencil

μόλυνση (η) [molinsi (i)] infection

ΜΟΛΥΣΜΕΝΑ ΥΔΑΤΑ μολυσμένα ύδατα polluted water

μολυσμένος [molismenos] polluted

ΜΟΝΑΔΕΣ μονάδες units

ΜΟΝΑΔΙΚΗ ΕΥΚΑΙΡΙΑ μοναδική ευκαιρία (η) special offer

μονή [moni] monastery

μόνο [mono] only

ΜΟΝΟΔΡΟΜΟΣ μονόδρομος one-way street

ΜΟΝΟ ΔΩΜΑΤΙΟ μονό δωμάτιο (το) [mono thomatio (to)]

single room
ΜΟΝΟΚΛΙΝΟ ΔΩΜΑΤΙΟ
μονόκλινο δωμάτιο (το)
[monoklino thomatio (to)] single
room
μονό κρεβάτι [mono krevati]
single bed
μονοπάτι (το) [monopati (to)] path
μόνος [monos] alone
μοντέρνος [mondernos] modern
μοτοσυκλέτα (η) [motosikleta (i)]
motorbike
μου [moo] my
ΜΟΥΣΕΙΟ μουσείο (το) [moosio
(to)] museum
ΜΟΥΣΙΚΑ ΟΡΓΑΝΑ μουσικά
όργανα [moosika organa]
musical instruments
μουσική (η) [moosiki (i)] music
μουσική ποπ (η) [moosiki pop (i)]
pop music
μουστάκι (το) [moostaki (to)]
moustache
μπαίνω [beno] go in, enter
ΜΠΑΚΑΛΙΚΟ μπακάλικο (το)
[bakaliko (to)] grocer's
μπαλκόνι (το) [balkoni (to)]
balcony
μπάλλα (η) [bala (i)] ball (large)
μπαλλάκι (το) [balaki (to)] ball
(small)
μπαμπάς (ο) [babas (o)] dad
μπανιέρα (η) [baniera (i)] bathtub
ΜΠΑΝΙΟ μπάνιο (το) [banio
(to)] bath
κάνω μπάνιο [kano banio] swim
(verb); have a bath
πάω για μπάνιο [pao ya banio]
go swimming

ΜΠΑΡ μπαρ (το) [bar (to)] bar
μπάρμαν (ο) [barman (o)] barman
μπάρ γούμαν (η) [bar woman (i)]
barmaid
μπαταρία (η) [bataria (i)] battery
μπεζ [bez] beige
μπέιμπι-σίττερ (η) [baby-sitter (i)]
babysitter
μπερδεμένος [berthemenos]
complicated
μπικίνι (το) [bikini (to)] bikini
μπλε [bleh] blue
μπλούζα (η) [blooza (i)] blouse
μπλουζάκι (το) [bloozaki (to)]
T-shirt
μπόρα (η) [bora (i)] shower (rain)
μπορείς [boris] you can
μπορείς να ...; [boris na ...?] can
you ...?
μπορείτε [boriteh] you can
μπορείτε να ...; [boriteh na ...?]
can you ...?
μπρος [bros] forwards; in front
of
βάζω μπρος [vazo bros] switch
on (engine)
μπορώ [boro] I can
μπότα (η) [bota (i)] boot (shoe)
μπουγάδα (η) [boogatha (i)]
washing
βάζω μπουγάδα [vazo boogatha]
do the washing
μπουζί (το) [boozi (to)] spark
plug
ΜΠΟΥΖΟΥΚΙΑ μπουζούκια
(τα) [boozookia (ta)] club with
bouzouki music
μπουκάλι (το) [bookali (to)] bottle
μπουκιά (η) [bookia (i)] bite

μπούτι (το) [booti (to)] thigh
ΜΠΟΥΤΙΚ μπουτίκ (η) [bootik (i)] boutique
μπροστινό μέρος (το) [brostino meros (to)] front (part)
ΜΠΥΡΑ μπύρα [bira] beer, lager
μπωλ (το) [bol (to)] bowl
μύγα (η) [miga (i)] fly
μυθιστόρημα (το) [miTHistorima (to)] novel
μυρίζω [mirizo] smell (verb)
μυρμήγκι (το) [mirmingi (to)] ant
μυρωδιά (η) [mirothia (i)] smell
μυστικός [mistikos] secret
μυς (ο) [mis (o)] muscle
μύτη (η) [miti (i)] nose
μύωπας [miopas] shortsighted
μωβ [mov] purple
μωρό (το) [moro (to)] baby

N

να [na] here is/are
ναι [neh] yes
ναι, ναι! [neh neh!] oh yes I do!
νάιτκλαμπ (το) [nightclub (to)] nightclub
ΝΑ ΛΑΜΒΑΝΕΤΑΙ ΜΟΝΟΝ ΑΠΟ ΤΟ ΣΤΟΜΑ να λαμβάνεται μόνον από το στόμα to be taken orally only
ΝΑ ΛΑΜΒΑΝΕΤΑΙ ... ΦΟΡΕΣ ΗΜΕΡΗΣΙΩΣ να λαμβάνεται ... φορές ημερησίως to be taken ... times daily
ναρκωτικά (τα) [narkotika (ta)] drugs (narcotics)

ΝΑ ΦΥΛΑΣΣΕΤΑΙ ΜΑΚΡΙΑ ΑΠΟ ΠΑΙΔΙΑ να φυλάσσεται μακριά από παιδιά keep out of reach of children
νέα (η) [nea (i)] teenager
νέα (τα) [nea (ta)] news
ΝΕΑ ΖΗΛΑΝΔΙΑ Νέα Ζηλανδία (η) [Nea Zilanthia (i)] New Zealand
ΝΕΚΡΟΤΑΦΕΙΟ νεκροταφείο (το) [nekrotafio (to)] cemetery
Νέο Έτος (το) [Neo Etos (to)] New Year
ΝΕΟΖΗΛΑΝΔΕΖΑ Νεοζηλανδέζα (η) [Neozilantheza (i)] New Zealander
ΝΕΟΖΗΛΑΝΔΟΣ Νεοζηλανδός (ο) [Neozilanthos (o)] New Zealander
νέοι (οι) [nei (i)] young people
νέος (ο) [neos (o)] teenager
νέος [neos] new; young
ΝΕΡΟ νερό (το) [nero (to)] water
νεροχύτης (ο) [nerokhitis (o)] sink
νευρικός [nevrikos] nervous
νεφρά (τα) [nefra (ta)] kidneys
νησί (το) [nisi (to)] island
νιπτήρας (ο) [niptiras (o)] washbasin
νιώθω [nioTHo] feel
ΝΟΕΜΒΡΙΟΣ Νοέμβριος (ο) [Noemvrios (o)] November
νοικιάζω [nikiazo] rent (verb)
ΝΟΜΑΡΧΙΑ νομαρχία (η) local government office
νομίζω [nomizo] think
ΝΟΜΟΣ νομός (ο) [nomos (o)] county
νόμος (ο) [nomos (o)] law

ΝΟΣΟΚΟΜΕΙΟ νοσοκομείο (το)
[nosokomio (to)] hospital

νόστιμο [nostimo] tasty

νοστιμώτατο [nostimotato]
delicious

ΝΟΥΜΕΡΟ νούμερο (το)
[noomero (to)] number

ΝΤΕΜΙ ΠΑΝΣΙΟΝ ντεμί
πανσιόν (η) [demi pansion (i)]
half board

ντεπόζιτο (το) [ndepozito (to)]
tank

ΝΤΗΖΕΛ ντήζελ (το) [dizel (to)]
diesel

ντισκοτέκ (η) [ndiskotek (i)] disco

ντιστριμπυτέρ (το) [ndIstribiter
(to)] distributor

ντουλάπι (το) [ndoolapi (to)]
cupboard

ΝΤΟΥΣ ντους (το) [doos (to)]
shower (in bathroom)

ΝΤΡΑΙΒ - ΙΝ ντραιβ - ιν
drive-in

ντροπαλός [ndropalos] shy

ντύνομαι [ndinomeh] dress
(oneself)

ντύνω [ndino] dress (verb:
someone)

νύφη (η) [nifi (i)] daughter-in-
law; sister-in-law; bride

νύχι (το) [nikhi (to)]
fingernail

νυχοκόπτης (ο) [nikhokoptis (o)]
nail clippers

νύχτα (η) [nikhta (i)] night

ΝΥΧΤΕΡΙΝΟ ΚΕΝΤΡΟ
νυχτερινό κέντρο [nikhterino
kendro] nightclub

νυχτικό (το) [nikhtiko (to)]
nightdress

νωρίς [noris] early

Ξ

ξαδέλφη (η) [xathelfi (i)] cousin

ξάδελφος (ο) [xathelfos (o)] cousin

ξανά [xana] again

ξανθός [xanthos] blond

ξαπλώνω [xaplono] lie down

ξαφνικά [xafnika] suddenly

ξεκουράζομαι [xekoorazomeh]
relax

ξεναγός (ο/η) [xenagos (o/i)] guide

ΞΕΝΟΔΟΧΕΙΟ ξενοδοχείο (το)
[xenothokhio (to)] hotel

ξένος [xenos] foreign

ΞΕΝΩΝΑΣ ξενώνας (ο) [xenonas
(o)] guesthouse

ΞΕΝΩΝΑΣ ΝΕΟΤΗΤΑΣ
ξενώνας νεότητας [xenonas
neotitas] youth hostel

ΞΕΝΩΝΑΣ ΝΕΩΝ ξενώνας νέων
[xenonas neon] youth hostel

ΞΕΠΟΥΛΗΜΑ ξεπούλημα
closing-down sale

ξέρω [xero] know

δεν ξέρω [then xero] I don't
know

ξεφωνίζω [xefonizo] scream (verb)

ξεχνώ [xekhno] leave (verb);
forget

ξεχωριστά [xekhorista] separately

ξηρός [xiros] dry

ξοδεύω [xothevo] spend

ξύλο (το) [xilo (to)] wood

ξυνός [xinos] sour

ξυπνάω [xipnao] wake up

ξυπνητήρι (το) [xipnitiri (to)] alarm clock

ξύπνιος [xipnios] awake

ξυραφάκι (το) [xirafaki (to)] razor

ξυρίζομαι [xirizomeh] shave (verb)

ξύρισμα (το) [xirisma (to)] shave

ξυριστική μηχανή (η) [xiristiki mikhani (i)] electric shaver

Ο

ο [o] the

Ο.Α. Olympic Airways

Ο/Γ ferry

ογδόντα [ogthonda] eighty

όγδοος [ogthoos] eighth

οδηγάω [othigao] drive

οδηγός (ο/η) [othigos (o/i)] driver

ΟΔΙΚΑ ΕΡΓΑ οδικά έργα roadworks

ΟΔΟΝΤΙΑΤΡΟΣ οδοντίατρος (ο/η) [othondiatros (o/i)] dentist

οδοντόβουρτσα (η) [othondovoortsa (i)] toothbrush

ΟΔΟΝΤΟΓΙΑΤΡΟΣ οδοντογιατρός (ο/η) [othondoyatros (o/i)] dentist

ΟΔΟΝΤΙΑΤΡΕΙΟ οδοντιατρείο (το) [othondiatrio (to)] dentist's

ΟΔΟΝΤΟΚΡΕΜΑ οδοντόκρεμα (η) [othondokrema (i)] toothpaste

ΟΔΟΣ οδός (η) [othos (i)] road, street

ΟΔΟΣ ΑΝΕΥ ΣΗΜΑΝΣΕΩΣ ΣΕ ΜΗΚΟΣ ... ΧΙΛ. οδός άνευ σημάνσεως σε μήκος ... χιλ. no road markings for ...

kms

οδυνηρός [othiniros] painful

όζα (η) [oza (i)] nail polish

Ο.Η.Ε. UN

ΟΧΙ ΕΠΙΤΑΓΕΣ όχι επιταγές no cheques/checks

οι [i] the

οικογένεια (η) [ikoyenia (i)] family

ΟΚΤΩΒΡΙΟΣ Οκτώβριος (ο) [Oktovrios (o)] October

όλα [ola] all

όλα καλά [ola kala] that'll do nicely, everything's fine

όλα πληρωμένα [ola pliromena] all inclusive

όλες, όλη [oles, oli] all

ΟΛΙΣΘΗΡΟ ΟΔΟΣΤΡΩΜΑ ολισθηρό οδόστρωμα slippery road surface

όλο [olo] αμμ

όλοι [oli] everyone; all

ολόκληρος [olokliros] whole

όλος [olos] all

Ο.Λ.Π. Piraeus Port Authorities

ΟΛΥΜΠΙΑΚΗ ΑΕΡΟΠΟΡΙΑ Ολυμπιακή Αεροπορία Olympic Airways

ομάδα (η) [omatha (i)] group; team

ομάδα αίματος (η) [omatha ematos (i)] blood group

ομίχλη (η) [omikhli (i)] fog

όμοιος [omios] similar

όμορφος [omorfos] fine, beautiful

ομοφυλόφιλος (ο) [omofilofilos (o)] gay

ομπρέλλα (η) [ombrella (i)]

umbrella

όνειρο (το) [oniro (to)] dream

ΟΝΟΜΑ όνομα (το) [onoma (to)] name; first name

οπά! [opa!] watch it!

ΟΠΕΡΑ όπερα (η) [opera (i)] opera

όπισθεν (η) [opisтнen (i)] reverse (gear)

όπλο (το) [oplo (to)] gun; rifle

ΟΠΤΙΚΑ οπτικά (τα) [optika (ta)] optician's

ΟΠΤΙΚΟΣ οπτικός (ο) [optikos (o)] optician

ΟΠΩΡΟΠΩΛΕΙΟ οπωροπωλείο (το) [oporopolio (to)] grocer's

όπως [opos] like; as

όπως και νάναι [opos keh naneh] anyway

ΟΡΓΑΝΙΣΜΟΣ ΗΝΩΜΕΝΩΝ ΕΘΝΩΝ Οργανισμός Ηνωμένων Εθνών United Nations Organization

οργανωμένη εκδρομή (η) [organomeni ekthromi (i)] package tour

οργανώνω [organono] organize

όρεξη (η) [orexi (i)] appetite

καλή όρεξη! [kali orexi!] enjoy your meal!, bon appetit!

ΟΡΘΙΩΝ ορθίων standing

ΟΡΙΟ ΤΑΧΥΤΗΤΑΣ όριο ταχύτητας (το) speed limit

ορίστε; [oristeh?] can I help you?

όροφος (ο) [orofos (o)] floor, storey

ΟΡΥΚΤΕΛΑΙΟ ορυκτέλαιο (το) [orikteleo (to)] engine oil

ορχήστρα (η) [orkhistra (i)] orchestra

Ο.Σ.Ε. Greek Railways

όταν [otan] when

Ο.Τ.Ε. Greek Telecommunications Company

ότι [oti] that

οτιδήποτε [otithipoteh] anything

Ο.Υ. water authorities

Ουαλλή (η) [Ooali (i)] Welshwoman

ΟΥΑΛΛΙΑ Ουαλλία (η) [Ooalia (i)] Wales

Ουαλλικός [Ooalikos] Welsh (adj)

Ουαλλός (ο) [Ooalos (o)] Welshman

ΟΥΖΕΡΙ ουζερί [oozeri] bar serving ouzo and beer with snacks or full meals

σύλο (το) [oolo (to)] gum (in mouth)

ΟΥΡΑ ουρά (η) [oora (i)] queue; tail; queue here

κάνω ουρά [kano oora] queue (verb)

ουρανός (ο) [ooranos (o)] sky

ούτε ... ούτε ... [oote ... oote ...] neither ... nor ...

ΟΦΘΑΛΜΙΑΤΡΟΣ οφθαλμίατρος (ο/η) eye specialist

όχημα (το) [okhima (to)] vehicle

ΟΧΙ όχι [okhi] no; not

όχι άλλο [okhi allo] no more

ΟΧΙ ΥΠΕΡΑΣΤΙΚΑ όχι υπεραστικά no long-distance calls

οχτώ [okhto] eight

Π

ΠΑΓΟΣ πάγος (ο) [pagos (o)] ice

παγωτο παγωτό (το) [pagoto (to)] ice cream

παγωτο ξυλακι παγωτό ξυλάκι (το) [pagoto xilaki (to)] ice lolly

πάει: πώς πάει; [pos pai?] how are things?

ΠΑΖΑΡΙ παζάρι (το) [pazari (to)] bazaar

ΠΑΘΟΛΟΓΟΣ παθολόγος (ο/η) [paтHologos (o/i)] doctor, general practitioner

ΠΑΙΔΙ παιδί (το) [pethi (to)] child

ΠΑΙΔΙΑΤΡΟΣ παιδίατρος (ο/η) paediatrician

ΠΑΙΔΙΚΑ παιδικά (τα) [pethika (ta)] children's wear

ΠΑΙΔΙΚΑ ΕΙΔΗ παιδικά είδη (τα) [pethika ithi (ta)] children's department

ΠΑΙΔΙΚΑ ΕΣΩΡΟΥΧΑ παιδικά εσώρουχα [pethika esorookha] children's underwear

ΠΑΙΔΙΚΑ ΦΟΡΜΑΚΙΑ παιδικά φορμάκια [pethika formakia] babywear, toddlers' clothes

ΠΑΙΔΙΚΟ παιδικό [pethiko] children's (adj)

παίζω [pezo] play (verb)

παίρνω [perno] get; take

παίρνω τηλέφωνο [perno tilefono] phone (verb)

ΠΑΙΧΝΙΔΙ παιχνίδι (το) [pekhnithi (to)] game; toy

ΠΑΚΕΤΟ πακέτο (το) [paketo (to)] package; packet

ΠΑΛΑΙΟΠΩΛΕΙΟ παλαιοπωλείο (το) [paleopolio (to)] antique shop

παλαιός [paleos] old, ancient, antique

παλάτι (το) [palati (to)] palace

παλίρροια (η) [paliria (i)] tide

παλτό (το) [palto (to)] coat

πάνα (η) [pana (i)] nappy, diaper

ΠΑΝΕΠΙΣΤΗΜΙΟ πανεπιστήμιο (το) [panepistimio (to)] university

ΠΑΝΗΓΥΡΙ πανηγύρι (το) [paniyiri (to)] fair, funfair

πανί (το) [pani (to)] sail

ΠΑΝ/ΜΙΟ παν/μιο university

ΠΑΝΣΙΟΝ πανσιόν (η) [pansion (i)] guesthouse

πάντα [panda] always; still

πανταλόνι (το) [pandaloni (to)] trousers, (US) pants

παντζούρια (τα) [pandzooria (ta)] shutters

ΠΑΝΤΟΠΩΛΕΙΟ παντοπωλείο (το) [pandopolio (to)] grocery store

πάντοτε [pandoteh] always

παντού [pandoo] everywhere

παντόφλες (οι) [pandofles (i)] slippers

παντρεμένος [pandremenos] married

παντρεμένη [pandremeni] married

πάνω [pano] on; up; upstairs

πάνω από [pano apo] above

παξιμάδι (το) [paximathi (to)] nut (for bolt)

παπάς (ο) [papas (o)] priest

πάπια (η) [papia (i)] duck

πάπλωμα (το) [paploma (to)] quilt

παπούτσι (το) [papootsi (to)] shoe

παππούς (ο) [pappoos (o)] grandfather

παραγγελία (η) [parangelia (i)] message

παραγγέλνω [paragelno] order (verb: in restaurant)

παράδειγμα (το) [parathigma (to)] example

παραδείγματος χάρι [parathigmatos khari] for example

παράδοση (η) [parathosi (i)] tradition

παραδοσιακός [parathosiakos] traditional

παράθυρο (το) [paraThiro (to)] window

παρακαλώ [parakalo] please; excuse me; don't mention it

παρακαλώ; [parakalo?] can I help you?

ΠΑΡΑΚΑΜΠΤΗΡΙΟΣ παρακαμπτήριος (η) diversion

ΠΑΡΑΛΑΒΗ ΑΠΟΣΚΕΥΩΝ παραλαβή αποσκευών (η) [paralavi aposkevon (i)] baggage claim

ΠΑΡΑΛΙΑ παραλία (η) [paralia (i)] beach

κοντά στην παραλία [konda stin paralia] at the seaside

παραμάνα (η) [paramana (i)] safety pin

παραμένω [parameno] stay (verb), remain

παράξενος [paraxenos] strange

παραπονούμαι [paraponoomeh] complain

ΠΑΡΑΣΚΕΥΗ Παρασκευή (η) [Paraskevi (i)] Friday

παρατηρώ [paratiro] watch (verb)

παρατσούκλι (το) [paratsookli (to)] nickname

παρεξήγηση (η) [parexiyisi (i)] misunderstanding

παρκάρω [parkaro] park (verb)

ΠΑΡΚΙΝΓΚ πάρκινγκ (το) [parking (to)] car park, parking lot

πάρκο (το) [parko (to)] park

ΠΑΡΟΔΟΣ πάροδος (η) [parothos (i)] side street

παρμπρίζ (το) [parpriz (to)] windscreen

πάρτυ (το) [parti (to)] party, celebration

παστίλιες λαιμού (οι) [pastili-es lemoo (i)] throat pastilles

Πάσχα (το) [Paskha (to)] Easter

πατέρας (ο) [pateras (o)] father

πατερίτσες (οι) [pateritses (i)] crutches

πάτωμα (το) [patoma (to)] floor (of room)

ΠΑΥΣΙΠΟΝΟ παυσίπονο (το) [pafsipono (to)] painkiller

πάχος (το) [pakhos (to)] fat (on meat)

παχύς [pakhis] fat; thick

πάω [pao] go (verb)

πεζοδρόμιο (το) [pezothromio (to)] pavement, sidewalk

ΠΕΖΟΔΡΟΜΟΣ πεζόδρομος (ο) pedestrian precinct

ΠΕΖΟΙ πεζοί pedestrians
πεθαίνω [peΤΗeno] die
πεθαμένος [peΤΗamenos] dead
πεθερά (η) [peΤΗera (i)] mother-in-law
πεθερός (ο) [peΤΗeros (o)] father-in-law
πειράζει [pirazi] it matters
  θα σε πείραζε αν ...; [ΤΗa seh pirazeh an ...?] do you mind if I ...?
  δεν πειράζει [then pirazi] it doesn't matter
ΠΕΙΡΑΙΑΣ Πειραιάς [Pireas] Piraeus
ΠΕΜΠΤΗ Πέμπτη (η) [Pempti (i)] Thursday
πέμπτος [pemptos] fifth
πενήντα [peninda] fifty
ΠΕΝΗΝΤΑΡΙΚΟ
  πενηντάρικο (το) [penindariko (to)] 50-drachma coin or note/bill
πενικιλλίνη (η) [penikilini (i)] penicillin
πέννα (η) [pena (i)] pen
πένσα (η) [pensa (i)] pliers
ΠΕΝΤΑΚΟΣΑΡΙΚΟ
  πεντακοσάρικο (το) [pendakosariko (to)] 500-drachma note/bill
πέντε [pendeh] five
πέος (το) [peos (to)] penis
περάστε [perasteh] come in; come back
ΠΕΡΙΕΧΟΜΕΝΟ περιεχόμενο contains
περίμενε [perimeneh] wait
περιμένω [perimeno] wait (for); expect
ΠΕΡΙΟΔΙΚΟ περιοδικό (το) [periothiko (to)] magazine
περίοδος (η) [periothos (i)] period
περιοχή (η) [periokhi (i)] area
περίπατος (ο) [peripatos (o)] walk
  πάω περίπατο [pao peripato] go for a walk
περίπου [peripoo] about, approximately
ΠΕΡΙΠΤΕΡΟ περίπτερο [periptero] newspaper kiosk
ΣΕ ΠΕΡΙΠΤΩΣΗ ΑΝΑΓΚΗΣ ΣΠΑΣΤΕ ΤΟ ΤΖΑΜΙ σε περίπτωση ανάγκης σπάστε το τζάμι [seh periptosi anangis spasteh to tzami] in emergency break glass
περισσότερο [perisotero] more, most (of)
περισσότερος [perisoteros] more, most (of)
ΠΕΡΜΑΝΑΝΤ περμανάντ (η) [permanand (i)] perm
περνάω [pernao] cross, go through
περπατάω [perpatao] walk (verb)
πέρσυ [persi] last year
πετάλι (το) [petali (to)] pedal
πετάω [petao] throw away (verb)
πέτρα (η) [petra (i)] stone
πετσέτα (η) [petseta (i)] napkin; towel
πετσέτα κουζίνας [petseta koozinas] tea towel
πετώ [peto] fly (verb)
πέφτω [pefto] fall (verb)
πηγή (η) [piyi (i)] fountain
πηγούνι (το) [pigooni (to)] chin

πηδάω [pithao] jump (verb)
πηρούνι (το) [pirooni (to)] fork
πιάνω [piano] catch (verb)
πιατάκι (το) [piataki (to)] saucer
πιατικά (τα) [piatika (ta)] crockery
πιάτο (το) [piato (to)] dish; plate
ΠΙΕΣΗ ΑΙΜΑΤΟΣ πίεση αίματος (η) [piesi ematos (i)] blood pressure
πιθανώς [piTHanos] probably
πικάντικος [pikandikos] spicy
πικάπ (το) [pikap (to)] record player
πικνίκ (το) [piknik (to)] picnic
πικρός [pikros] bitter
πιλότυς (ο) [pilotos (o)] pilot
πινακίδες (οι) [pinakithes (i)] number plates
ΠΙΝΑΚΟΘΗΚΗ πινακοθήκη (η) [pinakoTHiki (i)] art gallery
πινγκ-πονγκ (το) [ping-pong (to)] table tennis
πινέλο (το) [pinelo (to)] paintbrush
πινέλο για ξύρισμα [pinelo ya xirisma] shaving brush
πίνω [pinno] drink (verb)
πίπα (η) [pipa (i)] pipe (for smoking)
ΠΙΣΙΝΑ πισίνα (η) [pisina (i)] swimming pool
πιστεύω [pistevo] believe
πιστολάκι (το) [pistolaki (to)] hairdryer
πιστόλι (το) [pistoli (to)] gun, pistol
πιστοποιητικό (το) [pistopi-itiko (to)] certificate
ΠΙΣΤΩΤΙΚΗ ΚΑΡΤΑ

πιστωτική κάρτα (η) [pistotiki karta (i)] credit card
πίσω [piso] back; behind
πίσω φώτα (τα) [piso fota (ta)] rear lights
ΠΙΤΣΑΡΙΑ πιτσαρία (η) [pitsaria (i)] pizzeria
πλαστική σακούλα (η) [plastiki sakoola (i)] plastic bag
πλαστικός [plastikos] plastic
ΠΛΑΤΕΙΑ πλατεία (η) [platia (i)] square (in town); stalls (in theatre)
πλάτη (η) [plati (i)] back (of person)
πλατύς [platis] wide
ΠΛΑΤΦΟΡΜΑ πλατφόρμα (η) [platforma (i)] platform, (US) track
πλέκω [pleko] knit
πλένομαι [plenomeh] wash (oneself)
πλένω [pleno] wash (verb: something)
πλευρά (η) [plevra (i)] side
πλευρό (το) [plevro (to)] rib
πληγή (η) [pliyi (i)] wound
πλήθος (το) [pliTHos (to)] crowd
ΠΛΗΡΕΣ πλήρες no vacancies, full
ΠΛΗΡΟΦΟΡΙΕΣ πληροφορίες (οι) [plirofories (i)] information; directory enquiries
ΠΛΗΡΩΜΑ πλήρωμα (το) crew
πληρώνω [plirono] pay (verb)
πλοίο (το) [plio (to)] boat, ship
πλούσιος [ploosios] rich
πλυντήριο (το) [plindirio (to)] washing machine
ΠΛΥΝΤΗΡΙΟ ΑΥΤΟΚΙΝΗΤΩΝ

πλυντήριο αυτοκινήτων car wash

ΠΛΥΝΤΗΡΙΟ ΡΟΥΧΩΝ

πλυντήριο ρούχων [plindirio **rook**hon] launderette, laundromat

ΠΛΥΣΙΜΟ ΜΕ ΤΟ ΧΕΡΙ

πλύσιμο με το χέρι handwash only

πλύσιμο των πιάτων (το) [**pl**isimo ton piaton (to)] washing up

πνεύμονες (οι) [**pnev**mones (i)] lungs

ποδηλασία (η) [pothi**la**sia (i)] cycling

ποδηλάτης (ο/η) [pothi**la**tis (o/i)] cyclist

ΠΟΔΗΛΑΤΟ ποδήλατο (το) [po**thi**lato (to)] bicycle

πόδι (το) [**po**thi (to)] foot; leg

με τα πόδια [meh ta **po**thia] on foot

ποδόσφαιρο (το) [po**thos**fero (to)] football

ποιά; [pia?] who?

ποιανού; [pia**noo**?] whose?

ποιό; [pio?] which?

ποιός; [pios?] who?

ποιός είναι; [**pi**os **i**neh?] who is it?

πόλεμος (ο) [**po**lemos (o)] war

πόλη (η) [**po**li (i)] city, town

πολιτεία (η) [poli**ti**a (i)] state

πολιτικά (τα) [poli**ti**ka (ta)] politics

πολιτικός [politi**kos**] political; politician

πολλά, πολλές, πολλή, πολλοί [po**la**, po**les**, po**li**, po**li**] many, a lot (of)

πολύ [po**li**] a lot of; very; too much

πάρα πολύ [**pa**ra po**li**] too much; very much

πολυσύχναστος [polisi**khnas**tos] busy (place)

πολύς [po**lis**] a lot (of)

ΠΟΛΥΤΕΛΕΙΑΣ πολυτελείας luxury class, four-star (hotel)

πονάει [po**na**i] hurt

πονόδοντος (ο) [pono**thon**dos (o)] toothache

πονοκέφαλος (ο) [pono**ke**falos (o)] headache

πόνος (ο) [**po**nos (o)] ache, pain

ποντίκι (το) [pon**di**ki (to)] mouse

πόνυ (το) [**po**ni (to)] pony

πορεία (η) [po**ri**a (i)] route

πόρτα (η) [**por**ta (i)] door

πορτ-μπαγκάζ (το) [port-ban**gaz** (to)] boot (car), (US) trunk

πορτ-μπε-μπέ (το) [port-be-**be** (to)] carrycot

πορτοκαλί [porto**ka**li] orange (colour)

πορτοφολάς (ο) [portofo**las** (o)] pickpocket

πορτοφόλι (το) [porto**fo**li (to)] wallet

πόσα;, πόσες;, [**po**sa?, **po**ses?] how many?

ΠΟΣΙΜΟ ΝΕΡΟ πόσιμο νερό (το) [**po**simo ne**ro** (to)] drinking water

πόσο; [**po**so?] how much?

πόσοι; [**po**si?] how many?

πόστερ (το) [**pos**ter (to)] poster

ΠΟΣΤ ΡΕΣΤΑΝΤ ποστ ρεστάντ

[post restant] poste restante
ποτάμι (το) [potami (to)] river
ποτέ [poteh] never
πότε; [poteh?] when?
έχετε ποτέ ...; [ekheteh poteh ...?] have you ever ...?
ποτήρι (το) [potiri (to)] glass
ΠΟΤΟΠΩΛΕΙΟ ποτοπωλείο (το) [potopolio (to)] off-licence, liquor store
που [poo] who, which, that
πού; [poo?] where?
πούδρα ταλκ (η) [poothra talk (i)] talcum powder
πουθενά [poothena] nowhere
πουκάμισο (το) [pookamiso (to)] shirt
πουλί (το) [pooli (to)] bird
ΠΟΥΛΜΑΝ πούλμαν (το) [poolman (to)] bus, coach
πουλόβερ (το) [poolover (to)] jumper
πουλώ [poolo] sell
πούρο (το) [pooro (to)] cigar
πράγμα (το) [pragma (to)] thing
πραγματικά [pragmatika] really
πρακτικός [praktikos] practical
πρακτορείο (το) [praktorio (to)] agency
ΠΡΑΚΤΟΡΕΙΟ ΕΦΗΜΕΡΙΔΩΝ πρακτορείο εφημερίδων newsagent, news vendor
ΠΡΑΚΤΟΡΕΙΟ ΛΕΩΦΟΡΕΙΩΝ πρακτορείο λεωφορείων [praktorio leoforion] bus station
πράσινος [prasinos] green
ΠΡΑΤΗΡΙΟ ΒΕΝΖΙΝΗΣ πρατήριο βενζίνης (το) [pratirio venzinis (to)] petrol station, gas

station
πρέπει να ... [prepi na ...] I must ...
ΠΡΕΣΒΕΙΑ πρεσβεία (η) [presvia (i)] embassy
πρησμένος [prismenos] swollen
πρίγκηπας (ο) [pringipas (o)] prince
πριγκίπισσα (η) [pringipisa (i)] princess
πρίζα (η) [priza (i)] socket; plug
πρίζα ταυ (η) [priza taf (i)] adaptor
πριν [prin] before; ago
πριν τρεις μέρες [prin tris meres] three days ago
προάστια (τα) [proastia (ta)] suburbs
πρόβατο (το) [provato (to)] sheep
πρόβλημα (το) [provlima (to)] problem
ΠΡΟΒΛΗΤΑ προβλήτα (η) [provlita (i)] quay
προβολείς (οι) [provolis (i)] headlights
ΠΡΟΓΕΥΜΑ πρόγευμα (το) [proyevma (to)] breakfast
πρόγονος (ο/η) [proyonos (o/i)] ancestor
ΠΡΟΓΡΑΜΜΑ πρόγραμμα (το) [programa (to)] timetable, (US) schedule; programme
προκαταβάλλω [prokatavalo] advance (verb)
προκαταβολικά [prokatavolika] in advance
ΠΡΟΞΕΝΕΙΟ προξενείο (το) [proxenio (to)] consulate
ΠΡΟΟΡΙΣΜΟΣ προορισμός

[pro-orism**os**] destination

προσβάλλω [pros**v**alo] offend

ΠΡΟΣ ΓΚΑΡΑΖ προς γκαράζ to car deck

ΠΡΟΣΔΕΘΗΤΕ προσδεθήτε fasten your seat belt

προσεκτικός [prosektik**os**] careful

πρόσεξε! [pr**o**sexeh!] look out!

ΠΡΟΣΕΧΕ! πρόσεχε! [pr**o**sekheh!] look out!

προσέχω [pros**e**kho] take care of

ΠΡΟΣΕΧΩΣ προσεχώς coming soon

πρόσθετο (το) [pr**o**sTHeto (to)] supplementary

προσκαλώ [proskal**o**] invite

πρόσκληση (η) [pr**o**sklisi (i)] invitation

ΠΡΟΣ ΟΡΟΦΟΥΣ προς ορόφους to all floors

ΠΡΟΣΟΧΗ! προσοχή! caution!

ΠΡΟΣΟΧΗ ΑΡΓΑ προσοχή αργά caution: slow

ΠΡΟΣΟΧΗ ΕΞΟΔΟΣ ΟΧΗΜΑΤΩΝ προσοχή έξοδος οχημάτων caution: vehicle exit

ΠΡΟΣΟΧΗ ΕΥΦΛΕΚΤΟΝ προσοχή εύφλεκτον caution: highly inflammable

ΠΡΟΣΟΧΗ ΚΙΝΔΥΝΟΣ προσοχή κίνδυνος caution: danger

προσοχή παρακαλώ [prosokh**i** parakal**o**] attention please

ΠΡΟΣΟΧΗ ΣΚΥΛΟΣ προσοχή σκύλος beware of the dog

ΠΡΟΣ ΠΑΡΑΣΚΗΝΙΑ προς παρασκήνια to dressing rooms

προσπέκτους (το) [prosp**e**ktoos (to)] brochure

προσπερνώ [prospern**o**] overtake

προστατεύω [prostat**e**vo] protect

ΠΡΟΣΤΙΜΟ πρόστιμο (το) [pr**o**stimo (to)] fine

προσφέρω [prosf**e**ro] offer (verb); give

ΠΡΟΣΦΟΡΑ προσφορά special bargain

πρόσωπο (το) [pr**o**sopo (to)] face

προς [pros] towards

προτείνω [prot**i**no] recommend

ΠΡΟΤΕΡΑΙΟΤΗΤΑ προτεραιότητα (η) right of way

προτιμώ [protim**o**] prefer

προφανής [profan**i**s] obvious

προφέρω [prof**e**ro] pronounce

προφορά (η) [profor**a** (i)] accent

προφυλακτήρας (ο) [profilakt**i**ras (o)] bumper, fender

ΠΡΟΦΥΛΑΚΤΙΚΑ προφυλακτικά contraceptives

ΠΡΟΦΥΛΑΚΤΙΚΟ προφυλακτικό (το) [profilaktik**o** (to)] condom

προχτές [pro**k**htes] the day before yesterday

πρωί (το) [proi (to)] morning
το πρωί [to proi] in the morning

ΠΡΩΙΝΟ πρωινό (το) [pro-in**o** (to)] breakfast

πρώτα [pr**o**ta] first, firstly

ΠΡΩΤΕΣ ΒΟΗΘΕΙΕΣ πρώτες βοήθειες (οι) [pr**o**tes voiTHi-es (i)] first aid

ΠΡΩΤΗ ΘΕΣΗ πρώτη θέση first class

πρώτο! [proto!] great!
ΠΡΩΤΟ ΠΑΤΩΜΑ πρώτο
πάτωμα (το) [proto patoma (to)]
first floor, (US) second floor
πρώτος [protos] first
ΠΡΩΤΟΣ ΟΡΟΦΟΣ πρώτος
όροφος [protos orofos] first
floor, (US) second floor
Πρωτοχρονιά (η) [Protokhronia (i)]
New Year's Day
ΠΤΗΣΕΙΣ ΕΞΩΤΕΡΙΚΟΥ
πτήσεις εξωτερικού
international flights
ΠΤΗΣΕΙΣ ΕΣΩΤΕΡΙΚΟΥ
πτήσεις εσωτερικού domestic
flights
ΠΤΗΣΗ πτήση (η) [ptisi (i)]
flight
ΠΤΗΣΗ ΤΣΑΡΤΕΡ πτήση
τσάρτερ charter flight
πυζάμες (οι) [pizames (i)] pyjamas
πυξίδα (η) [pixitha (i)] compass
πύργος (ο) [pirgos (o)] tower
πυρετός (ο) [piretos (o)] fever
πυρκαγιά (η) [pirkaya (i)] fire
ΠΥΡΟΣΒΕΣΤΗΡ πυροσβεστήρ
(ο) fire extinguisher
ΠΥΡΟΣΒΕΣΤΗΡΑΣ
πυροσβεστήρας (ο) fire
extinguisher
ΠΥΡΟΣΒΕΣΤΙΚΗ ΣΩΛΗΝΑ
πυροσβεστική σωλήνα (η) fire
hose
ΠΥΡΟΣΒΕΣΤΙΚΗ (ΥΠΗΡΕΣΙΑ)
πυροσβεστική (υπηρεσία) (η)
[pirosvestiki ipiresia (i)] fire
brigade
πυροτεχνήματα (τα)
[pirotekhnimata (ta)] fireworks

πυτζάμες (οι) [pitzames (i)]
pyjamas
ΠΩΛΕΙΤΑΙ πωλείται for sale
ΠΩΛΗΣΗ πώληση (η) sale
πώς; [pos?] how?; what?

Ρ

ράβω [ravo] sew
ραδιόφωνο (το) [rathiofono (to)]
radio
ραντεβού (το) [randevoo (to)]
appointment
ράντζο (το) [randzo (to)] campbed
ΡΑΦΕΙΟ ραφείο (το) [rafio (to)]
tailor's
ρεζέρβα (η) [rezerva (i)] spare
tyre
ΡΕΣΕΨΙΟΝ ρεσεψιόν (η)
[resepsion (i)] reception
ρεσεψιονίστ (ο/η) [resepsionist
(o/i)] receptionist
ρε συ! [reh si!] you there!, oy
you!
ρεύμα (το) [revma (to)] current;
draught
ρευματισμοί (οι) [revmatismi (i)]
rheumatism
ρίχνω [rikhno] throw (verb)
ρόδα (η) [rotha (i)] wheel
ροζ [roz] pink
ρόκ (η) [rok (i)] rock music
ρολόι (το) [roloi (to)] clock;
watch
ρόμπα (η) [roba (i)] dressing
gown
ΡΟΥΦ - ΓΚΑΡΝΤΕΝ Ρουφ
- Γκάρντεν [Roof - garden] roof

garden

ρούχα (τα) [**roo**kha (ta)] clothes

ροχαλίζω [**ro**khalizo] snore

ρυμούλκα (η) [ri**moo**lka (i)] trailer (for car)

ρυμουλκό [rimool**ko**] trailer (for car etc)

ρωτώ [ro**to**] ask

Σ

ΣΑΒΒΑΤΟ Σάββατο (το) [**Sa**vato (to)] Saturday

σαββατοκύριακο (το) [savatoki**ri**ako (to)] weekend

ΣΑΓΙΟΝΑΡΕΣ σαγιονάρες [sayo**na**res] beach sandals, flip-flops

σαγόνι (το) [sa**go**ni (to)] jaw

σακάκι (το) [sa**ka**ki (to)] jacket

σακβουαγιάζ (το) [sakvooa**yaz** (to)] hand luggage, hand baggage

σακίδιο (το) [sa**ki**thio (to)] rucksack

σάκος (ο) [**sa**kos (o)] backpack, rucksack

ΣΑΛΟΝΙ σαλόνι (το) [sa**lo**ni (to)] lounge

ΣΑΜΠΟΥΑΝ σαμπουάν (το) [sampoo**an** (to)] shampoo

σαμπρέλα (η) [sa**bre**la (i)] inner tube

σαν [san] like, as

σανδάλια (τα) [san**tha**lia (ta)] sandals

σάουνα (η) [**sa**oona (i)] sauna

σάπιος [**sa**pios] rotten

ΣΑΠΟΥΝΙ ΠΙΑΤΩΝ σαπούνι

πιάτων (το) [sa**poo**ni **pia**ton (to)] washing-up liquid

ΣΑΠΟΥΝΙ σαπούνι (το) [sa**poo**ni (to)] soap

σαράντα [sa**ran**da] forty

σας [sas] you; your

σβήνω [**svi**no] switch off (engine); put out (fire)

ΣΒΗΣΤΕ ΤΗΝ ΜΗΧΑΝΗ σβήστε την μηχανή switch off engine

σβήστρα (η) [**svi**stra (i)] rubber, eraser

σγουρά [**sgoo**ra] curly

σε [seh] you; to; at; in

σεζ λόνγκ (η) [sez long (i)] deckchair

ΣΕΙΡΑ σειρά (η) [si**ra** (i)] row (of seats)

σελίδα (η) [se**li**tha (i)] page

ΣΕΛΛΟΤΕΗΠ σέλλοτέηπ (το) [**se**lloteip (to)] Sellotape®, Scotch tape®

ΣΕΛΦ ΣΕΡΒΙΣ σελφ σέρβις [self **ser**vis] self-service

σεντόνι (το) [sen**do**ni (to)] sheet

σέξυ [**se**xi] sexy

ΣΕ ΠΕΡΙΠΤΩΣΗ ΑΝΑΓΚΗΣ ΣΠΑΣΤΕ ΤΟ ΤΖΑΜΙ σε περίπτωση ανάγκης σπάστε το τζάμι in emergency break glass

ΣΕΠΤΕΜΒΡΙΟΣ Σεπτέμβριος (ο) [Sep**tem**vrios (o)] September

ΣΕΡΒΙΕΤΕΣ σερβιέτες (οι) [ser**vie**tes (i)] sanitary towels/ napkins

σερβιτόρα (η) [servi**to**ra (i)] barmaid; waitress

σερβιτόρος (ο) [servitoros (o)] waiter

ΣΗΚΩΣΤΕ ΤΟ ΑΚΟΥΣΤΙΚΟ σηκώστε το ακουστικό lift receiver

σημαδούρα (η) [simathoora (i)] buoy

σημαία (η) [simea (i)] flag

σημειωματάριο (το) [simiomatario (to)] notebook

ΣΗΜΕΡΑ σήμερα [simera] today

ΣΗΜΕΡΟΝ σήμερον showing today

σήραγγα (η) [siranga (i)] tunnel

σιγά-σιγά [siga-siga] slowly; slow down

σίγουρος [sigooros] sure

σίδερο (το) [sithero (to)] iron

σιδερώνω [sitherono] iron (verb)

ΣΙΔΗΡΟΔΡΟΜΙΚΟΣ ΣΤΑΘΜΟΣ σιδηροδρομικός σταθμός (ο) [sithirothromikos staTHmos (o)] railway station

σιδηρόδρομος (ο) [sithirothromos (o)] railway

ΣΙΔΗΡΟΥΡΓΕΙΟ σιδηρουργείο (το) [sithirooryio (to)] hardware store

ΣΙΝΕΜΑ σινεμά (το) [sinema (to)] cinema, movie theater

σιωπή (η) [siopi (i)] silence

σκάλα (η) [skala (i)] ladder

ΣΚΑΛΕΣ σκάλες (οι) [skales (i)] stairs

σκέπτομαι [skeptomeh] think

ΣΚΗΝΗ σκηνή (η) [skini (i)] tent

σκιά (η) [skia (i)] shade, shadow

στη σκιά [sti skia] in the shade

ΣΚΙΑ ΜΑΤΙΩΝ σκιά ματιών (η) [skia mation (i)] eye shadow

ΣΚΛΗΡΟΙ ΦΑΚΟΙ σκληροί φακοί (οι) [skliri faki (i)] hard lenses

σκληρός [skliros] hard

ΣΚΟΝΗ ΠΛΥΝΤΗΡΙΟΥ σκόνη πλυντηρίου (η) [skoni plindirioo (i)] washing powder

σκοτεινός [skotinos] dark

σκοτώνω [skotono] kill (verb)

σκουλαρίκια (τα) [skoolarikia (ta)] earrings

σκούπα [skoopa] broom

σκουπίδια (τα) [skoopithia (ta)] rubbish, garbage

σκουπιδοντενεκές (ο) [skoopithondenekes (o)] dustbin, trashcan

σκύλος (ο) [skilos (o)] dog

σκωληκοειδίτις (η) [skoliko-ithitis (i)] appendicitis

ΣΚΩΤΙΑ Σκωτία (η) [Skotia (i)] Scotland

Σκωτσέζικος [Skotsezikos] Scottish

σλάιντ (το) [slaid (to)] slide

σλίπ (το) [slip (to)] underpants; panties

ΣΛΙΠΙΝΓΚ ΜΠΑΓΚ σλίπινγκ μπαγκ (το) [sliping bag (to)] sleeping bag

σοβαρός [sovaros] serious

σοκ (το) [sok (to)] shock

ΣΟΚΟΛΑΤΑ σοκολάτα (η) [sokolata (i)] chocolate

ΣΟΚΟΛΑΤΑ ΓΑΛΑΚΤΟΣ σοκολάτα γάλακτος (η) [sokolata galaktos (i)] milk chocolate

ΣΟΚΟΛΑΤΑΚΙΑ σοκολατάκια
(τα) [sokolatakia (ta)] chocolates

σόλα (η) [sola (i)] sole (of shoe)

σόμπα (η) [soba (i)] oil heater

σορτς (το) [sorts (to)] shorts

σου [soo] you; your

σουγιάς (ο) [sooyas (o)] penknife

ΣΟΥΠΕΡ ΒΕΝΖΙΝΗ σούπερ
βενζίνη (η) [sooper venzini (i)]
four-star petrol, premium

ΣΟΥΠΕΡΜΑΡΚΕΤ
σούπερμάρκετ (το) [soopermarket
(to)] supermarket

σουτιέν (το) [sootien (to)] bra

ΣΠΑΓΓΟΣ σπάγγος (ο) [spangos
(o)] string

σπασμένος [spasmenos] broken

σπάω [spao] break (verb)

σπηλιά (το) [spilia (to)] cave

σπιράλ (το) [spiral (to)] spiral;
IUD; incense coil (mosquito
repellent)

σπίρτα (τα) [spirta (ta)] matches

σπίτι (το) [spiti (to)] house

στο σπίτι [sto spiti] at home

σπορ (το) [spor (to)] sport

σπουδαίος [spootheos] important

σπρώχνω [sprokhno] push (verb)

σταγόνα (η) [stagona (i)] drop

ΣΤΑΓΟΝΕΣ σταγόνες drops

ΣΤΑΔΙΟ στάδιο (το) [stathio (to)]
stadium

ΣΤΑΘΜΟΣ σταθμός (ο)
[staTHmos (o)] station

ΣΤΑΘΜΟΣ ΑΝΕΦΟΔΙΑΣΜΟΥ
ΘΑΛΑΜΗΓΩΝ σταθμός
ανεφοδιασμού θαλαμηγών yacht
refuelling station

ΣΤΑΘΜΟΣ ΛΕΩΦΟΡΕΙΩΝ

σταθμός λεωφορείων [staTHmos
leoforion] bus station

ΣΤΑΘΜΟΣ ΠΡΩΤΩΝ
ΒΟΗΘΕΙΩΝ σταθμός πρώτων
βοηθειών [staTHmos proton vo-
iTHion] first aid post

ΣΤΑΘΜΟΣ ΤΑΞΙ σταθμός ταξί
[staTHmos taxi] taxi stand

ΣΤΑΘΜΟΣ ΥΠΕΡΑΣΤΙΚΩΝ
ΛΕΩΦΟΡΕΙΩΝ σταθμός
υπεραστικών λεωφορείων
[staTHmos iperastikon leoforion]
bus station (long distance)

ΣΤΑΘΜΟΣ ΧΩΡΟΦΥΛΑΚΗΣ
σταθμός χωροφυλακής
[staTHmos khorofilakis] police
station

σταματάω [stamatao] stop (verb)

ΣΤΑΣΗ στάση (η) [stasi (i)] stop
(for bus, train)

ΣΤΑΣΗ ΑΣΤΙΚΩΝ
ΣΥΓΚΟΙΝΩΝΙΩΝ στάση
αστικών συγκοινωνιών city
bus stop

ΣΤΑΣΗ ΛΕΩΦΟΡΕΙΟΥ στάση
λεωφορείου bus stop

ΣΤΑΣΗ ΤΑΞΙ στάση ταξί [stasi
taxi] taxi stand

ΣΤΑΣΙΣ στάσις (η) [stasis (i)]
bus stop

στέγη (η) [steyi (i)] roof

ΣΤΕΓΝΟ ΚΑΘΑΡΙΣΜΑ
ΜΟΝΟΝ στεγνό καθάρισμα
μόνον dryclean only

ΣΤΕΓΝΟΚΑΘΑΡΙΣΤΗΡΙΟ
στεγνοκαθαριστήριο (το)
[stegnokaTHaristirio (to)] dry
cleaner's

στεγνός [stegnos] dry

στεγνώνω [stegnono] dry (verb)
στέλνω [stelno] send
στενός [stenos] narrow; tight
στενοχώρια (η) [stenokhoria (i)] worry (verb)
στήθος (το) [stiTHos (to)] breast; chest
στην [stin] at; in; to; on
ΣΤΙΒΟΣ στίβος (ο) [stivos (o)] athletics stadium
στο [sto] at; in; to
στόμα (το) [stoma (to)] mouth
στομάχι (το) [stomakhi (to)] stomach
στον [ston] at; in; to;
ΣΤΟΠ! στοπ! stop!
στριφτό (το) [strifto (to)] hand-rolled cigarette
στρογγυλός [strongilos] round
στρόφαλος (ο) [strofalos (o)] crankshaft
στροφή (η) [strofi (i)] bend
στρώμα (το) [stroma (to)] mattress
στυλό (το) [stilo (to)] biro®
συγγενείς (οι) [singenis (i)] relatives
συγγνώμη [signomi] sorry; excuse me
συγγνώμη; [signomi?] pardon (me)?, sorry?
σύγκρουση (η) [singroosi (i)] crash
συγχαρητήρια! [sinkharitiria!] congratulations!
συγχωρείτε: με συγχωρείτε [meh sinkhoriteh] excuse me
σύζυγος (ο) [sizigos (o)] husband
συκότι (το) [sikoti (to)] liver
συλλαμβάνω [silamvano] arrest

συλλογή (η) [siloyi (i)] collection
συμβαίνω [simveno] happen
συμβουλεύω [simvoolevo] advise
ΣΥΜΠΕΡΙΛΑΜΒΑΝΕΤΑΙ συμπεριλαμβάνεται included
συμπλέκτης (ο) [siblektis (o)] clutch
συμφωνώ [simfono] agree
ΣΥΝΑΓΕΡΜΟΣ συναγερμός (ο) [sinayermos (o)] alarm
συναίσθημα (το) [sinesTHima (to)] feeling
ΣΥΝΑΛΛΑΓΜΑ συνάλλαγμα (το) [sinalagma (to)] foreign exchange
ΣΥΝΑΛΛΑΓΜΑΤΙΚΗ ΙΣΟΤΙΜΙΑ συναλλαγματική ισοτιμία (η) [sinalagmatiki isotimia (i)] exchange rate
συνάντηση (η) [sinandisi (i)] meeting
συναντώ [sinando] meet
συναρπαστικός [sinarpastikos] exciting
συναυλία (η) [sinavlia (i)] concert
ΣΥΝ/ΓΕΙΟ συν/γειο auto repairs
σύνδεση (η) [sinTHesi (i)] connection (electrical)
ΣΥΝΕΡΓΕΙΟ (ΑΥΤΟΚΙΝΗΤΩΝ) συνεργείο (αυτοκινήτων) (το) auto repairs
συνήθεια (η) [siniTHia (i)] habit
συνηθισμένος [siniTHismenos] usual
συνήθως [siniTHos] usually
ΣΥΝΘΕΤΙΚΟ συνθετικό synthetic
συννεφιασμένος [sinefiasmenos]

cloudy
σύννεφο (το) [sinefo (to)] cloud
συνοδεύω [sinothevo]
accompany
ΣΥΝΟΙΚΙΑ συνοικία (η) [sinikia
(i)] district
συνολικά [sinolika] altogether
σύνορα (τα) [sinora (ta)] border
συνταγή (η) [sindayi (i)]
prescription; recipe
συνταξιούχος (ο/η) [sindaxioookhos
(o/i)] old-age pensioner
ΣΥΝΤΗΡΗΤΙΚΟ ΔΙΑΛΥΜΑ
συντηρητικό διάλυμα (το)
[sindiritiko thialima (to)] soaking
solution
σύντομα [sindoma] soon
ΣΥΡΑΤΕ σύρατε pull
σύρμα (το) [sirma (to)] wire
ΣΥΣΤΑΤΙΚΑ συστατικά
ingredients
ΣΥΣΤΗΜΕΝΑ συστημένα
[sistimena] registered mail
συστήνω [sistino] introduce;
recommend
συχνά [sikhna] often
σφήγγα (η) [sfinga (i)] wasp
σφράγισμα (το) [sfrayisma (to)]
filling (in tooth)
σφυρί (το) [sfiri (to)] hammer
σχάρα αυτοκινήτου (η) [skhara
aftokinitoo (i)] roof rack
σχέδιο (το) [skhethio (to)] plan
σχεδόν [skhethon] almost
σχοινί (το) [skhini (to)] rope
ΣΧΟΛΕΙΟ σχολείο (το) [skholio
(to)] school
σωλήνας (ο) [solinas (o)] pipe
(water)

σώμα (το) [soma (to)] body
ΣΩΣΙΒΙΑ σωσίβια lifejackets
σωστός [sostos] correct

T

τα [ta] the; them
ταβάνι (το) [tavani (to)] ceiling
ΤΑΒΕΡΝΑ ταβέρνα (η) [taverna
(i)] restaurant
τακούνι (το) [takooni (to)] heel
(of shoe)
ΤΑΛΗΡΟ τάληρο (το) [taliro (to)]
5-drachma coin
ΤΑΜΕΙΟ ταμείο (το) [tamio (to)]
box office; cash desk, till,
cashier
ΤΑΜΙΕΥΤΗΡΙΟ ταμιευτήριο
(το) [tami-eftirio (to)] savings
bank
ΤΑΜΠΛΕΤΑ ταμπλέτα (η)
[tableta (i)] tablet
ΤΑΜΠΟΝ ταμπόν (τα) [tampon
(ta)] tampons
τάξη (η) [taxi (i)] class
ΤΑΞΙ ταξί (το) [taxi (to)] taxi
ταξιδεύω [taxithevo] travel (verb)
ταξίδι (το) [taxithi (to)] journey,
trip
  καλό ταξίδι! [kalo taxithi!] have a
  good journey!, bon voyage!
ταξίδι για δουλειές [taxithi ya
thoolies] business trip
ΤΑΞΙΔΙΩΤΙΚΗ ΕΠΙΤΑΓΗ
ταξιδιωτική επιταγή (η)
[taxithiotiki epitayi (i)] traveller's
cheque/traveler's check
ΤΑΞΙΔΙΩΤΙΚΟ ΓΡΑΦΕΙΟ

ταξιδιωτικό γραφείο (το)
[taxithiotikó grafío (to)] travel
agent's

τάπα (η) [tapa (i)] plug (in sink)

ΤΑ ΡΕΣΤΑ ΣΑΣ τα ρέστα σας
your change

ΤΑΡΙΦΑ ταρίφα [tarifa] taxi
tariff

τασάκι (το) [tasaki (to)] ashtray

ταύρος (ο) [tavros (o)] bull

ΤΑΥΤΟΤΗΤΑ ταυτότητα (η)
[taftotita (i)] pass, identity card

ΤΑΧΥΔΡΟΜΕΙΟ ταχυδρομείο
(το) [takhithromio (to)] post
office

ΤΑΧΥΔΡΟΜΙΚΟΣ ΤΟΜΕΥΣ
ταχυδρομικός τομεύς (ο)
[takhithromikos tomefs (o)]
postcode, zipcode

ταχυδρόμος (ο) [takhithromos (o)]
postman

ταχυδρομώ [takhithromo] post,
mail (verb)

ταχύτητα (η) [takhitita (i)] gear
(in car)

ταχύτητα (η) [takhitita (i)] speed

τέλειος [tellius] perfect

τελειώνω [teliono] finish (verb)

ΤΕΛΕΥΤΑΙΑ ΠΑΡΑΣΤΑΣΗ
τελευταία παράσταση last
performance

τελευταίος [telefteos] last

τελεφερίκ (το) [teleferik (to)]
cable car

ΤΕΛΟΣ τέλος (το) [telos (to)] end

ΤΕΛΩΝΕΙΟ Τελωνείο (το)
[Telonio (to)] Customs

τεμπέλης [tebelis] lazy

τέννις (το) [tenis (to)] tennis

τέντα (η) [tenda (i)] tent,
marquee

τέσσερα [tesera] four

ΤΕΤΑΡΤΗ Τετάρτη (η) [Tetarti
(i)] Wednesday

τέταρτο (το) [tetarto (to)]
quarter

τέταρτος [tetartos] fourth

τέχνη (η) [tekhni (i)] art

τεχνητός [tekhnitos] artificial

ΤΕΧΝΗΤΟ ΧΡΩΜΑ τεχνητό
χρώμα artificial colouring

τζαζ (η) [tzaz (i)] jazz

τζηνς (τα) [tzins (ta)] jeans

τζόγγιγκ (το) [tzoging (to)]
jogging

τη [ti] the

τηγάνι (το) [tigani (to)] frying
pan

τηγανίζω [tiganizo] fry

ΤΗΛΕΓΡΑΦΗΜΑ τηλεγράφημα
(το) [tilegrafima (to)] telegram

ΤΗΛΕΓΡΑΦΗΜΑΤΑ
τηλεγραφήματα telegrams

ΤΗΛΕΓΡΑΦΙΚΗ ΕΝΤΟΛΗ
τηλεγραφική εντολή [tilegrafiki
endoli] telegram

ΤΗΛΕΚΑΡΤΑ τηλεκάρτα (η)
[tilekarta (i)] phonecard

ΤΗΛΕΟΡΑΣΗ τηλεόραση (η)
[tileorasi (i)] television

ΤΗΛΕΦΩΝΗΜΑ τηλεφώνημα
[tilefonima] call

ΤΗΛΕΦΩΝΗΜΑ ΚΟΛΛΕΚΤ
τηλεφώνημα κολλέκτ (το)
[tilefonima kollekt (to)] reverse
charge call

ΤΗΛΕΦΩΝΙΚΗ ΕΝΤΟΛΗ
τηλεφωνική εντολή operator-

A
B
Γ
Δ
E
Z
H
Θ
I
K
Λ
M
N
Ξ
O
Π
P
Σ
T
Y
Φ
X
Ψ
Ω

controlled phone call

ΤΗΛΕΦΩΝΙΚΟΣ ΘΑΛΑΜΟΣ
τηλεφωνικός θάλαμος (ο)
[tilefonikos THalamos (o)] phone box

ΤΗΛΕΦΩΝΙΚΟΣ ΚΑΤΑΛΟΓΟΣ
τηλεφωνικός κατάλογος (ο)
[tilefonikos katalogos (o)] phone book

ΤΗΛΕΦΩΝΟ τηλέφωνο (το)
[tilefono (to)] phone

ΤΗΛΕΦΩΝΩ τηλεφωνώ
[tilefono] ring, phone (verb)

την [tin] her; on; per; the
την εβδομάδα [tin evthomatha] per week

της [tis] her; to her; of her

τι; [ti?] what?

ΤΙΜΗ τιμή (η) [timi (i)] price

ΤΙΜΗ ΑΓΟΡΑΣ τιμή αγοράς
buying rate

ΤΙΜΗ ΑΝΕΥ ΠΟΣΟΣΤΩΝ τιμή
άνευ ποσοστών price exclusive of extras

ΤΙΜΗ ΔΩΜΑΤΙΟΥ τιμή
δωματίου room price

ΤΙΜΗ ΚΑΤ' ΑΤΟΜΟ τιμή κατ'
άτομο price per person

ΤΙΜΗ ΚΛΙΝΗΣ τιμή κλίνης
price per bed

ΤΙΜΗ ΜΕΤΑ ΠΟΣΟΣΤΩΝ τιμή
μετά ποσοστών price inclusive of extras

ΤΙΜΗ ΠΩΛΗΣΗΣ τιμή
πώλησης selling rate

τίμιος [timios] honest

τιμόνι (το) [timoni (to)] steering wheel

τίνος; [tinos?] whose

τίποτε [tipoteh] nothing

ΤΙΠΟΤΕ ΠΡΟΣ ΔΗΛΩΣΗ
τίποτε προς δήλωση nothing to declare

τις [tis] them

ΤΜΗΜΑ τμήμα (το) [tmima (to)]
department

το [to] in; it; the; per

τοις εκατό [tis ekato] per cent

ΤΟΙΣ ΜΕΤΡΗΤΟΙΣ τοις
μετρητοίς cash only, no credit cards

τοίχος (ο) [tikhos (o)] wall

**ΤΟ ΚΑΤΑΣΤΗΜΑ
ΜΕΤΑΦΕΡΘΗΚΕ ΕΙΣ ...** το
κατάστημα μεταφέρθηκε εις ...
we have moved to ...

ΤΟ ΚΟΜΜΑΤΙ το κομμάτι per item

ΤΟΚΟΣ τόκος (ο) [tokos (o)]
interest

τολμάω [tolmao] dare (verb)

τον [ton] him; the

ΤΟΞΙΚΟ τοξικό toxic

ΤΟΠΙΚΗ ΩΡΑ τοπική ώρα local time

ΤΟΠΙΚΟ (ΤΗΛΕΦΩΝΗΜΑ)
τοπικό (τηλεφώνημα) (το)
[topiko tilefonima (to)] local call

τοπίο (το) [topio (to)] landscape

τόσο [toso] so (much); that much

τότε [toteh] then

του [too] his; its; to him

ΤΟΥΑΛΕΤΑ τουαλέτα (η)
[tooaleta (i)] toilet, rest room

ΤΟΥΑΛΕΤΑ ΤΩΝ ΓΥΝΑΙΚΩΝ
τουαλέτα των γυναικών (η)
[tooaleta ton yinekon (i)] ladies'

toilet, ladies' room

ΤΟΥΑΛΕΤΕΣ τουαλέτες
[tooaletes] toilets, rest room

τουλάχιστον [toolakhiston] at least

του οποίου [too opíoo] whose

τουρίστας (o) [tooristas (o)]
tourist

ΤΟΥΡΙΣΤΙΚΗ ΑΣΤΥΝΟΜΙΑ
Τουριστική Αστυνομία (η)
[Tooristiki Astinomia (i)] Tourist
Police

τουριστικός οδηγός (o) [tooristikos
othigos (o)] guidebook

τουρίστρια (η) [tooristria (i)]
tourist

ΤΟΥΡΚΑΛΑ τουρκάλα (η)
[toorkala (i)] Turk

ΤΟΥΡΚΙΑ Τουρκία (η) [Toorkia
(i)] Turkey

Τούρκος (o) [Toorkos (o)] Turk

ΤΟΥΡΚΙΚΟΣ Τουρκικός
[Toorkikos] Turkish (adj)

τους [toos] them; to them

τραβάω [travao] pull (verb)

τραγούδι (το) [tragoothi (to)] song

τραγουδώ [tragootho] sing

ΤΡΑΠΕΖΑΡΙΑ τραπεζαρία (η)
[trapezaria (i)] dining room

ΤΡΑΠΕΖΑ τράπεζα (η) [trapeza
(i)] bank

τραπέζι (το) [trapezi (to)] table

τραπεζομάντηλο (το)
[trapezomandilo (to)] tablecloth

τραυματίζομαι [travmatizomeh]
hurt, injure

τραυματισμένος [travmatismenos]
injured

τρελλός [trelos] mad

ΤΡΕΝΟ τρένο (το) [treno (to)]

train

τρέχω [trekho] run (verb)

τρία [tria] three

τριακόσια [triakosia] three
hundred

τριάντα [trianda] thirty

τριαντάφυλλο (το) [triandafilo
(to)] rose

ΤΡΙΚΛΙΝΟ ΔΩΜΑΤΙΟ τρίκλινο
δωμάτιο (το) [triklino thomatio
(to)] triple room

ΤΡΙΤΗ Τρίτη (η) [Triti (i)]
Tuesday

ΤΡΙΤΗ ΘΕΣΗ τρίτη θέση third
class

τρίτος [tritos] third

τρόλλεϋ (το) [troleh-i (to)] trolley,
trolleybus

τρομερός [tromeros] tremendous

ΤΡΟΦΗ ΓΙΑ ΔΙΑΒΗΤΙΚΟΥΣ
τροφή γιά διαβητικούς [trofi ya
thiavitikoos] diabetic foods

τροφική δηλητηρίαση (η) [trofiki
thilitiriasi (i)] food poisoning

ΤΡΟΧΑΙΑ τροχαία (η) traffic
police

τροχονόμος (o) [trokhonomos (o)]
traffic warden

τροχόσπιτο (το) [trokhospito (to)]
caravan, (US) trailer

ΤΡΟΧΟΣΠΙΤΑ τροχόσπιτα (το)
caravans, (US) trailers

τρύπα (η) [tripa (i)] hole

τρώω [troo] eat; have dinner

τσαγιέρα (η) [tsayera (i)] teapot

ΤΣΑΓΚΑΡΗΣ τσαγκάρης (o)
[tsangaris (o)] shoe repairer's

τσάντα (η) [tsanda (i)] bag;
handbag, (US) purse

A
B
Γ
Δ
E
Z
H
Θ
I
K
Λ
M
N
Ξ
O
Π
P
Σ
T
Y
Φ
X
Ψ
Ω

ΤΣΑΝΤΕΣ ΜΠΑΝΙΟΥ τσάντες μπάνιου beach bags

τσέπη (η) [tsepi (i)] pocket

ΤΣΙΓΑΡΟ τσιγάρο (το) [tsigaro (to)] cigarette

τσίμπημα (το) [tsibima (to)] bite (insect)

τσιμπιδάκι (το) [tsibithaki (to)] tweezers

τσιμπώ [tsibo] sting (verb)

ΤΣΙΠΣ τσιπς (τα) [tsips (ta)] crisps, (US) potato chips

ΤΣΙΧΛΑ τσίχλα (η) [tsikhla (i)] chewing gum

τσόκ (το) [tsok (to)] choke (on car)

τσούχτρα (η) [tsookhtra (i)] jellyfish

τυλίγω [tiligo] wrap (verb)

τυφλός [tiflos] blind

τύχη (η) [tikhi (i)] luck

καλή τύχη! [kali tikhi!] good luck!

των [ton] of them

τώρα [tora] now

Υ

υαλοκαθαριστήρας (o) [ialokaтнaristiras (o)] windscreen wiper

υγεία: στην υγειά σας/σου! [stin iya sas/soo!] your health!, cheers!

υγιής [iyi-is] healthy

ΥΓΡΑΕΡΙΟ υγραέριο (το) [igraerio (to)] camping gas

υγρός [igros] damp, wet

ΥΔΡΑΥΛΙΚΑ υδραυλικά (τα)

[ithravlika (ta)] plumber

ΥΔΡΑΥΛΙΚΟΣ υδραυλικός (o) [ithravlikos (o)] plumber

υπάρχει [iparkhi] there is

υπάρχουν [iparkhoon] there are

ΥΠΕΡΑΣΤΙΚΟ (ΤΗΛΕΦΩΝΗΜΑ) υπεραστικό (τηλεφώνημα) (το) [iperastiko tilefonima (to)] long-distance call, international call

υπερβάλλω [ipervallo] exaggerate

υπέρβαρο (το) [ipervaro (to)] excess baggage

υπερβολικά [ipervolika] too

υπερήφανος [iperifanos] proud

ΥΠΕΡΠΟΛΥΤΕΛΕΙΑΣ υπερπολυτελειας five-star (hotel)

υπεύθυνος [ipefтнinos] responsible

ΥΠΗΡΕΣΙΑ υπηρεσία (η) [ipiresia (i)] service

ύπνο: πάω για ύπνο [pao ya ipno] go to bed

υπνοδωμάτιο (το) [ipnothomatio (to)] bedroom

ύπνος (o) [ipnos (o)] sleep

ΥΠΝΩΤΙΚΟ ΧΑΠΙ υπνωτικό χάπι (το) [ipnotiko khapi (to)] sleeping pill

ΥΠΟΓΕΙΑ ΔΙΑΒΑΣΗ ΠΕΖΩΝ υπόγεια διάβαση πεζών (η) pedestrian subway

ΥΠΟΓΕΙΟ υπόγειο (το) [ipoyio (to)] basement

ΥΠΟΓΕΙΟΣ υπόγειος (o) [ipoyios (o)] underground, (US) subway

υπογράφω [ipografo] sign (verb)

ΥΠΟΔΗΜΑΤΑ υποδήματα (τα) [ipothimata (ta)] shoes

ΥΠΟΔΗΜΑΤΑ ΓΥΝΑΙΚΕΙΑ
υποδήματα γυναικεία [ipothimata yinekia] ladies' shoes

ΥΠΟΔΗΜΑΤΟΠΟΙΕΙΟ
υποδηματοποιείο (το) [ipothimatopi-io (to)] shoe shop

υπολογιστής (ο) [ipoloyistis (o)] computer

υπόλοιπο (το) [ipolipo (to)] rest, remainder

υπόσχομαι [iposkhomeh] promise (verb)

ΥΠΟΥΡΓΕΙΟ υπουργείο (το) ministry

ύφασμα (το) [ifasma (to)] material

ΥΦΑΣΜΑΤΑ υφάσματα [ifasmata] clothing; cloth, material

Φ

ΦΑΓΗΤΟ φαγητό (το) [fayito (to)] food; meal; lunch

φαγούρα (η) [fagoora (i)] itch

φάκελος (ο) [fakelos (o)] envelope

ΦΑΚΟΙ ΕΠΑΦΗΣ φακοί επαφής (οι) [faki epafis (i)] contact lenses

φακός (ο) [fakos (o)] lens; torch

φαλακρός [falakros] bald

φαλλοκράτης (ο) [falokratis (o)] male chauvinist

φανάρια τροχαίας (τα) [fanaria trokheas (ta)] traffic lights

φανταστικός [fandastikos] fantastic

ΦΑΡΜΑΚΕΙΟ φαρμακείο (το) [farmakio (to)] chemist's, pharmacy

φάρμακο (το) [farmako (to)] medicine

φαρμακοποιός (ο) [farmakopios (o)] chemist, pharmacist

φασαρία (η) [fasaria (i)] noise

ΦΕΒΡΟΥΑΡΙΟΣ Φεβρουάριος (ο) [Fevrooarios (o)] February

φεγγάρι (το) [fengari (to)] moon

φεμινίστρια (η) [feministria (i)] feminist

φερμουάρ (το) [fermooar (to)] zip

φέρνω [ferno] bring

ΦΕΡΡΥ ΜΠΩΤ φέρρυ μπωτ (το) [feri bot (to)] ferry

φέτα (η) [feta (i)] slice

φεύγω [fevgo] go away

φθινόπωρο (το) [fthinoporo (to)] autumn, (US) fall

φίδι (το) [fithi (to)] snake

φιλενάδα (η) [filenatha (i)] girlfriend; friend

φιλί (το) [fili (to)] kiss

ΦΙΛΜ φιλμ (το) [film (to)] film, movie

ΦΙΛΟΔΩΡΗΜΑ φιλοδώρημα (το) [filothorima (to)] service charge; tip

φιλοξενία (η) [filoxenia (i)] hospitality

φιλοξενούμενη (η) [filoxenoomeni (i)] guest

φιλοξενούμενος (ο) [filoxenoomenos (o)] guest

φίλος (ο) [filos (o)] boyfriend; friend

φιλοφρόνηση (η) [filofronisi (i)] compliment

φίλτρο (το) [filtro (to)] filter

φιλώ [filo] kiss (verb)

φλας (το) [flas (to)] flash; indicator

φλέβα (η) [fleva (i)] vein

φλυτζάνι (το) [flitzani (to)] cup

φοβάμαι [fovameh] be afraid

φοβερός [foveros] terrible

φόβος (ο) [fovos (o)] fear

φοιτητής (ο) [fititis (o)] student

ΦΟΙΤΗΤΙΚΑ ΕΙΣΙΤΗΡΙΑ φοιτητικά εισιτήρια [fititika isitiria] student tickets

φοιτήτρια (η) [fititria (i)] student

φορά (η) [fora (i)] time, occasion

φόρεμα (το) [forema (to)] dress

φορτηγό (το) [fortigo (to)] lorry

ΦΟΥΑΓΙΕ φουαγιέ (το) [fooaye (to)] foyer

ΦΟΥΛ ΠΑΝΣΙΟΝ φουλ πανσιόν (η) [fool pansion (i)] full board

ΦΟΥΛ-ΣΑΙΖΟΝ φουλ-σαιζόν high season

ΦΟΥΡΝΟΣ φούρνος (ο) [foornos (o)] baker's; oven

φουσκάλα (η) [fooskala (i)] blister

φούστα (η) [foosta (i)] skirt

φρακαρισμένος [frakarismenos] blocked; stuck

φράκτης (ο) [fraktis (o)] fence

φρενάρω [frenaro] brake (verb)

φρένο (το) [freno (to)] brake

ΦΡΕΣΚΟΣ φρέσκος [freskos] fresh

φρικτός [friktos] horrible

φρύδι (το) [frithi (to)] eyebrow

φτάνει [ftani] that's enough

φτάνω [ftano] arrive

φτέρνα (η) [fterna (i)] heel (of foot)

φτερνίζομαι [fternizomeh] sneeze

(verb)

φτερό (το) [ftero (to)] wing

ΦΤΗΝΟΣ φτηνός [ftinos] cheap, inexpensive

φτιάχνω τις βαλίτσες [ftiakhno tis valitses] pack (verb)

φτυάρι (το) [ftiari (to)] spade

φτωχός [ftokhos] poor

φύγε! [fiyeh!] go away!

φύκια (τα) [fikia (ta)] seaweed

ΦΥΛΑΚΗ φυλακή (η) [filaki (i)] prison

ΦΥΛΑΞΗ ΑΠΟΣΚΕΥΩΝ φύλαξη αποσκευών [filaxi aposkevon] left luggage, baggage check

φύλλο (το) [filo (to)] leaf

φύλο (το) [filo (to)] gender

φύση (η) [fisi (i)] nature

ΦΥΣΙΚΟ ΠΡΟΪΟΝ φυσικό προϊόν natural product

ΦΥΣΙΚΟΣ φυσικός [fisikos] natural

ΦΥΣΙΚΟ ΧΡΩΜΑ φυσικό χρώμα natural colouring

φυσιολογικός [fisioloyikos] normal

ΦΥΤΟ φυτό (το) [fito (to)] plant

φωνάζω [fonazo] call; shout (verb)

φωνή (η) [foni (i)] voice

ΦΩΣ φως (το) [fos (to)] light

φώτα (τα) [fota (ta)] lights (on car)

ΦΩΤΙΑ φωτιά (η) [fotia (i)] fire έχεις φωτιά; [ekhis fotia?] have you got a light?

φωτογραφία (η) [fotografia (i)] photograph

ΦΩΤΟΓΡΑΦΙΚΑ φωτογραφικά

cameras

φωτογραφική μηχανή (η)
[fotografiki mikhani (i)] camera

φωτόμετρο (το) [fotometro (to)]
light meter

χαίρετε [khereteh] hello

χαλάκι (το) [khalaki (to)] rug

χαλί (το) [khali (to)] carpet

χάλια [khalia] awful

χαμηλά φώτα (τα) [khamila fota
(ta)] sidelights

χαμηλός [khamilos] low

χαμόγελο (το) [khamoyelo (to)]
smile

χαμογελώ [khamoyelo] smile
(verb)

χάνω [khano] lose; miss

ΧΑΠΙ *χάπι (το)* [khapi (to)] pill

χάρηκα! [kharika!] pleased to
meet you!

ΧΑΡΠΙΚ *χάρπικ (το)* [kharpik
(to)] bleach (for toilet)

ΧΑΡΤΗΣ *χάρτης (ο)* [khartis
(o)] map

ΧΑΡΤΙ *χαρτί (το)* [kharti (to)]
paper

χαρτιά (τα) [khartia (ta)] playing
cards

ΧΑΡΤΙ ΑΛΛΗΛΟΓΡΑΦΙΑΣ
χαρτί αλληλογραφίας (το) [kharti
alilografias (to)] writing paper

ΧΑΡΤΙΚΑ *χαρτικά (τα)* [khartika
(ta)] stationery

ΧΑΡΤΙ ΠΕΡΙΤΥΛΙΓΜΑΤΟΣ
χαρτί περιτυλίγματος [kharti

peritiligmatos] wrapping paper

ΧΑΡΤΙ ΥΓΕΙΑΣ *χαρτί υγείας*
[kharti iyias] toilet paper

ΧΑΡΤΟΜΑΝΤΗΛΑ
χαρτομάντηλα (τα)
[khartomandila (ta)] tissues,
Kleenex®

χαρτόνι (το) [khartoni (to)]
cardboard

χαρτονόμισμα [khartonomisma]
banknote, (US) bill

ΧΑΡΤΟΠΩΛΕΙΟ *χαρτοπωλείο
(το)* [khartopolio (to)] stationer's

χαρτοφύλακας (ο) [khartofilakas
(o)] briefcase

ΧΑΣΑΠΗΣ *χασάπης (ο)*
[khasapis (o)] butcher's

χείλι (το) [khili (to)] lip

ΧΕΙΜΕΡΙΝΟΣ *χειμερινός*
[khimerinos] (winter) cinema/
movie theater

χειμώνας (ο) [khimonas (o)]
winter

ΧΕΙΡΟΠΟΙΗΤΟ *χειροποίητο*
[khiropi-ito] handmade

χειρότερος [khiroteros] worse

χειρότερος (ο) [khiroteros (o)]
worst

ΧΕΙΡΟΤΕΧΝΙΑ *χειροτεχνία (η)*
crafts

χειρόφρενο (το) [khirofreno (to)]
handbrake

χέρι (το) [kheri (to)] arm; hand

χερούλι (το) [kherooli (to)] handle

χήρα (η) [khira (i)] widow

χήρος (ο) [khiros (o)] widower

χθες [khThes] yesterday

ΧΙΛ. *χιλ.* thousand, thousands

ΧΙΛΙΑ *χίλια* [khilia] thousand,

thousands

ΧΙΛΙΑΔΕΣ χιλιάδες [khiliathes] thousand, thousands

ΧΙΛΙΑΡΙΚΟ χιλιάρικο (το) [khiliariko (to)] 1,000-drachma note/bill

χιλιόμετρο (το) [khiliometro (to)] kilometre

χιούμορ (το) [khioomor (to)] humour

χλιαρός [khliaros] lukewarm; cool

ΧΛΩΡΙΝΗ χλωρίνη (η) [khlorini (i)] bleach

χόμπυ (το) [khobi (to)] hobby

ΧΟΝΔΡΙΚΗΣ χονδρικής wholesale

χορεύω [khorevo] dance (verb)

χορός (ο) [khoros (o)] dance

χορτάρι (το) [khortari (to)] grass

χορτοφαγικός [khortofayikos] vegetarian

χορτοφάγος (ο/η) [khortofagos (o/i)] vegetarian

χρειάζομαι [khriazomeh] need (verb)

ΧΡΗΜΑΤΙΣΤΗΡΙΟ χρηματιστήριο (το) [khrimatistirio (to)] currency exchange; stock exchange

χρήση (η) [khrisi (i)] use

χρησιμοποιώ [khrisimopio] use (verb)

χρήσιμος [khrisimos] useful

Χριστούγεννα (τα) [KHristooyena (ta)] Christmas

Καλά Χριστούγεννα! [Kala KHristooyena!] Happy Christmas!

χρονιά (η) [khronia (i)] year

Χρόνια Πολλά! [khronia pola!] Happy Birthday!

του χρόνου [too khronoo] next year

πόσο χρονών είσαι; [poso khronon iseh?] how old are you?

χρόνος (ο) [khronos (o)] time; year

ΧΡΥΣΟΣ χρυσός (ο) [khrisos (o)] gold

ΧΡΥΣΟΣ ΟΔΗΓΟΣ χρυσός οδηγός (ο) [khrisos othigos (o)] yellow pages

ΧΡΥΣΟΧΟΕΙΟ χρυσοχοείο (το) [khrisokhoio (to)] jeweller's

χρώμα (το) [khroma (to)] colour

ΧΡΩΜΑΤΑ - ΣΙΔΕΡΙΚΑ χρώματα - σιδερικά paint and hardware store

χτένα (η) [khtena (i)] comb

χτυπώ [khtipo] hit (verb)

χώμα (το) [khoma (to)] earth

χώρα (η) [khora (i)] country

χωράφι (το) [khorafi (to)] field

ΧΩΡΗΤΙΚΟΤΗΤΟΣ ... ΑΤΟΜΩΝ χωρητικότητος ... ατόμων max load ... persons

χωριό (το) [khorio (to)] village

χωρίς [khoris] without

ΧΩΡΙΣ ΕΙΣΠΡΑΚΤΟΡΑ χωρίς εισπράκτορα no ticket collector

χωρισμένος [khorismenos] divorced

ΧΩΡΙΣ ΜΠΑΝΙΟ χωρίς μπάνιο [khoris banio] without bathroom

ΧΩΡΙΣ ΝΤΟΥΣ χωρίς ντους

[khoris doos] without shower
ΧΩΡΙΣ ΣΥΝΤΗΡΗΤΙΚΑ
  χωρίς συντηρητικά no
  preservatives
χωριστός [khoristos] separate
ΧΩΡΟΣ ΔΙΑ ΠΟΔΗΛΑΤΕΣ
  χώρος διά ποδηλάτες cycle path
χώρος φύλαξης αποσκευών (ο)
  [khoros filaxis aposkevon (o)] left
  luggage, baggage check

Ψ

ψαλίδι (το) [psalithi (to)] scissors
ΨΑΡΑΔΙΚΟ ψαράδικο (το)
  [psarathiko (to)] fishmonger's
ψάρεμα (το) [psarema (to)]
  fishing
ΨΑΡΟΤΑΒΕΡΝΑ ψαροταβέρνα
  (η) [psarotaverna (i)] restaurant
  specializing in seafood
ψάχνω [psakhno] look for
ψέματα: λέω ψέματα [leo
  psemata] lie (say untruth)
ψεύτικος [pseftikos] false
ψήνω [psino] bake
ΨΗΣΤΑΡΙΑ ψησταριά (η)
  [psistaria (i)] restaurant
  specializing in charcoal-
  grilled food
ψιλά (τα) [psila (ta)] small
  change
ΨΙΛΙΚΑ ψιλικά (τα) [psilika (ta)]
  small shop
ψυγείο (το) [psiyio (to)] fridge
ψυγείο αυτοκινήτου (το) [psiyio
  aftokinitoo (to)] radiator (car)
ΨΩΜΑΔΙΚΟ ψωμάδικο

[psomathiko] baker's
ψωμάς (ο) [psomas (o)] baker
ψηλός [psilos] high; tall
ψώνια (τα) [psonia (ta)] shopping
  πάω για ψώνια [pao ya psonia]
  go shopping

Ω

ΩΘΗΣΑΤΕ ωθήσατε push
ώμος (ο) [omos (o)] shoulder
ώρα (η) [ora (i)] hour
  τι ώρα είναι; [ti ora ineh?] what
  time is it?
  σε λίγη ώρα [seh liyi ora] soon
  στην ώρα του [stin ora too] on
  time
ωραίος [oreos] beautiful;
  handsome; lovely
ΩΡΕΣ ΕΠΙΣΚΕΨΕΩΣ ώρες
  επισκέψεως visiting hours
ΩΡΕΣ ΛΕΙΤΟΥΡΓΕΙΑΣ ώρες
  λειτουργείας opening hours
ως [os] as, since
ΩΤΟΡΙΝΟΛΑΡΥΓΓΟΛΟΓΟΣ
  ωτορινολαρυγγολόγος (ο/η) ear,
  nose and throat specialist
ωτοστόπ (το) [otostop (to)]
  hitchhiking
ωτοστόπ: κάνω ωτοστόπ [kano
  otostop] hitchhike

Menu Reader:
Food

Essential Terms

bread to psomi
butter to vootiro
cup to flidzani
dessert to glikisma
fish to psari
fork to pirooni
glass to potiri
knife to makheri
main course to kirio piato
meat to kreas
menu to menoo
pepper to piperi
plate to piato
salad i salata
salt to alati
set menu to tabl-dot
soup i soopa
spoon to kootali
starter to proto piato
table to trapezi

another ..., please ali mia ..., parakalo
excuse me! parakalo
could I have the bill, please? boro na ekho ton logariasmo,
  parakalo?

ΑΓΓΙΝΑΡΕΣ ΑΥΓΟΛΕΜΟΝΟ αγγινάρες αυγολέμονο [aginares avgolemono] artichokes in egg and lemon sauce

ΑΓΓΟΥΡΑΚΙΑ αγγουράκια [agoorakia] cucumbers

ΑΓΓΟΥΡΙ αγγούρι [agoori] cucumber

ΑΓΓΟΥΡΙΑ ΚΑΙ ΝΤΟΜΑΤΕΣ ΣΑΛΑΤΑ αγγούρια και ντομάτες σαλάτα [agooria keh domates salata] cucumber and tomato salad

ΑΚΤΙΝΙΔΙΟ ακτινίδιο [aktinithio] kiwi fruit

ΑΛΑΤΙ αλάτι [alati] salt

ΑΛΕΥΡΙ αλεύρι [alevri] flour

ΑΛΕΥΡΙ ΚΑΛΑΜΠΟΚΙΟΥ αλεύρι καλαμποκιού [alevri kalabokioo] cornflour

ΑΛΕΥΡΙ ΣΤΑΡΙΟΥ αλεύρι σταριού [alevri starioo] wheat flour

ΑΛΛΑΝΤΙΚΑ αλλαντικά [alandika] sausages, salami, ham etc

ΑΜΥΓΔΑΛΑ αμύγδαλα [amigthala] almonds

ΑΜΥΓΔΑΛΩΤΑ αμυγδαλωτά [amigthalota] macaroons; almond pastries

ΑΝΑΝΑΣ ανανάς [ananas] pineapple

ΑΝΘΟΤΥΡΟ ανθότυρο [anTHotiro] type of cottage cheese

ΑΝΤΖΟΥΓΙΑ ΣΤΟ ΛΑΔΙ αντζούγια στο λάδι [andsoo-yia sto lathi] anchovies in oil

ΑΡΑΚΑΣ αρακάς [arakas] peas

ΑΡΑΚΑΣ ΛΑΔΕΡΟΣ αρακάς λαδερός [arakas latheros] peas cooked with tomato and oil

ΑΡΑΚΑΣ ΣΩΤΕ αρακάς σωτέ [arakas soteh] peas fried in butter

ΑΡΝΑΚΙ αρνάκι [arnaki] lamb

ΑΡΝΑΚΙ ΕΞΟΧΙΚΟ αρνάκι εξοχικό [arnaki exohiko] leg of lamb baked in greaseproof paper

ΑΡΝΑΚΙ ΜΕ ΜΠΑΜΙΕΣ αρνάκι με μπάμιες [arnaki meh bami-es] lamb and okra stew

ΑΡΝΑΚΙ ΜΕ ΠΑΤΑΤΕΣ ΣΤΟ ΦΟΥΡΝΟ αρνάκι με πατάτες στο φούρνο [arnaki meh patates sto foorno] roast lamb and potatoes

ΑΡΝΑΚΙ ΤΑΣ ΚΕΜΠΑΠ αρνάκι τας κεμπάπ [arnaki tas kebap] lamb in tomato sauce

ΑΡΝΑΚΙ ΤΗΣ ΣΟΥΒΛΑΣ αρνάκι της σούβλας [arnaki tis soovlas] spit-roast lamb

ΑΡΝΑΚΙ ΦΡΙΚΑΣΕ αρνάκι φρικασέ με μαρούλια [arnaki frikaseh meh maroolia] lamb and lettuce in egg and lemon sauce

ΑΡΝΙ αρνί [arni] mutton, lamb

ΑΡΝΙ ΓΕΜΙΣΤΟ ΣΤΟ ΦΟΥΡΝΟ αρνί γεμιστό στο φούρνο [arni yemisto sto foorno] oven-cooked stuffed lamb

ΑΡΝΙ ΕΞΟΧΙΚΟ αρνί εξοχικό [arni exohiko] lamb cooked in

greased foil with cheese and spices

ΑΡΝΙ ΚΟΚΚΙΝΙΣΤΟ αρνί κοκκινιστό [arni kokinisto] lamb in tomato sauce

ΑΡΝΙ ΛΑΔΟΡΙΓΑΝΗ ΣΤΟ ΦΟΥΡΝΟ αρνί λαδορίγανη στο φούρνο [arni lathorigani sto foorno] oven-cooked lamb with oil and oregano

ΑΡΝΙ ΜΕ ΑΡΑΚΑ αρνί με αρακά [arni meh araka] lamb with peas

ΑΡΝΙ ΜΕ ΚΟΛΟΚΥΘΑΚΙΑ ΑΥΓΟΛΕΜΟΝΟ αρνί με κολοκυθάκια αυγολέμονο [arni meh kolokiTHakia avgolemono] lamb with courgettes/zucchini in egg and lemon sauce

ΑΡΝΙ ΜΕ ΚΡΙΘΑΡΑΚΙ αρνί με κριθαράκι [arni meh kriTHaraki] lamb with pasta

ΑΡΝΙ ΜΕ ΜΑΚΑΡΟΝΙΑ αρνί με μακαρόνια [arni meh makaronia] lamb with spaghetti

ΑΡΝΙ ΜΕ ΜΕΛΙΤΖΑΝΕΣ αρνί με μελιτζάνες [arni meh melitzanes] lamb with aubergines/eggplants

ΑΡΝΙ ΜΕ ΜΠΑΜΙΕΣ αρνί με μπάμιες [arni meh bami-es] lamb with okra

ΑΡΝΙ ΜΕ ΠΑΤΑΤΕΣ ΡΑΓΟΥ αρνί με πατάτες ραγού [arni meh patates ragoo] lamb with potatoes cooked in tomato sauce

ΑΡΝΙ ΜΕ ΦΑΣΟΛΑΚΙΑ ΦΡΕΣΚΑ αρνί με φασολάκια φρέσκα [arni meh fasolakia freska] lamb with runner beans

ΑΡΝΙ ΜΕ ΧΥΛΟΠΙΤΕΣ αρνί με χυλοπίτες [arni meh khilopites] lamb with a type of lasagne

ΑΡΝΙ ΜΠΟΥΤΙ ΣΤΟ ΦΟΥΡΝΟ αρνί μπούτι στο φούρνο [arni booti sto foorno] oven-cooked leg of lamb

ΑΡΝΙ ΜΠΡΙΖΟΛΕΣ αρνί μπριζόλες [arni brizoles] lamb chops

ΑΡΝΙ ΠΑΪΔΑΚΙΑ αρνί παϊδάκια [arni paithakia] grilled lamb chops

ΑΡΝΙ ΤΑΣ ΚΕΜΠΑΠ αρνί τας κεμπάπ [arni tas kebab] chopped lamb kebab with tomato sauce

ΑΡΝΙ ΤΗΣ ΚΑΤΣΑΡΟΛΑΣ ΜΕ ΠΑΤΑΤΕΣ αρνί της κατσαρόλας με πατάτες [arni tis katsarolas meh patates] casseroled lamb cooked with potatoes

ΑΡΝΙ ΤΗΣ ΣΟΥΒΛΑΣ αρνί της σούβλας [arni tis soovlas] spit-roast lamb

ΑΡΝΙ ΦΡΙΚΑΣΕ αρνί φρικασέ [arni frikaseh] lamb fricassee

ΑΣΤΑΚΟΣ αστακός [astakos] lobster

ΑΣΤΑΚΟΣ ΜΕ ΛΑΔΟΛΕΜΟΝΟ αστακός με λαδολέμονο [astakos meh latholemono] lobster cooked in lemon and oil sauce

ΑΣΤΑΚΟΣ ΜΕ ΜΑΓΙΟΝΕΖΑ αστακός με μαγιονέζα [astakos meh mayoneza] lobster with mayonnaise

ΑΤΖΕΜ ΠΙΛΑΦΙ ατζέμ πιλάφι [atzem pilafi] rice pilaf

ΑΥΓΑ αυγά [avga] eggs

ΑΥΓΑ ΒΡΑΣΤΑ αυγά βραστά [avga vrasta] boiled eggs

ΑΥΓΑ ΒΡΑΣΤΑ ΣΦΙΧΤΑ αυγά βραστά σφιχτά [avga vrasta sfikhta] hard-boiled eggs

ΑΥΓΑ ΓΕΜΙΣΤΑ αυγά γεμιστά [avga yemista] stuffed eggs

ΑΥΓΑ ΓΕΜΙΣΤΑ ΜΕ ΜΑΓΙΟΝΕΖΑ αυγά γεμιστά με μαγιονέζα [avga yemista meh mayoneza] stuffed eggs with mayonnaise

ΑΥΓΑ ΜΑΤΙΑ αυγά μάτια [avga matia] fried eggs

ΑΥΓΑ ΜΕΛΑΤΑ αυγά μελάτα [avga melata] soft-boiled eggs

ΑΥΓΑ ΜΕ ΜΑΝΙΤΑΡΙΑ αυγά με μανιτάρια [avga meh manitaria] mushroom omelette

ΑΥΓΑ ΜΕ ΜΠΕΙΚΟΝ αυγά με μπέικον [avga meh bacon] bacon and eggs

ΑΥΓΑ ΜΕ ΝΤΟΜΑΤΕΣ αυγά με ντομάτες [avga meh domates] eggs cooked in tomato sauce

ΑΥΓΑ ΜΕ ΤΥΡΙ αυγά με τυρί [avga meh tiri] cheese omelette

ΑΥΓΑ ΟΜΕΛΕΤΑ αυγά ομελέτα [avga omeleta] plain omelette

ΑΥΓΑ ΟΜΕΛΕΤΑ ΜΕ

ΠΑΤΑΤΕΣ αυγά ομελέτα με πατάτες [avga omeleta meh patates] omelette with chips/ fries

ΑΥΓΑ ΠΟΣΕ αυγά ποσέ [avga poseh] poached eggs

ΑΥΓΑ ΣΦΙΧΤΑ αυγά σφιχτά [avga sfikhta] hard-boiled eggs

ΑΥΓΑ ΤΗΓΑΝΗΤΑ αυγά τηγανητά [avga tiganita] fried eggs

ΑΥΓΑ Ω ΓΚΡΑΤΕΝ αυγά ω γκρατέν [avga o graten] eggs au gratin

ΑΥΓΟ αυγό [avgo] egg

ΑΥΓΟΛΕΜΟΝΟ αυγολέμονο [avgolemono] egg and lemon sauce

ΑΥΓΟΛΕΜΟΝΟ ΣΟΥΠΑ αυγολέμονο σούπα [avgolemono soopa] chicken broth with egg and lemon

ΑΥΓΟΤΑΡΑΧΟ αυγοτάραχο [avgotarakho] roe

ΑΧΛΑΔΙ αχλάδι [akhlathi] pear

ΒΑΝΙΛΙΑ βανίλια [vanilia] vanilla

ΒΑΤΟΜΟΥΡΟ βατόμουρο [vatomooro] blackberry

ΒΕΡΙΚΟΚΟ βερίκοκο [verikoko] apricot

ΒΟΔΙΝΟ βοδινό [vothino] beef

ΒΟΔΙΝΟ ΒΡΑΣΤΟ βοδινό βραστό [vothino vrasto] boiled beef

ΒΟΔΙΝΟ ΡΟΣΜΠΙΦ βοδινό ροσμπίφ [vothino rosbif] roast beef

A
B
Γ
Δ
E
Z
H
Θ
I
K
Λ
M
N
Ξ
O
Π
P
Σ
T
Y
Φ
X
Ψ
Ω

BOTANA βότανα [votana] herbs

BOYTYPO βούτυρο [vootiro] butter

BPAΣTO βραστό [vrasto] boiled

BYΣΣINO βύσσινο [visino] sour cherries

ΓΑΛΑΚΤΟΜΠΟΥΡΕΚΟ γαλακτομπούρεκο [galaktobooreko] cream-filled sweet filo pastry with honey

ΓΑΛΟΠΟΥΛΑ γαλοπούλα [galopoola] turkey

ΓΑΛΟΠΟΥΛΑ ΓΕΜΙΣΤΗ γαλοπούλα γεμιστή [galopoola yemisti] stuffed turkey

ΓΑΛΟΠΟΥΛΑ ΚΟΚΚΙΝΙΣΤΗ γαλοπούλα κοκκινιστή [galopoola kokinisti] turkey cooked with tomatoes

ΓΑΛΟΠΟΥΛΑ ΨΗΤΗ ΣΤΟ ΦΟΥΡΝΟ γαλοπούλα ψητή στο φούρνο [galopoola psiti sto foorno] roast turkey

ΓΑΡΔΟΥΜΠΑ γαρδούμπα [garthoomba] spit-roast rolled lamb offal

ΓΑΡΙΔΕΣ γαρίδες [garithes] prawns

ΓΑΡΙΔΕΣ ΒΡΑΣΤΕΣ γαρίδες βραστές [garithes vrastes] boiled shrimps

ΓΑΡΙΔΕΣ ΚΟΚΤΑΙΗΛ γαρίδες κοκταίηλ [garithes cocktail] shrimp cocktail

ΓΑΡΙΔΕΣ ΠΙΛΑΦΙ γαρίδες πιλάφι [garithes pilafi] shrimp pilaf

ΓΑΡΙΔΟΠΙΛΑΦΟ γαριδοπίλαφο [garithopilafo] prawns with rice cooked in butter

ΓΑΡΝΙΤΟΥΡΑ γαρνιτούρα [garnitoora] vegetables

ΓΑΡΝΙΤΟΥΡΑ ΚΑΡΟΤΑ ΣΩΤΕ γαρνιτούρα καρότα σωτέ [garnitoora karota soteh] sautéed carrots

ΓΑΡΝΙΤΟΥΡΑ ΚΟΥΝΟΥΠΙΔΙ ΣΩΤΕ γαρνιτούρα κουνουπίδι σωτέ [garnitoora koonoopithi soteh] sautéed cauliflower

ΓΑΡΝΙΤΟΥΡΑ ΠΑΤΑΤΕΣ γαρνιτούρα πατάτες [garnitoora patates] potatoes

ΓΑΡΝΙΤΟΥΡΑ ΣΠΑΝΑΚΙ ΣΩΤΕ γαρνιτούρα σπανάκι σωτέ [garnitoora spanaki soteh] sautéed spinach

ΓΑΡΝΙΤΟΥΡΑ ΦΑΣΟΛΙΑ ΠΡΑΣΙΝΑ ΣΩΤΕ γαρνιτούρα φασόλια πράσινα σωτέ [garnitoora fasolia prasina soteh] sautéed runner beans

ΓΕΜΙΣΤΑ γεμιστά [yemista] stuffed, usually with rice and/or minced meat

ΓΕΜΙΣΤΕΣ γεμιστές [yemistes] stuffed vegetables

ΓΙΑΛΑΝΤΖΗ ΝΤΟΛΜΑΔΕΣ γιαλαντζή ντολμάδες [yalantzi dolmathes] vine leaves stuffed with rice

ΓΙΑΟΥΡΤΙ γιαούρτι [ya-oorti] yoghurt

ΓΙΓΑΝΤΕΣ γίγαντες [yigandes] white haricot beans; butter

beans

ΓΙΟΥΒΑΡΛΑΚΙΑ γιουβαρλάκια [yoovarlakia] meatballs, rice and seasoning in a sauce

ΓΙΟΥΒΑΡΛΑΚΙΑ ΑΥΓΟΛΕΜΟΝΟ γιουβαρλάκια αυγολέμονο [yoovarlakia avgolemono] meatballs with egg and lemon sauce

ΓΙΟΥΒΑΡΛΑΚΙΑ ΜΕ ΣΑΛΤΣΑ ΝΤΟΜΑΤΑΣ γιουβαρλάκια με σάλτσα ντομάτας [yoovarlakia meh saltsa domatas] meatballs with rice cooked with tomatoes

ΓΙΟΥΒΕΤΣΙ γιουβέτσι [yoovetsi] oven-roasted lamb with pasta

ΓΚΡΕΙΠΦΡΟΥΤ γκρέιπφρουτ [grapefruit] grapefruit

ΓΛΥΚΑ γλυκά [glika] cakes, desserts

ΓΛΥΚΙΣΜΑ γλύκισμα [glikisma] dessert

ΓΛΥΚΟ γλυκό [gliko] sweet, dessert

ΓΛΥΚΟ ΒΥΣΣΙΝΟ γλυκό βύσσινο [gliko visino] candied cherries in syrup

ΓΛΥΚΟ ΚΑΡΥΔΑΚΙ ΦΡΕΣΚΟ γλυκό καρυδάκι φρέσκο [gliko karithaki fresko] dried fresh green walnuts in syrup

ΓΛΥΚΟ ΜΑΣΤΙΧΑ γλυκό μαστίχα [gliko mastikha] vanilla-flavoured fudge

ΓΛΥΚΟ ΜΕΛΙΤΖΑΝΑΚΙ γλυκό μελιτζανάκι [gliko melitzanaki] dried small

aubergine/eggplant in syrup

ΓΛΥΚΟ ΝΕΡΑΝΤΖΑΚΙ γλυκό νεραντζάκι [gliko nerantzaki] dried bitter orange in syrup

ΓΛΥΚΟ ΣΥΚΟ γλυκό σύκο [gliko siko] candied figs in syrup

ΓΛΥΚΟ ΣΥΚΟ ΦΡΕΣΚΟ γλυκό σύκο φρέσκο [gliko siko fresko] dried fig in syrup

ΓΛΥΚΟ ΤΡΙΑΝΤΑΦΥΛΛΟ γλυκό τριαντάφυλλο [gliko triandafilo] dried rose petals in syrup

ΓΛΩΣΣΑ γλώσσα [glosa] sole; tongue

ΓΛΩΣΣΕΣ ΤΗΓΑΝΗΤΕΣ γλώσσες τηγανητές [gloses tiganites] fried sole

ΓΟΥΡΟΥΝΟΠΟΥΛΟ ΣΤΟ ΦΟΥΡΝΟ ΜΕ ΠΑΤΑΤΕΣ γουρουνόπουλο στο φούρνο με πατάτες [gooroonopoolo sto foorno meh patates] oven-cooked pork with potatoes

ΓΡΑΒΙΕΡΑ γραβιέρα [gravi-era] hard cheese like gruyère

ΓΡΑΝΙΤΑ γρανίτα [granita] sorbet

ΓΡΑΝΙΤΑ ΛΕΜΟΝΙ γρανίτα λεμόνι [granita lemoni] lemon sorbet

ΓΡΑΝΙΤΑ ΜΠΑΝΑΝΑ γρανίτα μπανάνα [granita banana] banana sorbet

ΓΡΑΝΙΤΑ ΠΟΡΤΟΚΑΛΙ γρανίτα πορτοκάλι [granita portokali] orange sorbet

ΓΡΑΝΙΤΑ ΦΡΑΟΥΛΕΣ γρανίτα

φράουλες [granita fraooles]
strawberry sorbet

ΔΑΜΑΣΚΗΝΑ δαμάσκηνα
[thamaskina] prunes
ΔΑΜΑΣΚΗΝΟ δαμάσκηνο
[thamaskino] plum
ΔΙΠΛΕΣ δίπλες [thiples]
pancakes

ΕΛΑΙΟΛΑΔΟ ελαιόλαδο
[eleolatho] olive oil
ΕΛΙΕΣ ελιές [eli-es] olives
ΕΝΤΟΣΘΙΑ ΑΡΝΙΟΥ
ΛΑΔΟΡΙΓΑΝΗ εντόσθια
αρνιού λαδορίγανη [endosthia
arnioo lathorigani] lambs'
intestines cooked in lemon
and oil
ΕΠΙΔΟΡΠΙΟ επιδόρπιο
[epithorpio] dessert
ΕΣΚΑΛΟΠ ΜΕ ΖΑΜΠΟΝ
ΚΑΙ ΣΑΛΤΣΑ ΝΤΟΜΑΤΑΣ
εσκαλόπ με ζαμπόν και σάλτσα
ντομάτας [eskalop meh zabon
keh saltsa domatas] escalope of
veal with ham and tomato
sauce

ΖΑΜΠΟΝ ζαμπόν [zabon] ham
ΖΑΧΑΡΗ ζάχαρη [zakhari] sugar
ΖΕΛΕ ζελέ [zeleh] jelly
ΖΥΜΑΡΙΚΑ ζυμαρικά
[zimarika] pasta and rice

ΘΑΛΑΣΣΙΝΑ θαλασσινά
[THalasina] seafood

ΚΑΒΟΥΡΙΑ καβούρια

[kavooria] crab
ΚΑΚΑΒΙΑ κακαβιά [kakavia]
mixed fish soup
ΚΑΚΑΒΙΑ ΨΑΡΟΣΟΥΠΑ
κακαβιά ψαρόσουπα [kakavia
psarosoopa] fish soup
ΚΑΛΑΜΑΡΑΚΙΑ καλαμαράκια
[kalamarakia] baby squid
ΚΑΛΑΜΑΡΑΚΙΑ ΓΕΜΙΣΤΑ
καλαμαράκια γεμιστά
[kalamarakia yemista] stuffed
baby squid
ΚΑΛΑΜΑΡΑΚΙΑ ΤΗΓΑΝΗΤΑ
καλαμαράκια τηγανητά
[kalamarakia tiganita] fried baby
squid
ΚΑΛΑΜΑΡΙΑ καλαμάρια
[kalamaria] squid
ΚΑΝΑΠΕ καναπέ [kanapeh]
canapés
ΚΑΝΑΠΕ ΜΕ ΖΑΜΠΟΝ
καναπέ με ζαμπόν [kanapeh meh
zabon] ham canapés
ΚΑΝΑΠΕ ΜΕ ΚΡΕΑΣ ΨΗΤΟ
καναπέ με κρέας ψητό [kanapeh
meh kreas psito] meat canapés
ΚΑΝΑΠΕ ΜΕ ΜΑΥΡΟ
ΧΑΒΙΑΡΙ καναπέ με μαύρο
χαβιάρι [kanapeh meh mavro
haviari] black caviar canapés
ΚΑΝΑΠΕ ΜΕ
ΤΑΡΑΜΟΣΑΛΑΤΑ καναπέ με
ταραμοσαλάτα [kanapeh meh
taramosalata] taramosalata
canapés
ΚΑΝΕΛΛΑ κανέλλα [kanela]
cinnamon
ΚΑΝΕΛΛΟΝΙΑ ΓΕΜΙΣΤΑ
κανελλόνια γεμιστά [kanelonia

yemista] stuffed canelloni

ΚΑΝΤΑΪΦΙ κανταΐφι [kanda-ifi] shredded and rolled filo pastry in syrup

ΚΑΠΑΜΑΣ ΑΡΝΙ καπαμάς αρνί [kapamas arni] lamb cooked in spices and tomato sauce

ΚΑΠΝΙΣΤΟ καπνιστό [kapnisto] smoked

ΚΑΠΠΑΡΗ κάππαρη [kapari] caper

ΚΑΡΑΒΙΔΕΣ καραβίδες [karavithes] king prawns; crayfish

ΚΑΡΟΤΑ καρότα [karota] carrots

ΚΑΡΠΟΥΖΙ καρπούζι [karpoozi] watermelon

ΚΑΡΥΔΙ καρύδι [karithi] nut

ΚΑΡΥΔΟΠΙΤΤΑ καρυδόπιττα [karithopita] walnut cake; cake with nuts and syrup

ΚΑΡΧΑΡΙΑΣ καρχαρίας [karkharias] shark

ΚΑΣΕΡΙ κασέρι [kaseri] Cheddar-type cheese

ΚΑΣΤΑΝΑ κάστανα [kastana] chestnuts

ΚΑΣΤΑΝΑ ΓΛΑΣΕ κάστανα γλασέ [kastana glaseh] glazed chestnuts, marrons glacés

ΚΑΤΑΪΦΙ καταΐφι [kata-ifi] shredded filo pastry with honey and nuts

ΚΑΤΑΛΟΓΟΣ κατάλογος [katalogos] menu

ΚΕΙΚ κέικ [cake] cake

ΚΕΙΚ ΚΑΝΕΛΛΑΣ κέικ κανέλλας [cake kanelas] cinammon cake

ΚΕΙΚ ΜΕ ΑΜΥΓΔΑΛΑ κέικ με αμύγδαλα [cake meh amigthala] almond cake

ΚΕΙΚ ΜΕ ΚΑΡΥΔΙΑ ΚΑΙ ΣΤΑΦΙΔΕΣ κέικ με καρύδια και σταφίδες [cake meh karithia keh stafithes] nut and sultana cake

ΚΕΙΚ ΣΟΚΟΛΑΤΑΣ κέικ σοκολάτας [cake sokolatas] chocolate cake

ΚΕΙΚ ΦΡΟΥΤΩΝ κέικ φρούτων [cake frooton] fruit cake

ΚΕΡΑΣΙΑ κεράσια [kerasia] cherries

ΚΕΦΑΛΟΤΥΡΙ κεφαλοτύρι [kefalotiri] very salty, hard cheese

ΚΕΦΤΕΔΕΣ κεφτέδες [keftethes] meatballs

ΚΕΦΤΕΔΕΣ ΜΕ ΣΑΛΤΣΑ κεφτέδες με σάλτσα [keftethes meh saltsa] meatballs in tomato sauce

ΚΕΦΤΕΔΕΣ ΣΤΟ ΦΟΥΡΝΟ κεφτέδες στο φούρνο [keftethes sto foorno] oven-cooked meatballs

ΚΕΦΤΕΔΕΣ ΤΗΓΑΝΗΤΟΙ κεφτέδες τηγανητοί [keftethes tiganiti] fried meatballs

ΚΙΜΑΣ κιμάς [kimas] minced meat

ΚΛΕΦΤΙΚΟ κλέφτικο [kleftiko] meat, potatoes and

vegetables cooked together in a pot or foil

ΚΟΚΚΙΝΙΣΤΟ κοκκινιστό [kokinisto] in tomato sauce

ΚΟΚΟΡΕΤΣΙ κοκορέτσι [kokoretsi] spit-roast rolled lamb offal

ΚΟΛΙΟΙ κολιοί [koli-i] mackerel

ΚΟΛΙΟΙ ΨΗΤΟΙ κολιοί ψητοί [koli-i psiti] fried mackerel

ΚΟΛΟΚΥΘΑΚΙΑ κολοκυθάκια [kolokiTHakia] courgettes/ zucchini

ΚΟΛΟΚΥΘΑΚΙΑ ΓΕΜΙΣΤΑ ΜΕ ΚΙΜΑ κολοκυθάκια γεμιστά με κιμά [kolokiTHakia yemista meh kima] courgettes/ zucchini stuffed with minced meat

ΚΟΛΟΚΥΘΑΚΙΑ ΓΕΜΙΣΤΑ ΜΕ ΡΥΖΙ κολοκυθάκια γεμιστά με ρύζι [kolokiTHakia yemista meh rizi] courgettes/ zucchini stuffed with rice

ΚΟΛΟΚΥΘΑΚΙΑ ΓΙΑΧΝΙ κολοκυθάκια γιαχνί [kolokiTHakia yakhni] courgettes/zucchini and onions in a tomato sauce

ΚΟΛΟΚΥΘΑΚΙΑ ΛΑΔΕΡΑ κολοκυθάκια λαδερά [kolokiTHakia lathera] courgettes/zucchini cooked in oil

ΚΟΛΟΚΥΘΑΚΙΑ ΜΕ ΚΡΕΑΣ κολοκυθάκια με κρέας [kolokiTHakia meh kreas] courgette/zucchini and beef stew

ΚΟΛΟΚΥΘΑΚΙΑ ΜΕ ΠΑΤΑΤΕΣ κολοκυθάκια με πατάτες [kolokiTHakia meh patates] courgettes/zucchini with potatoes

ΚΟΛΟΚΥΘΑΚΙΑ ΜΟΥΣΑΚΑΣ κολοκυθάκια μουσακάς [kolokiTHakia moosakas] courgettes/zucchini with minced meat and béchamel

ΚΟΛΟΚΥΘΑΚΙΑ ΠΑΠΟΥΤΣΑΚΙΑ κολοκυθάκια παπουτσάκια [kolokiTHakia papootsakia] courgettes/ zucchini with minced meat and onions

ΚΟΛΟΚΥΘΑΚΙΑ ΤΗΓΑΝΗΤΑ κολοκυθάκια τηγανητά [kolokiTHakia tiganita] fried courgettes/zucchini

ΚΟΛΟΚΥΘΟΚΕΦΤΕΔΕΣ κολοκυθοκεφτέδες [kolokiTHokeftethes] fried courgette/zucchini balls

ΚΟΛΟΚΥΘΟΤΥΡΟΠΙΤΤΑ κολοκυθοτυρόπιττα [kolokiTHotiropita] courgette/ zucchini and cheese pie

ΚΟΜΠΟΣΤΑ κομπόστα [kobosta] fruit compote

ΚΟΤΑ κότα [kota] chicken

ΚΟΤΑ ΒΡΑΣΤΗ κότα βραστή [kota vrasti] boiled chicken

ΚΟΤΑ ΨΗΤΗ ΣΤΟ ΦΟΥΡΝΟ κότα ψητή στο φούρνο [kota psiti sto foorno] roast chicken

ΚΟΤΑ ΨΗΤΗ ΤΗΣ ΚΑΤΣΑΡΟΛΑΣ κότα ψητή της κατσαρόλας [kota psiti tis katsar**ol**as] chicken casserole

ΚΟΤΑ ΨΗΤΗ ΤΗΣ ΣΟΥΒΛΑΣ
κότα ψητή της σούβλας [k**o**ta
psiti tis s**oo**vlas] spit-roast
chicken

**ΚΟΤΟΛΕΤΕΣ ΑΡΝΙΣΙΕΣ
ΠΑΝΕ** κοτολέτες αρνίσιες πανέ
[kotol**e**tes arn**i**si-es pan**eh**] lamb
cutlets

**ΚΟΤΟΛΕΤΕΣ ΜΟΣΧΑΡΙΣΙΕΣ
ΠΑΝΕ** κοτολέτες μοσχαρίσιες
πανέ [kotol**e**tes moskhar**i**si-es
pan**eh**] veal cutlets

ΚΟΤΟΠΙΤΤΑ κοτόπιττα
[kot**o**pita] chicken pie

ΚΟΤΟΠΟΥΛΟ κοτόπουλο
[kot**o**poolo] chicken

**ΚΟΤΟΠΟΥΛΟ ΓΙΟΥΒΕΤΣΙ
ΜΕ ΧΥΛΟΠΙΤΤΕΣ** κοτόπουλο
γιουβέτσι με χυλοπίττες
[kot**o**poolo yioov**e**tsi meh hil**o**pites]
chicken with pasta

ΚΟΤΟΠΟΥΛΟ ΚΟΚΚΙΝΙΣΤΟ
κοτόπουλο κοκκινιστό
[kot**o**poolo kokinist**o**] chicken in
tomato sauce

ΚΟΤΟΠΟΥΛΟ ΜΕ ΜΠΑΜΙΕΣ
κοτόπουλο με μπάμιες [kot**o**poolo
meh b**a**mi-es] chicken with
okra

**ΚΟΤΟΠΟΥΛΟ ΜΕ
ΜΠΙΖΕΛΙΑ** κοτόπουλο με
μπιζέλια [kot**o**poolo meh biz**e**lia]
chicken with peas

ΚΟΤΟΠΟΥΛΟ ΠΑΝΕ
κοτόπουλο πανέ [kot**o**poolo
pan**eh**] breaded chicken

ΚΟΤΟΠΟΥΛΟ ΠΙΛΑΦΙ
κοτόπουλο πιλάφι [kot**o**poolo

pil**a**fi] chicken pilaf

**ΚΟΤΟΠΟΥΛΟ ΤΗΣ
ΣΟΥΒΛΑΣ** κοτόπουλο της
σούβλας [kot**o**poolo tis s**oo**vlas]
spit-roast chicken

ΚΟΤΟΣΟΥΠΑ κοτόσουπα
[kot**o**soopa] chicken soup

ΚΟΥΚΙΑ ΛΑΔΕΡΑ κουκιά
λαδερά [k**oo**kia lath**e**ra] broad
beans in tomato sauce

ΚΟΥΝΕΛΙ κουνέλι [k**oo**neli]
rabbit

ΚΟΥΝΕΛΙ ΜΕ ΣΑΛΤΣΑ
κουνέλι με σάλτσα [k**oo**neli meh
s**a**ltsa] rabbit with tomato
sauce

ΚΟΥΝΕΛΙ ΣΤΙΦΑΔΟ κουνέλι
στιφάδο [k**oo**neli stif**a**tho] rabbit
with onions

ΚΟΥΝΟΥΠΙΔΙ κουνουπίδι
[koon**oo**pithi] cauliflower

**ΚΟΥΝΟΥΠΙΔΙ ΒΡΑΣΤΟ
ΣΑΛΑΤΑ** κουνουπίδι βραστό
σαλάτα [koon**o**pithi vrast**o** sal**a**ta]
boiled cauliflower salad

ΚΟΥΡΑΜΠΙΕΔΕΣ
κουραμπιέδες [koor**a**bi-ethes]
Greek shortbread

**ΚΟΥΡΑΜΠΙΕΔΕΣ ΜΕ
ΑΜΥΓΔΑΛΟ** κουραμπιέδες
με αμύγδαλο [koorabi-ethes meh
amigthal**o**] shortbread-type
biscuits with sesame seeds
and icing sugar

ΚΡΑΚΕΡΣ ΑΛΜΥΡΑ κράκερς
αλμυρά [kr**a**kers alm**i**ra] salted
crackers

ΚΡΑΣΑΤΟ κρασάτο [kras**a**to]
cooked in wine sauce

A
B
Γ
Δ
E
Z
H
Θ
I
K
Λ
M
N
Ξ
O
Π
P
Σ
T
Y
Φ
X
Ψ
Ω

ΚΡΕΑΣ κρέας [kreas] meat,
usually beef
ΚΡΕΑΣ ΜΕ ΑΝΤΙΔΙΑ
ΑΥΓΟΛΕΜΟΝΟ κρέας με
αντίδια αυγολέμονο [kreas meh
antithia avgolemono] beef with
endives in egg and lemon
sauce
ΚΡΕΑΣ ΜΕ ΦΑΣΟΛΙΑ ΞΕΡΑ
κρέας με φασόλια ξερά [kreas
meh fasolia xera] beef with
butter beans
ΚΡΕΑΤΙΚΑ κρεατικά [kreh-
atika] meat dishes
ΚΡΕΑΤΟΠΙΤΤΑ κρεατόπιττα
[kreh-atopita] minced meat in
filo pastry
ΚΡΕΜΑ κρέμα [krema] cream
ΚΡΕΜΑ ΚΑΡΑΜΕΛΕ κρέμα
καραμελέ [krema karameleh]
crème caramel
ΚΡΕΜΑ ΜΕ ΜΗΛΑ κρέμα με
μήλα [krema meh mila] apples
with cream
ΚΡΕΜΑ ΜΕ ΜΠΑΝΑΝΕΣ
κρέμα με μπανάνες [krema meh
bananes] bananas with cream
ΚΡΕΜΜΥΔΑΚΙΑ ΦΡΕΣΚΑ
κρεμμυδάκια φρέσκα
[kremithakia freska] spring
onions
ΚΡΕΜΜΥΔΙΑ κρεμμύδια
[kremithia] onions
ΚΡΕΜΜΥΔΟΣΟΥΠΑ
κρεμμυδόσουπα [kremithosoopa]
onion soup
ΚΡΕΠΑ κρέπα [krepa] pancake
ΚΡΟΚΕΤΕΣ κροκέτες
[kroketes] croquettes

ΚΡΟΚΕΤΕΣ ΑΠΟ ΚΡΕΑΣ
κροκέτες από κρέας [kroketes
apo kreas] meat croquettes
ΚΡΟΚΕΤΕΣ ΜΕ ΑΥΓΑ ΚΑΙ
ΤΥΡΙ κροκέτες με αυγά και
τυρί [kroketes meh avga keh tiri]
egg and cheese croquettes
ΚΡΟΚΕΤΕΣ ΜΠΑΚΑΛΙΑΡΟΥ
κροκέτες μπακαλιάρου
[kroketes bakaliaroo] cod
croquettes
ΚΡΟΚΕΤΕΣ ΠΑΤΑΤΕΣ
κροκέτες πατάτες [kroketes
patates] potato croquettes
ΚΡΟΥΑΣΑΝ κρουασάν
[croissants] croissants
ΚΥΔΩΝΙΑ κυδώνια [kithonia]
quinces
ΚΥΔΩΝΟΠΑΣΤΟ
κυδωνόπαστο [kithonopasto]
thick jelly made from
quince
ΚΥΝΗΓΙ κυνήγι [kiniyi] game
ΚΥΡΙΟ ΠΙΑΤΟ κύριο πιάτο
[kirio piato] main course
ΚΩΚ κωκ [kok] cake with
cream and chocolate
topping

ΛΑΓΟΣ λαγός [lagos] hare
ΛΑΓΟΣ ΜΕ ΣΑΛΤΣΑ λαγός
με σάλτσα [lagos meh saltsa]
hare in tomato sauce
ΛΑΓΟΣ ΣΤΙΦΑΔΟ λαγός
στιφάδο [lagos stifatho] hare
and shallot stew
ΛΑΔΕΡΑ λαδερά [lathera] in
olive oil and tomato sauce
ΛΑΔΙ λάδι [lathi] oil

ΛΑΔΟΛΕΜΟΝΟ λαδολέμονο [latholemono] olive oil and lemon dressing

ΛΑΔΟΞΥΔΟ λαδόξυδο [lathoxitho] oil and vinegar salad dressing

ΛΑΖΑΝΙΑ λαζάνια [lazania] lasagne

ΛΑΧΑΝΙΚΑ λαχανικά [lakhanika] vegetables

ΛΑΧΑΝΙΚΑ ΜΙΚΤΑ λαχανικά μικτά [lakhanika mikta] vegetables

ΛΑΧΑΝΑΚΙΑ ΒΡΥΞΕΛΛΩΝ λαχανάκια Βρυξελλών [lakhanakia vrixelon] Brussels sprouts

ΛΑΧΑΝΟ λάχανο [lakhano] cabbage

ΛΑΧΑΝΟ ΚΟΚΚΙΝΟ λάχανο κόκκινο [lakhano kokino] red cabbage

ΛΑΧΑΝΟ ΝΤΟΛΜΑΔΕΣ ΑΥΓΟΛΕΜΟΝΟ λάχανο ντολμάδες αυγολέμονο [lakhano dolmathes avgolemono] cabbage leaves stuffed with rice in egg and lemon sauce

ΛΑΧΑΝΟ ΝΤΟΛΜΑΔΕΣ λάχανο ντολμάδες [lakhano dolmathes] cabbage leaves stuffed with minced meat and rice

ΛΑΧΑΝΟ ΝΤΟΛΜΑΔΕΣ ΜΕ ΣΑΛΤΣΑ ΝΤΟΜΑΤΑΣ λάχανο ντολμάδες με σάλτσα ντομάτας [lakhano dolmathes meh saltsa domatas] vine leaves stuffed with rice in tomato sauce

ΛΑΧΑΝΟΣΑΛΑΤΑ λαχανοσαλάτα [lakhanosalata] cabbage salad

ΛΕΜΟΝΙ λεμόνι [lemoni] lemon

ΛΙΘΡΙΝΙ λιθρίνι [liTHrini] red snapper

ΛΙΘΡΙΝΙ ΨΗΤΟ λιθρίνι ψητό [liTHrini psito] grilled red snapper

ΛΟΥΚΑΝΙΚΑ λουκάνικα [lookanika] sausages

ΛΟΥΚΑΝΙΚΑ ΒΡΑΣΤΑ λουκάνικα βραστά [lookanika vrasta] boiled sausages

ΛΟΥΚΑΝΙΚΑ ΚΑΠΝΙΣΤΑ ΣΤΗ ΣΧΑΡΑ λουκάνικα καπνιστά στη σχάρα [lookanika kapnista sti skhara] grilled smoked sausages

ΛΟΥΚΑΝΙΚΑ ΤΗΓΑΝΗΤΑ λουκάνικα τηγανητά [lookanika tiganita] fried sausages

ΛΟΥΚΟΥΜΑΔΕΣ λουκουμάδες [lookoomathes] doughnuts

ΛΟΥΚΟΥΜΙΑ λουκούμια [lookoomia] Turkish delight

ΜΑΓΕΙΡΙΤΣΑ μαγειρίτσα [mayiritsa] traditional Easter soup made from lambs' intestines

ΜΑΓΙΑ μαγιά [maya] yeast

ΜΑΓΙΟΝΕΖΑ μαγιονέζα [mayoneza] mayonnaise

ΜΑΪΝΤΑΝΟΣ μαϊντανός [maindanos] parsley

A
B
Γ
Δ
E
Z
H
Θ
I
K
Λ
M
N
Ξ
O
Π
P
Σ
T
Y
Φ
X
Ψ
Ω

185

ΜΑΚΑΡΟΝΑΚΙ ΚΟΦΤΟ
μακαρονάκι κοφτό [makaronaki kofto] macaroni

ΜΑΚΑΡΟΝΙΑ μακαρόνια [makaronia] pasta

ΜΑΚΑΡΟΝΙΑ ΜΕ ΚΙΜΑ
μακαρόνια με κιμά [makaronia meh kima] spaghetti bolognaise

ΜΑΚΑΡΟΝΙΑ ΜΕ ΦΡΕΣΚΟ ΒΟΥΤΥΡΟ ΚΑΙ ΠΑΡΜΕΖΑΝΑ μακαρόνια με φρέσκο βούτυρο και παρμεζάνα [makaronia meh fresko vootiro keh parmezana] spaghetti with butter and parmesan cheese

ΜΑΚΑΡΟΝΙΑ ΠΑΣΤΙΤΣΙΟ ΜΕ ΚΙΜΑ μακαρόνια παστίτσιο με κιμά [makaronia pastitsio meh kima] baked pasta dish with minced meat and béchamel

ΜΑΝΙΤΑΡΙΑ μανιτάρια [manitaria] mushrooms

ΜΑΝΙΤΑΡΙΑ ΤΗΓΑΝΗΤΑ μανιτάρια τηγανητά [manitaria tiganita] fried mushrooms

ΜΑΝΟΥΡΙ μανούρι [manoori] hard cheese

ΜΑΝΤΑΡΙΝΙ μανταρίνι [mandarini] satsuma, tangerine

ΜΑΡΓΑΡΙΝΗ μαργαρίνη [margarini] margarine

ΜΑΡΙΔΕΣ ΤΗΓΑΝΗΤΕΣ μαρίδες τηγανητές [marithes tiganites] small fried fish

ΜΑΡΜΕΛΑΔΑ μαρμελάδα [marmelatha] jam, marmalade

ΜΑΡΜΕΛΑΔΑ ΒΕΡΥΚΟΚΚΑ μαρμελάδα βερύκοκκα [marmelatha verikoka] apricot jam

ΜΑΡΜΕΛΑΔΑ ΠΟΡΤΟΚΑΛΙ μαρμελάδα πορτοκάλι [marmelatha portokali] orange jam

ΜΑΡΜΕΛΑΔΑ ΡΟΔΑΚΙΝΑ μαρμελάδα ροδάκινα [marmelatha pothakina] peach jam

ΜΑΡΜΕΛΑΔΑ ΦΡΑΟΥΛΕΣ μαρμελάδα φράουλες [marmelatha fraooles] strawberry jam

ΜΑΡΟΥΛΙ μαρούλι [marooli] lettuce

ΜΑΡΟΥΛΙΑ ΣΑΛΑΤΑ μαρούλια σαλάτα [maroolia salata] green salad

ΜΕ ΛΑΔΟΛΕΜΟΝΟ με λαδολέμονο [meh latholemono] with olive oil and lemon dressing

ΜΕΛΙ μέλι [meli] honey

ΜΕΛΙΤΖΑΝΕΣ μελιτζάνες [melidzanes] aubergines/ eggplants

ΜΕΛΙΤΖΑΝΕΣ ΓΕΜΙΣΤΕΣ ΜΕ ΚΙΜΑ μελιτζάνες γεμιστές με κιμά [melitzanes yemistes meh kima] aubergines/eggplants stuffed with minced meat

ΜΕΛΙΤΖΑΝΕΣ ΓΙΑΧΝΙ μελιτζάνες γιαχνί [melitzanes yakhni] aubergines/eggplants with tomato and onions

ΜΕΛΙΤΖΑΝΕΣ ΙΜΑΜ

ΜΠΑΪΛΝΤΙ μελιτζάνες ιμάμ μπαϊλντί [melitzanes imam baildi] aubergines/eggplants with garlic and tomato

ΜΕΛΙΤΖΑΝΕΣ ΜΟΥΣΑΚΑ μελιτζάνες μουσακά [melidzanes moosaka] layers of aubergine/eggplant and minced meat topped with béchamel

ΜΕΛΙΤΖΑΝΕΣ ΠΑΠΟΥΤΣΑΚΙΑ μελιτζάνες παπουτσάκια [melidzaness papootsakia] stuffed aubergines/eggplants

ΜΕΛΙΤΖΑΝΕΣ ΤΗΓΑΝΗΤΕΣ μελιτζάνες τηγανητές [melitzanes tiganites] fried aubergines/eggplants

ΜΕΛΙΤΖΑΝΟΣΑΛΑΤΑ μελιτζανοσαλάτα [melidzanosalata] puréed aubergine/eggplant dip

ΜΕΛΟΜΑΚΑΡΟΝΑ μελομακάρονα [melomakarona] sweet cakes with cinammon, nuts and syrup

ΜΕΝΟΥ μενού [menoo] menu

ΜΕ ΣΑΛΤΣΑ με σάλτσα [meh saltsa] with sauce, usually tomato sauce

ΜΗΛΑ ΓΕΜΙΣΤΑ μήλα γεμιστά [mila yemista] stuffed apples with cinammon

ΜΗΛΟ μήλο [milo] apple

ΜΗΛΟΠΙΤΤΑ μηλόπιττα [milopita] apple pie μισοψημένο [misopsimeno] medium (steak)

ΜΟΣΧΑΡΙ μοσχάρι [moskhari] veal; tender beef

ΜΟΣΧΑΡΙ ΒΡΑΣΤΟ μοσχάρι βραστό [moskhari vrasto] veal stew

ΜΟΣΧΑΡΙ ΚΟΚΚΙΝΙΣΤΟ μοσχάρι κοκκινιστό [moskhari kokinisto] veal in tomato sauce

ΜΟΣΧΑΡΙ ΜΕ ΑΡΑΚΑ μοσχάρι με αρακά [moskhari meh araka] veal with peas

ΜΟΣΧΑΡΙ ΜΕ ΚΡΙΘΑΡΑΚΙ μοσχάρι με κριθαράκι [moskhari meh kriTHaraki] veal with pasta

ΜΟΣΧΑΡΙ ΜΕ ΜΕΛΙΤΖΑΝΕΣ μοσχάρι με μελιτζάνες [moskhari meh melitzanes] veal with aubergines/eggplants

ΜΟΣΧΑΡΙ ΜΕ ΜΠΑΜΙΕΣ μοσχάρι με μπάμιες [moskhari meh bami-es] veal with okra

ΜΟΣΧΑΡΙ ΜΕ ΠΑΤΑΤΕΣ μοσχάρι με πατάτες [moskhari meh patates] veal with potatoes

ΜΟΣΧΑΡΙ ΜΕ ΠΑΤΑΤΕΣ ΣΤΟ ΦΟΥΡΝΟ μοσχάρι με πατάτες στο φούρνο [moskhari meh patates sto foorno] veal with potatoes cooked in the oven

ΜΟΣΧΑΡΙ ΜΕ ΠΟΥΡΕ μοσχάρι με πουρέ [moskhari meh pooreh] veal with mashed potatoes

ΜΟΣΧΑΡΙ ΜΕ ΦΑΣΟΛΑΚΙΑ μοσχάρι με φασολάκια [moskhari meh fasolakia] veal and green beans

ΜΟΣΧΑΡΙ ΡΟΣΜΠΙΦ
μοσχάρι ροσμπίφ [moskhari rosbif] roast beef

ΜΟΣΧΑΡΙΣΙΟΣ ΚΙΜΑΣ
μοσχαρίσιος κιμάς [moskharisios kimas] minced meat

ΜΟΣΧΑΡΙ ΣΝΙΤΖΕΛ ΜΕ ΠΑΤΑΤΕΣ ΤΗΓΑΝΗΤΕΣ
μοσχάρι σνίτζελ με πατάτες τηγανητές [moskhari schnitzel meh patates tiganites] steak and chips/fries

ΜΟΣΧΑΡΙ ΣΝΙΤΖΕΛ ΜΕ ΠΟΥΡΕ μοσχάρι σνίτζελ με πουρέ [moskhari schnitzel meh patates pooreh] steak with mashed potatoes

ΜΟΣΧΑΡΙ ΨΗΤΟ μοσχάρι ψητό [moskhari psito] veal pot roast

ΜΟΥΣΑΚΑΣ μουσακάς [moosakas] moussaka – layers of vegetables and minced meat topped with béchamel sauce

ΜΟΥΣΑΚΑΣ ΠΑΤΑΤΕΣ
μουσακάς πατάτες [moosakas patates] potatoes with minced meat and béchamel

ΜΟΥΣΤΑΡΔΑ μουστάρδα [moostartha] mustard

ΜΟΥΣΤΟΚΟΥΛΟΥΡΑ
μουστοκούλουρα [moostokooloora] Greek biscuits

ΜΠΑΚΑΛΙΑΡΟΣ μπακαλιάρος [bakaliaros] cod; salt cod; haddock

ΜΠΑΚΑΛΙΑΡΟΣ ΚΡΟΚΕΤΕΣ
μπακαλιάρος κροκέτες [bakaliaros kroketes] haddock croquettes

ΜΠΑΚΑΛΙΑΡΟΣ ΠΛΑΚΙ
μπακαλιάρος πλακί [bakaliaros plaki] salted cod cooked in tomato sauce

ΜΠΑΚΑΛΙΑΡΟΣ ΤΗΓΑΝΗΤΟΣ μπακαλιάρος τηγανητός [bakaliaros tiganitos] fried salted cod

ΜΠΑΚΛΑΒΑΔΕΣ μπακλαβάδες [baklavathes] baklava – layers of thin pastry with nuts and syrup

ΜΠΑΚΛΑΒΑΔΕΣ ΜΕ ΚΑΡΥΔΙΑ μπακλαβάδες με καρύδια [baklavathes meh karithia] baklava – layers of thin pastry with walnuts and syrup

ΜΠΑΚΛΑΒΑΣ μπακλαβάς [baklavas] baklava – filo pastry with nuts and syrup

ΜΠΑΜΙΕΣ μπάμιες [bami-es] okra

ΜΠΑΜΙΕΣ ΛΑΔΕΡΕΣ
μπάμιες λαδερές [bami-es latheres] okra in olive oil and tomato sauce

ΜΠΑΝΑΝΑ μπανάνα [banana] banana

ΜΠΑΡΜΠΟΥΝΙΑ μπαρμπούνια [barboonia] red mullet

ΜΠΑΡΜΠΟΥΝΙΑ ΠΑΝΕ
μπαρμπούνια πανέ [barboonia paneh] breaded red mullet

ΜΠΑΧΑΡΙΚΟ μπαχαρικό [bakhariko] spice

ΜΠΕΖΕΔΕΣ μπεζέδες [bezethes] meringues with cream

ΜΠΕΙΚΟΝ μπέικον [bacon] bacon

ΜΠΕΙΚΟΝ ΚΑΠΝΙΣΤΟ μπέικον καπνιστό [bacon kapnisto] smoked bacon

ΜΠΕΣΑΜΕΛ ΣΑΛΤΣΑ μπεσαμέλ σάλτσα [besamel saltsa] béchamel sauce

ΜΠΙΖΕΛΙΑ μπιζέλια [bizelia] peas

ΜΠΙΣΚΟΤΑ μπισκότα [biskota] biscuits

ΜΠΙΣΚΟΤΑΚΙΑ ΑΛΜΥΡΑ μπισκοτάκια αλμυρά [biskotakia almira] savoury crackers

ΜΠΙΣΚΟΤΑ ΣΟΚΟΛΑΤΑΣ μπισκότα σοκολάτας [biskota sokolatas] chocolate biscuits

ΜΠΙΦΤΕΚΙ μπιφτέκι [bifteki] hamburger; grilled meatballs

ΜΠΟΝ ΦΙΛΕ μπον φιλέ [bon fileh] fillet steak

ΜΠΟΥΓΑΤΣΑ μπουγάτσα [boogatsa] puff pastry with various fillings

ΜΠΟΥΓΑΤΣΑ ΓΛΥΚΙΑ μπουγάτσα γλυκιά [boogatsa glikia] puff pastry with cream and icing sugar

ΜΠΟΥΡΕΚΑΚΙΑ μπουρεκάκια [boorekakia] cheese or minced meat pies

ΜΠΟΥΡΕΚΙ μπουρέκι [booreki] courgette, potato and cheese pie

ΜΠΡΙΑΜΙ μπριάμι [briami] ratatouille

ΜΠΡΙΑΜΙ ΜΕ ΚΟΛΟΚΥΘΑΚΙΑ μπριάμι με κολοκυθάκια [briami meh kolokiΤHakia] courgettes/ zucchini cooked with potatoes in the oven

ΜΠΡΙΖΟΛΑ μπριζόλα [brizola] chop; steak

ΜΠΡΙΖΟΛΑ ΜΟΣΧΑΡΙΣΙΑ μπριζόλα μοσχαρίσια [brizola moskharisia] beef steak

ΜΠΡΙΖΟΛΕΣ μπριζόλες [brizoles] chops; steaks

ΜΠΡΙΖΟΛΕΣ ΒΟΔΙΝΕΣ ΣΤΗ ΣΧΑΡΑ μπριζόλες βοδινές στη σχάρα [brizoles vothines sti skhara] grilled T-bone steak

ΜΠΡΙΖΟΛΕΣ ΣΤΟ ΤΗΓΑΝΙ μπριζόλες στο τηγάνι [brizoles sto tigani] fried T-bone steak

ΜΠΡΙΖΟΛΕΣ ΧΟΙΡΙΝΕΣ μπριζόλες χοιρινές [brizoles khirines] pork chops

ΜΠΡΙΖΟΛΕΣ ΧΟΙΡΙΝΕΣ ΣΤΗ ΣΧΑΡΑ μπριζόλες χοιρινές στη σχάρα [brizoles khirines sti skhara] charcoal-grilled pork chops

ΜΠΡΟΚΟΛΟ μπρόκολο [brokolo] broccoli

ΜΥΑΛΑ μυαλά [miala] brains

ΜΥΑΛΑ ΠΑΝΕ μυαλά πανέ [miala paneh] breaded cows' brains

ΜΥΔΙΑ μύδια [mithia] mussels

ΜΥΔΙΑ ΤΗΓΑΝΗΤΑ μύδια τηγανητά [mithia tiganita] fried mussels

ΝΕΦΡΑ νεφρά [nefra] kidneys
ΝΕΦΡΑ ΨΗΤΑ/ΤΗΓΑΝΗΤΑ νεφρά ψητά/τηγανητά [nefra psita/tiganita] grilled/fried kidneys
ΝΤΟΛΜΑΔΑΚΙΑ ντολμαδάκια [dolmathakia] vine leaves stuffed with minced meat, rice and herbs
ΝΤΟΛΜΑΔΕΣ ντολμάδες [dolmathes] vine or cabbage leaves stuffed with minced meat and/or rice
ΝΤΟΛΜΑΔΕΣ ΑΥΓΟΛΕΜΟΝΟ ΜΕ ΚΙΜΑ ντολμάδες αυγολέμονο με κιμά [dolmathes avgolemono meh kima] vine leaves with rice and minced meat in egg and lemon sauce
ΝΤΟΛΜΑΔΕΣ ΓΙΑΛΑΝΤΖΙ ντολμάδες γιαλαντζί [dolmathes yialantzi] vine leaves stuffed with rice
ΝΤΟΜΑΤΕΣ ντομάτες [domates] tomatoes
ΝΤΟΜΑΤΕΣ ΓΕΜΙΣΤΕΣ ΜΕ ΚΙΜΑ ντομάτες γεμιστές με κιμά [domates yemistes meh kima] stuffed tomatoes with minced meat
ΝΤΟΜΑΤΕΣ ΓΕΜΙΣΤΕΣ ΜΕ ΡΥΖΙ ντομάτες γεμιστές με ρύζι [domates yemistes meh rizi] tomatoes stuffed with rice

ΝΤΟΜΑΤΕΣ ΓΕΜΙΣΤΕΣ ντομάτες γεμιστές [domates yemistes] stuffed tomatoes
ΝΤΟΜΑΤΟΣΑΛΑΤΑ ντοματοσαλάτα [domatosalata] tomato salad
ΝΤΟΜΑΤΟΣΟΥΠΑ ντοματόσουπα [domatosoopa] tomato soup
ΝΤΟΝΑΤΣ ντόνατς [doughnuts] doughnuts

ΞΗΡΟΙ ΚΑΡΠΟΙ ξηροί καρποί [xiri karpi] nuts, dried fruit
ΞΙΦΙΑΣ ξιφίας [xifias] swordfish
ΞΥΔΙ ξύδι [xithi] vinegar

ΟΜΕΛΕΤΑ ομελέτα [omeleta] omelette
ΟΜΕΛΕΤΑ ΛΟΥΚΑΝΙΚΑ ομελέτα λουκάνικα [omeleta lookanika] omelette with sausages
ΟΡΕΚΤΙΚΑ ορεκτικά [orektika] hors d'oeuvres, starters
ΟΣΤΡΑΚΟΕΙΔΗ οστρακοειδή [ostrako-ithi] shellfish

ΠΑΓΩΤΟ παγωτό [pagoto] ice cream
ΠΑΓΩΤΟ ΒΕΡΥΚΟΚΚΟ παγωτό βερύκοκκο [pagoto verikoko] apricot ice cream
ΠΑΓΩΤΟ ΚΟΚΤΑΙΗΛ παγωτό κοκταίηλ [pagoto cocktail] ice cream cocktail
ΠΑΓΩΤΟ ΚΡΕΜΑ παγωτό

κρέμα [pagoto krema] vanilla ice cream

ΠΑΓΩΤΟ ΜΕ ΣΑΝΤΙΓΥ παγωτό με σαντιγύ [pagoto meh sandiyi] ice cream with whipped cream

ΠΑΓΩΤΟ ΜΟΚΚΑ παγωτό μόκκα [pagoto moka] coffee-flavoured ice cream

ΠΑΓΩΤΟ ΜΠΑΝΑΝΑ παγωτό μπανάνα [pagoto banana] banana ice cream

ΠΑΓΩΤΟ ΠΑΡΦΑΙ παγωτό παρφαί [pagoto parfeh] ice cream parfait

ΠΑΓΩΤΟ ΠΡΑΛΙΝΑ παγωτό πραλίνα [pagoto pralina] praline ice cream

ΠΑΓΩΤΟ ΣΟΚΟΛΑΤΑ παγωτό σοκολάτα [pagoto sokolata] chocolate ice cream

ΠΑΓΩΤΟ ΦΡΑΟΥΛΑ παγωτό φράουλα [pagoto fraoola] strawberry ice cream

ΠΑΓΩΤΟ ΦΥΣΤΙΚΙ παγωτό φυστίκι [pagoto fistiki] pistachio ice cream

ΠΑΞΙΜΑΔΙ παξιμάδι [paximathi] dried, hard bread

ΠΑΝΤΖΑΡΙ παντζάρι [pandzari] beetroot

ΠΑΠΙΑ πάπια [papia] duck

ΠΑΠΡΙΚΑ πάπρικα [paprika] paprika

ΠΑΡΜΕΖΑΝΑ παρμεζάνα [parmezana] parmesan

ΠΑΣΤΑ πάστα [pasta] cake

ΠΑΣΤΑ ΑΜΥΓΔΑΛΟΥ πάστα αμυγδάλου [pasta amigthaloo] almond gâteau

ΠΑΣΤΑ ΚΟΡΜΟΣ πάστα κορμός [pasta kormos] chocolate log

ΠΑΣΤΑ ΝΟΥΓΚΑΤΙΝΑ πάστα νουγκατίνα [pasta noogatin] cream gâteau

ΠΑΣΤΑ ΣΟΚΟΛΑΤΙΝΑ πάστα σοκολατίνα [pasta sokolatina] chocolate gâteau

ΠΑΣΤΑ ΦΡΑΟΥΛΑ πάστα φράουλα [pasta fraoola] strawberry gâteau

ΠΑΣΤΙΤΣΙΟ παστίτσιο [pastitsio] macaroni cheese or lasagne-type dish, with minced meat and white sauce

ΠΑΣΤΙΤΣΙΟ ΛΑΖΑΝΙΑ παστίτσιο λαζάνια [pastitsio lazania] lasagne

ΠΑΣΤΙΤΣΙΟ ΜΑΚΑΡΟΝΙΑ ΜΕ ΚΙΜΑ παστίτσιο μακαρόνια με κιμά [pastitsio makaronia meh kima] baked pasta dish with minced meat and béchamel

ΠΑΣΤΟ παστό [pasto] salted

ΠΑΤΑΤΕΣ πατάτες [patates] potatoes

ΠΑΤΑΤΕΣ ΓΑΡΝΙΤΟΥΡΑ πατάτες γαρνιτούρα [patates garnitoora] potatoes

ΠΑΤΑΤΕΣ ΓΙΑΧΝΙ πατάτες γιαχνί [patates yakhni] potatoes cooked with onion and tomato

ΠΑΤΑΤΕΣ ΚΑΙ ΚΟΛΟΚΥΘΑΚΙΑ ΣΤΟ

ΦΟΥΡΝΟ πατάτες και κολοκυθάκια στο φούρνο [patates keh kolokiTHakia sto foorno] potatoes, courgettes/zucchini and tomatoes baked in the oven

ΠΑΤΑΤΕΣ ΚΟΛΟΚΥΘΙΑ ΜΟΥΣΑΚΑΣ πατάτες κολοκύθια μουσακάς [patates kolokiTHia moosakas] potatoes with courgettes/zucchini, minced meat and cheese sauce

ΠΑΤΑΤΕΣ ΠΟΥΡΕ πατάτες πουρέ [patates pooreh] mashed potatoes

ΠΑΤΑΤΕΣ ΡΙΓΑΝΑΤΕΣ πατάτες ριγανάτες στο φούρνο [patates riganates sto foorno] oven-cooked potatoes with oregano

ΠΑΤΑΤΕΣ ΣΟΥΦΛΕ πατάτες σουφλέ [patates soofleh] potato soufflé

ΠΑΤΑΤΕΣ ΣΤΟ ΦΟΥΡΝΟ ΡΙΓΑΝΑΤΕΣ πατάτες στο φούρνο ριγανάτες [patates sto foorno riganates] potatoes baked in the oven with oregano, lemon and olive oil

ΠΑΤΑΤΕΣ ΤΗΓΑΝΙΤΕΣ πατάτες τηγανιτές [patates tiganites] chips, French fries

ΠΑΤΑΤΕΣ ΤΣΙΠΣ πατάτες τσιπς [patates tsips] chips, French fries

ΠΑΤΑΤΟΣΑΛΑΤΑ πατατοσαλάτα [patatosalata] potato salad

ΠΑΤΖΑΡΙΑ πατζάρια [patzaria] beetroot

ΠΑΤΣΑΣ πατσάς [patsas] tripe; soup made from lambs' intestines

ΠΑΤΣΑΣ ΣΟΥΠΑ πατσάς σούπα [patsas soopa] tripe soup

ΠΕΠΟΝΙ πεπόνι [peponi] melon

ΠΕΣΤΡΟΦΑ πέστροφα [pestrofa] trout

ΠΕΣΤΡΟΦΑ ΨΗΤΗ πέστροφα ψητή [pestrofa psiti] grilled trout

ΠΗΧΤΗ πηχτή [pikhti] potted meat

ΠΙΛΑΦΙ πιλάφι [pilafi] rice

ΠΙΛΑΦΙ ΜΕ ΓΑΡΙΔΕΣ πιλάφι με γαρίδες [pilafi meh garithes] shrimp pilaf

ΠΙΛΑΦΙ ΜΕ ΜΥΔΙΑ πιλάφι με μύδια [pilafi meh mithia] pilaf with mussels

ΠΙΛΑΦΙ ΜΕ ΣΑΛΤΣΑ ΝΤΟΜΑΤΑ πιλάφι με σάλτσα ντομάτα [pilafi meh saltsa domata] pilaf with tomato sauce

ΠΙΛΑΦΙ ΤΑΣ-ΚΕΜΠΑΠ πιλάφι τας-κεμπάπ [pilafi tas kebab] rice with cubes of beef in tomato sauce

ΠΙΠΕΡΙ πιπέρι [piperi] pepper (spice)

ΠΙΠΕΡΙΕΣ πιπεριές [piperi-es] peppers

ΠΙΠΕΡΙΕΣ ΓΕΜΙΣΤΕΣ ΜΕ ΚΙΜΑ πιπεριές γεμιστές με

κιμά [piperi-es yemistes meh kima] peppers stuffed with minced meat

ΠΙΠΕΡΙΕΣ ΓΕΜΙΣΤΕΣ ΜΕ ΡΥΖΙ πιπεριές γεμιστές με ρύζι [piperi-es yemistes meh rizi] peppers stuffed with rice

ΠΙΠΕΡΙΕΣ ΓΕΜΙΣΤΕΣ πιπεριές γεμιστές [piperi-es yemistes] stuffed peppers

ΠΙΠΕΡΙΕΣ ΚΟΚΚΙΝΕΣ πιπεριές κόκκινες [piperi-es kokines] red peppers

ΠΙΠΕΡΙΕΣ ΠΡΑΣΙΝΕΣ πιπεριές πράσινες [piperi-es prasines] green peppers

ΠΙΡΟΣΚΙ πιροσκί [piroski] minced meat or sausage rolls

ΠΙΤΣΑ πίτσα [pizza] pizza

ΠΙΤΣΑ ΜΕ ΖΑΜΠΟΝ πίτσα με ζαμπόν [pizza meh zabon] ham pizza

ΠΙΤΣΑ ΜΕ ΜΑΝΙΤΑΡΙΑ πίτσα με μανιτάρια [pizza meh manitaria] mushroom pizza

ΠΙΤΣΑ ΜΕ ΝΤΟΜΑΤΑ ΤΥΡΙ πίτσα με ντομάτα τυρί [pizza meh domata tiri] cheese and tomato pizza

ΠΙΤΣΑ ΣΠΕΣΙΑΛ πίτσα σπέσιαλ [pizza special] special pizza

ΠΙΤΤΑ πίττα [pita] pie

ΠΙΤΤΑ ΜΕ ΚΙΜΑ πίττα με κιμά [pita meh kima] minced meat pie

ΠΛΑΚΙ πλακί [plaki] baked in the oven in a tomato sauce

πολύ ψημένο [poli psimeno] overdone

ΠΟΡΤΟΚΑΛΙ πορτοκάλι [portokali] orange

ΠΟΥΛΕΡΙΚΑ πουλερικά [poulerika] poultry

ΠΟΥΤΙΓΚΑ πουτίγκα [pootiga] pudding

ΠΟΥΤΙΓΚΑ ΜΕ ΑΝΑΝΑ πουτίγκα με ανανά [pootiga meh anana] pineapple pudding

ΠΟΥΤΙΓΚΑ ΜΕ ΚΑΡΥΔΙΑ πουτίγκα με καρύδια [pootiga meh karithia] walnut pudding

ΠΟΥΤΙΓΚΑ ΜΕ ΣΤΑΦΙΔΕΣ πουτίγκα με σταφίδες [pootiga meh stafithes] sultana pudding

ΠΡΑΣΑ πράσα [prasa] leeks

ΠΡΑΣΟΠΙΤΤΑ πρασόπιττα [prasopita] leek pie

ΠΡΩΤΟ ΠΙΑΤΟ πρώτο πιάτο [proto piato] starter

ΡΑΒΑΝΙ ραβανί [ravani] very sweet sponge cake

ΡΑΒΙΟΛΙΑ ραβιόλια [raviolia] ravioli

ΡΙΓΑΝΗ ρίγανη [rigani] oregano

ΡΟΔΑΚΙΝΟ ροδάκινο [rothakino] peaches

ΡΟΣΜΠΙΦ ΑΡΝΙ ΜΟΣΧΑΡΙ ροσμπίφ αρνί μοσχάρι [rozbif arni moskhari] roast beef, veal or lamb

ΡΥΖΙ ρύζι [rizi] rice

ΡΥΖΟΓΑΛΟ ρυζόγαλο [rizogalo] rice pudding

A
B
Γ
Δ
E
Z
H
Θ
I
K
Λ
M
N
Ξ
O
Π
P
Σ
T
Y
Φ
X
Ψ
Ω

ΡΩΣΙΚΗ ΣΑΛΑΤΑ ρώσικη σαλάτα [rosiki salata] Russian salad

ΣΑΛΑΜΙ σαλάμι [salami] salami

ΣΑΛΑΤΑ σαλάτα [salata] salad

ΣΑΛΑΤΑ ΑΜΠΕΛΟΦΑΣΟΥΛΑ σαλάτα αμπελοφάσουλα [salata abelofasoola] runner bean salad

ΣΑΛΑΤΑ ΚΟΥΝΟΥΠΙΔΙ ΒΡΑΣΤΟ σαλάτα κουνουπίδι βραστό [salata koonoopithi vrasto] boiled cauliflower salad

ΣΑΛΑΤΑ ΜΑΡΟΥΛΙΑ σαλάτα μαρούλια [salata maroolia] lettuce salad

ΣΑΛΑΤΑ ΝΤΟΜΑΤΕΣ ΚΑΙ ΑΓΓΟΥΡΙΑ σαλάτα ντομάτες και αγγούρια [salata domates keh agooria] tomato and cucumber salad

ΣΑΛΑΤΑ ΝΤΟΜΑΤΕΣ-ΠΙΠΕΡΙΕΣ σαλάτα ντομάτες-πιπεριές [salata domates piperi-es] tomato and green pepper salad

ΣΑΛΑΤΑ ΣΠΑΡΑΓΓΙΑ σαλάτα σπαράγγια [salata sparagia] asparagus salad

ΣΑΛΑΤΑ ΦΑΣΟΛΙΑ ΞΗΡΑ σαλάτα φασόλια ξηρά [salata fasolia xira] butter bean salad

ΣΑΛΑΤΑ ΧΟΡΤΑ ΒΡΑΣΜΕΝΑ σαλάτα χόρτα βρασμένα [salata khorta vrasmena] chicory salad

ΣΑΛΑΤΑ ΧΩΡΙΑΤΙΚΗ σαλάτα χωριάτικη [salata khoriatiki] Greek salad – tomatoes,

cucumber, peppers, feta, olives and boiled eggs with olive oil and vinegar dressing

ΣΑΛΙΓΚΑΡΙΑ σαλιγκάρια [saligaria] snails

ΣΑΛΤΣΑ σάλτσα [saltsa] sauce

ΣΑΛΤΣΑ ΜΠΕΣΑΜΕΛ σάλτσα μπεσαμέλ [saltsa besamel] béchamel sauce

ΣΑΛΤΣΑ ΝΤΟΜΑΤΑ σάλτσα ντομάτα [saltsa domata] tomato sauce

ΣΑΜΑΛΙ σάμαλι [samali] semolina cake with honey

ΣΑΝΤΙΓΥ σαντιγύ [sandiyi] whipped cream

ΣΑΝΤΟΥΙΤΣ σάντουιτς [sandwich] sandwich

ΣΑΡΔΕΛΛΕΣ σαρδέλλες [sartheles] sardines

ΣΑΡΔΕΛΛΕΣ ΛΑΔΙΟΥ σαρδέλλες λαδιού [sartheles lathioo] sardines in oil

ΣΕΛΙΝΟ σέλινο [selino] celery

ΣΙΜΙΓΔΑΛΙ σιμιγδάλι [simigthali] semolina

ΣΙΡΟΠΙ σιρόπι [siropi] syrup

ΣΚΟΡΔΑΛΙΑ σκορδαλιά [skorthalia] thick garlic sauce

ΣΚΟΡΔΑΛΙΑ ΜΕ ΨΩΜΙ σκορδαλιά με ψωμί [skorthalia meh psomi] thick garlic sauce made with bread

ΣΚΟΡΔΟ σκόρδο [skortho] garlic

ΣΟΚΟΛΑΤΑΚΙΑ σοκολατάκια [sokolatakia] little chocolate cakes; milk chocolates

ΣΟΛΟΜΟΣ σολομός [solomos] salmon

ΣΟΛΟΜΟΣ ΚΑΠΝΙΣΤΟΣ σολομός καπνιστός [solomos kapnistos] smoked salmon

ΣΟΥΒΛΑΚΙΑ σουβλάκια [soovlakia] meat grilled on a skewer, served in pitta bread

ΣΟΥΒΛΑΚΙΑ ΑΠΟ ΚΡΕΑΣ ΑΡΝΙΣΙΟ σουβλάκια από κρέας αρνίσιο [soovlakia apo kreas arnisio] lamb souvlaki/ kebab

ΣΟΥΒΛΑΚΙΑ ΑΠΟ ΚΡΕΑΣ ΜΟΣΧΑΡΙΣΙΟ σουβλάκια από κρέας μοσχαρίσιο [soovlakia apo kreas moskharisio] veal souvlaki/kebab

ΣΟΥΒΛΑΚΙΑ ΑΠΟ ΚΡΕΑΣ ΧΟΙΡΙΝΟ σουβλάκια από κρέας χοιρινό [soovlakia apo kreas khirino] pork souvlaki/ kebab

ΣΟΥΒΛΑΚΙΑ ΝΤΟΝΕΡ ΜΕ ΠΙΤΤΑ σουβλάκια ντονέρ με πίττα [soovlaki doner meh pita] donner kebab with pitta bread

ΣΟΥΒΛΑΚΙ ΚΑΛΑΜΑΚΙ σουβλάκι καλαμάκι [soovlaki kalamaki] shish kebab

ΣΟΥΠΑ σούπα [soopa] soup

ΣΟΥΠΑ ΠΑΤΣΑΣ σούπα πατσάς [soopa patsas] tripe soup

ΣΟΥΠΑ ΡΕΒΥΘΙΑ σούπα ρεβύθια [soopa reviThia] chickpea soup

ΣΟΥΠΑ ΤΡΑΧΑΝΑΣ σούπα τραχανάς [soopa trakhanas] milk broth with flour

ΣΟΥΠΑ ΦΑΚΕΣ σούπα φακές [soopa fakes] lentil soup

ΣΟΥΠΑ ΦΑΣΟΛΙΑ σούπα φασόλια [soopa fasolia] bean soup

ΣΟΥΠΑ ΨΑΡΙ σούπα ψάρι [soopa psari] fish soup

ΣΟΥΠΑ ΨΑΡΙ ΑΥΓΟΛΕΜΟΝΟ σούπα ψάρι αυγολέμονο [soopa psari avgolemono] fish soup with egg and lemon

ΣΟΥΠΕΣ σούπες [soopes] soups

ΣΟΥΠΙΕΣ σουπιές [soopi-es] cuttlefish

ΣΟΥΠΙΕΣ ΜΕ ΣΠΑΝΑΚΙ σουπιές με σπανάκι [soopi-es meh spanaki] cuttlefish and spinach stew

ΣΟΥΠΙΕΣ ΤΗΓΑΝΗΤΕΣ σουπιές τηγανητές [soopi-es tiganites] fried cuttlefish

ΣΟΥΣΑΜΙ σουσάμι [soosami] sesame

ΣΟΥΤΖΟΥΚΑΚΙΑ σουτζουκάκια [sootzookakia] spicy meatballs in red sauce

ΣΟΥΦΛΕ σουφλέ [soofleh] soufflé

ΣΠΑΓΓΕΤΟ ΜΕ ΦΡΕΣΚΟ ΒΟΥΤΥΡΟ ΚΑΙ ΠΑΡΜΕΖΑΝΑ σπαγγέτο με φρέσκο βούτυρο και παρμεζάνα [spageto meh fresko vootiro keh parmezana] spaghetti with butter and parmesan cheese

ΣΠΑΝΑΚΙ σπανάκι [spanaki]
spinach

ΣΠΑΝΑΚΟΠΙΤΤΑ
σπανακόπιττα [spanakopita]
spinach (and sometimes feta)
in filo pastry

σπάνιος [spanios] rare
(steak)

ΣΠΑΡΑΓΓΙΑ ΣΑΛΑΤΑ
σπαράγγια σαλάτα [sparagia
salata] asparagus salad

ΣΠΕΣΙΑΛΙΤΕ σπεσιαλιτέ
[spesialiteh] speciality

ΣΠΛΗΝΑΝΤΕΡΟ σπληνάντερο
[splinandero] intestines stuffed
with spleen

ΣΤΑΦΙΔΕΣ σταφίδες [stafithes]
dried fruit

ΣΤΑΦΙΔΟΨΩΜΟ
σταφιδόψωμο [stafithopsomo]
bread with raisins

ΣΤΑΦΥΛΙΑ σταφύλια [stafilia]
grapes

ΣΤΙΦΑΔΟ στιφάδο [stifatho]
chopped meat with onions;
hare or rabbit stew with
onions

ΣΤΟ ΦΟΥΡΝΟ στο φούρνο
[sto foorno] baked in the
oven

ΣΤΡΕΙΔΙΑ στρείδια [strithia]
oysters

ΣΥΚΑ σύκα [sika] figs

ΣΥΚΩΤΑΚΙΑ συκωτάκια
[sikotakia] liver

ΣΥΚΩΤΑΚΙΑ ΜΑΡΙΝΑΤΑ
συκωτάκια μαρινάτα [sikotakia
marinata] liver cooked in
rosemary

ΣΥΚΩΤΑΚΙΑ ΠΙΛΑΦΙ
συκωτάκια πιλάφι [sikotakia
pilafi] liver pilaf

ΣΥΚΩΤΑΚΙΑ ΣΤΗ ΣΧΑΡΑ
συκωτάκια στη σχάρα [sikotakia
sti skhara] grilled liver

ΣΥΚΩΤΑΚΙΑ ΤΗΓΑΝΗΤΑ
συκωτάκια τηγανητά [sikotakia
tiganita] fried liver

ΣΥΚΩΤΙ ΨΗΤΟ συκώτι ψητό
[sikoti psito] charcoal-grilled
liver

ΣΥΝΑΓΡΙΔΑ ΨΗΤΗ συναγρίδα
ψητή [sinagritha psiti] grilled
sea bream

ΣΦΥΡΙΔΑ ΒΡΑΣΤΗ σφυρίδα
βραστή [sriritha vrasti] boiled
pike

ΣΩΤΕ σωτέ [soteh] lightly
fried, sautéed

ΤΑΡΑΜΑΣ ταραμάς [taramas]
cod roe

ΤΑΡΑΜΟΚΕΦΤΕΔΕΣ
ταραμοκεφτέδες
[taramokeftethes] roe pâté balls
with spices

ΤΑΡΑΜΟΣΑΛΑΤΑ
ταραμοσαλάτα [taramosalata]
cod roe dip

ΤΑΡΤΑ τάρτα [tarta] tart

ΤΑΡΤΑ ΜΕ ΚΕΡΑΣΙΑ τάρτα
με κεράσια [tarta meh kerasia]
cherry tart

ΤΑΡΤΑ ΜΕ ΚΡΕΜΑ ΚΑΙ
ΑΜΥΓΔΑΛΑ τάρτα με κρέμα
και αμύγδαλα [tarta meh krema
keh amigthala] cream and
almond tart

**ΤΑΡΤΑ ΜΕ ΚΡΕΜΑ ΚΑΙ
ΚΑΡΥΔΙΑ** τάρτα με κρέμα και
καρύδια [tarta meh krema keh
karithia] walnut and cream
tart

ΤΑΡΤΑ ΜΕ ΦΡΑΟΥΛΕΣ τάρτα
με φράουλες [tarta meh fraooles]
strawberry tart

ΤΑΡΤΑ ΜΗΛΟΥ τάρτα μήλου
[tarta miloo] apple tart

ΤΑΣ-ΚΕΜΠΑΠ τας-κεμπάπ
[tas kebab] spicy lamb cutlets

ΤΑΣ-ΚΕΜΠΑΠ ΠΙΛΑΦΙ τας-
κεμπάπ πιλάφι [tas kebab pilafi]
spicy lamb cutlets pilaf

ΤΖΑΤΖΙΚΙ τζατζίκι [dzadziki]
yoghurt, cucumber and
garlic dip

ΤΗΓΑΝΗΤΟΣ τηγανητός
[tiganitos] fried

ΤΗΓΑΝΙΤΕΣ τηγανίτες
[tiganites] pancakes

ΤΗΣ ΚΑΤΣΑΡΟΛΑΣ της
κατσαρόλας [tis katsarolas]
casseroled

ΤΗΣ ΣΟΥΒΛΑΣ της σούβλας
[tis soovlas] roast on a spit

ΤΗΣ ΣΧΑΡΑΣ της σχάρας [tls
skharas] grilled over charcoal

ΤΟΝΝΟΣ τόννος [tonos] tuna

ΤΟΝΝΟΣΑΛΑΤΑ τοννοσαλάτα
[tonosalata] tuna salad

ΤΟΣΤ τοστ [tost] toasted
sandwich

ΤΟΣΤ ΚΛΑΜΠ τοστ κλαμπ
[tost club] toasted club
sandwich

ΤΟΣΤ ΜΕ ΑΥΓΟ τοστ με αυγό
[tost meh avgo] toasted egg

sandwich

ΤΟΣΤ ΜΕ ΖΑΜΠΟΝ τοστ με
ζαμπόν [tost meh zabon] toasted
ham sandwich

ΤΟΣΤ ΜΕ ΚΟΤΟΠΟΥΛΟ
τοστ με κοτόπουλο [tost meh
kotopoolo] toasted chicken
sandwich

ΤΟΣΤ ΜΕ ΚΡΕΑΣ τοστ με
κρέας [tost meh kreas] toasted
meat sandwich

ΤΟΣΤ ΜΕ ΜΠΙΦΤΕΚΙ τοστ
με μπιφτέκι [tost meh bifteki]
toasted hamburger

ΤΟΣΤ ΜΕ ΤΥΡΙ τοστ με τυρί
[tost meh tiri] toasted cheese
sandwich

ΤΟΥ ΑΤΜΟΥ του ατμού [too
atmoo] steamed

ΤΟΥΡΣΙ τουρσί [toorsi] pickled

ΤΟΥΡΤΑ τούρτα [toorta]
gâteau

ΤΟΥΡΤΑ ΑΜΥΓΔΑΛΟΥ
τούρτα αμυγδάλου [toorta
amigthaloo] almond gâteau

**ΤΟΥΡΤΑ ΚΡΕΜΑ ΜΕ
ΦΡΑΟΥΛΕΣ** τούρτα κρέμα
με ψράουλες [toorta krema meh
fraooles] strawberry cream
gâteau

ΤΟΥΡΤΑ ΜΟΚΚΑ τούρτα
μόκκα [toorta moka] coffee
gâteau

ΤΟΥΡΤΑ ΝΟΥΓΚΑΤΙΝΑ
τούρτα νουγκατίνα [toorta
noogatina] nougat gâteau

ΤΟΥΡΤΑ ΣΑΝΤΙΓΥ τούρτα
σαντιγύ [toorta sandiyi]
whipped cream gâteau

ΤΟΥΡΤΑ ΣΟΚΟΛΑΤΑΣ τούρτα σοκολάτας [**toor**ta soko**latas**] chocolate gâteau

ΤΡΟΥΦΑΚΙΑ τρουφάκια [troo**fakia**] small chocolate fudge cake

ΤΣΙΠΟΥΡΕΣ τσιπούρες [tsi**poores**] sea bream

ΤΣΙΠΟΥΡΕΣ ΨΗΤΕΣ τσιπούρες ψητές [tsi**poores** psi**tes**] roast sea bream

ΤΣΙΠΣ τσιπς [tsips] crisps, (US) potato chips

ΤΣΟΥΡΕΚΙ τσουρέκι [tsoo**reki**] light sponge

ΤΣΟΥΡΕΚΙΑ τσουρέκια [tsoo**rekia**] sweet bread with fresh butter (Christmas/Easter dish)

ΤΥΡΙ τυρί [ti**ri**] cheese

ΤΥΡΙΑ τυριά [ti**ria**] cheese

ΤΥΡΟΠΙΤΤΑ τυρόπιττα [ti**ro**pita] cheese and egg in filo pastry

ΤΥΡΟΠΙΤΤΑΚΙΑ τυροπιττάκια [tiropit**akia**] small cheese pies

ΦΑΒΑ φάβα [**fava**] chick pea soup

ΦΑΚΕΣ φακές [fa**kes**] lentil soup

ΦΑΣΟΛΑΔΑ φασολάδα [faso**latha**] bean soup with celery, carrots and tomatoes

ΦΑΣΟΛΑΚΙΑ φασολάκια [faso**lakia**] green beans

ΦΑΣΟΛΑΚΙΑ ΛΑΔΕΡΑ φασολάκια λαδερά [faso**lakia lathera**] green beans in olive oil and tomato sauce

ΦΑΣΟΛΑΚΙΑ ΦΡΕΣΚΑ ΓΙΑΧΝΙ φασολάκια φρέσκα γιαχνί [faso**lakia freska yakhni**] runner beans with onion and tomato

ΦΑΣΟΛΑΚΙΑ ΦΡΕΣΚΑ ΣΑΛΑΤΑ φασολάκια φρέσκα σαλάτα [faso**lakia freska salata**] runner bean salad

ΦΑΣΟΛΙΑ φασόλια [fa**solia**] beans

ΦΑΣΟΛΙΑ ΓΙΓΑΝΤΕΣ ΓΙΑΧΝΙ φασόλια γίγαντες γιαχνί [fa**solia yigandes yakhni**] butter beans with onion and tomato

ΦΑΣΟΛΙΑ ΓΙΓΑΝΤΕΣ ΣΤΟ ΦΟΥΡΝΟ φασόλια γίγαντες στο φούρνο [fa**solia yigandes sto foorno**] oven-cooked butter beans

ΦΑΣΟΛΙΑ ΓΙΓΑΝΤΕΣ φασόλια γίγαντες [fa**solia yigandes**] large dried beans in tomato sauce

ΦΑΣΟΛΙΑ ΣΟΥΠΑ φασόλια σούπα [fa**solia soopa**] bean soup

ΦΕΤΑ φέτα [**feta**] feta cheese

ΦΙΛΕ ΜΙΝΙΟΝ φιλέ μινιόν [fi**leh** minion] thin fillet steak

ΦΙΛΕΤΟ φιλέτο [fi**leto**] fillet steak

ΦΛΟΓΕΡΕΣ ΜΕ ΚΡΕΜΑ φλογέρες με κρέμα [flo**yeres** meh **krema**] round sweets filled with cream

ΦΟΝΤΑΝ φοντάν [fondan] sweets

ΦΟΝΤΑΝ ΑΜΥΓΔΑΛΟΥ φοντάν αμυγδάλου [fondan amigthaloo] almond sweets

ΦΟΝΤΑΝ ΑΠΟ ΚΑΡΥΔΑ φοντάν από καρύδα [fondan apo karitha] coconut sweets

ΦΟΝΤΑΝ ΑΠΟ ΚΑΡΥΔΙΑ φοντάν από καρύδια [fondan apo karithia] walnut sweets

ΦΟΝΤΑΝ ΙΝΔΙΚΗΣ ΚΑΡΥΔΑΣ φοντάν ινδικής καρύδας [fondan inthikis karithas] coconut sweets

ΦΟΝΤΑΝ ΠΟΡΤΟΚΑΛΙΟΥ φοντάν πορτοκαλιού [fondan portokali-oo] orange sweets

ΦΟΥΝΤΟΥΚΙΑ φουντούκια [foondookia] hazelnuts

ΦΡΑΟΥΛΕΣ φράουλες [fra-ooles] strawberries

ΦΡΑΟΥΛΕΣ ΜΕ ΣΑΝΤΙΓΥ φράουλες με σαντιγύ [fra-ooles meh sandiyi] strawberries with whipped cream

ΦΡΙΚΑΣΕ ΑΡΝΙ φρικασέ αρνί [frikaseh arni] lamb cooked in lettuce with cream sauce

ΦΡΟΥΙ-ΓΚΛΑΣΕ φρουί-γκλασέ [frooi-glaseh] dried assorted fruits with sugar

ΦΡΟΥΤΑ φρούτα [froota] fruit

ΦΡΟΥΤΟΣΑΛΑΤΑ φρουτοσαλάτα [frootosalata] fruit salad

ΦΡΥΓΑΝΙΑ φρυγανιά [frigania] toast

ΦΡΥΓΑΝΙΕΣ φρυγανιές [friganies] French toast

ΦΥΛΛΟ ΠΙΤΤΑΣ φύλλο πίττας [filo pitas] filo pastry

ΦΥΣΤΙΚΙΑ φυστίκια [fistikia] peanuts

ΦΥΣΤΙΚΙΑ ΑΙΓΙΝΗΣ φυστίκια Αιγίνης [fistikia Eyinis] pistachios

ΧΑΒΙΑΡΙ χαβιάρι [khaviari] caviar

ΧΑΛΒΑΣ χαλβάς [khalvas] halva, sweet made from semolina, sesame seeds, nuts and honey

ΧΑΜΠΟΥΡΓΚΕΡ χάμπουργκερ [khamburger] hamburger

ΧΗΝΑ χήνα [khina] goose

ΧΟΙΡΙΝΟ χοιρινό [khirino] pork

ΧΟΙΡΙΝΟ ΜΕ ΣΕΛΙΝΟ χοιρινό με σέλινο [khirino meh selino] pork casserole with celery

ΧΟΙΡΙΝΟ ΠΑΣΤΟ χοιρινό παστό [khirino pasto] salted pork

ΧΟΙΡΙΝΟ ΣΟΥΒΛΑΣ χοιρινό σούβλας [khirino soovlas] pork on the spit

ΧΟΙΡΙΝΟ ΣΤΗ ΣΧΑΡΑ χοιρινό στη σχάρα [khirino sti skhara] grilled pork

ΧΟΙΡΙΝΟ ΦΟΥΡΝΟΥ ΜΕ ΠΑΤΑΤΕΣ χοιρινό φούρνου με πατάτες [khirino foornoo meh patates] roast pork with potatoes

ΧΟΡΤΑ ΒΡΑΣΜΕΝΑ ΣΑΛΑΤΑ
χόρτα βρασμένα σαλάτα [khorta vrasmena salata] boiled chicory salad

ΧΟΡΤΑΡΙΚΑ χορταρικά [khortarika] vegetables

ΧΟΡΤΟΣΟΥΠΑ χορτόσουπα [khortosoopa] vegetable soup

ΧΤΑΠΟΔΑΚΙ ΞΥΔΑΤΟ χταποδάκι ξυδάτο [khtapothaki xithato] pickled octopus

ΧΤΑΠΟΔΙ χταπόδι [khtapothi] octopus

ΧΤΑΠΟΔΙ ΒΡΑΣΤΟ χταπόδι βραστό [khtapothi vrasto] boiled octopus

ΧΤΑΠΟΔΙ ΚΡΑΣΑΤΟ χταπόδι κρασάτο [khtapothi krasato] octopus in wine

ΧΤΑΠΟΔΙ ΜΕ ΜΑΚΑΡΟΝΑΚΙ χταπόδι με μακαρονάκι [khtapothi meh makaronaki] octopus with macaroni

ΧΤΑΠΟΔΙ ΠΙΛΑΦΙ χταπόδι πιλάφι [khtapothi pilafi] octopus pilaf

ΧΤΑΠΟΔΙ ΣΤΙΦΑΔΟ χταπόδι στιφάδο [khtapothi stifatho] octopus with small onions

ΧΥΛΟΠΙΤΕΣ χυλοπίτες [khilopites] tagliatelle

ΧΥΛΟΠΙΤΕΣ ΜΕ ΒΟΥΤΥΡΟ ΚΑΙ ΤΥΡΙ χυλοπίτες με βούτυρο και τυρί [khilopites meh vootiro keh tiri] tagliatelle with butter and cheese

ΧΥΛΟΠΙΤΕΣ ΜΕ ΚΙΜΑ χυλοπίτες με κιμά [khilopites meh kima] tagliatelle with minced meat sauce

ΧΥΛΟΠΙΤΕΣ ΜΕ ΚΟΤΟΠΟΥΛΟ χυλοπίτες με κοτόπουλο [khilopites meh kotopoolo] tagliatelle with chicken

ΧΩΡΙΑΤΙΚΗ ΣΑΛΑΤΑ χωριάτικη σαλάτα [khoriatiki salata] Greek salad – tomatoes, cucumber, peppers, feta, olives and boiled eggs with olive oil and vinegar dressing

ΨΑΡΙ ψάρι [psari] fish

ΨΑΡΙ ΒΡΑΣΤΟ ΜΑΓΙΟΝΕΖΑ ψάρι βραστό μαγιονέζα [psari vrasto mayoneza] steamed fish with mayonnaise

ΨΑΡΙΑ ψάρια [psaria] fish

ΨΑΡΙΑ ΓΛΩΣΣΕΣ ΒΡΑΣΤΕΣ ΜΕ ΑΥΓΟΛΕΜΟΝΟ ψάρια γλώσσες βραστές με αυγολέμονο [psaria gloses vrastes meh avgolemono] steamed sole with oil and lemon

ΨΑΡΙΑ ΜΑΡΙΝΑΤΑ ψάρια μαρινάτα [psaria marinata] marinated fish

ΨΑΡΙΑ ΤΗΓΑΝΗΤΑ ψάρια τηγανητά [psaria tiganita] fried fish

ΨΑΡΙΑ ΨΗΤΑ ΣΤΗ ΣΧΑΡΑ ψάρια ψητά στη σχάρα [psaria psita sti skhara] charcoal-grilled fish

ΨΑΡΟΣΟΥΠΑ ψαρόσουπα [psarosoopa] fish soup

ΨΗΤΟ ψητό [psito] grilled
over charcoal; oven-roasted

ΨΗΤΟ ΣΤΗ ΣΧΑΡΑ
ψητό στη σχάρα [psito sti skhara]
grilled

ΨΩΜΑΚΙ ψωμάκι [psomaki]
roll

ΨΩΜΙ ψωμί [psomi] bread

ΨΩΜΙ ΑΣΠΡΟ ψωμί άσπρο
[psomi aspro] white bread

ΨΩΜΙ ΓΙΑ ΤΟΣΤ ψωμί γιά
τοστ [psomi ya tost] sliced
bread

ΨΩΜΙ ΜΑΥΡΟ ψωμί μαύρο
[psomi mavro] brown bread

ΩΜΟΣ ωμός [omos] raw

Menu Reader:
Drink

Essential Terms

beer i bira
bottle to bookali
brandy to koniak
coffee o kafes
cup: a cup of ... ena flidzani ...
fruit juice o khimos frooton
gin to tzin
 a gin and tonic ena tzin meh tonik
glass: a glass of ... ena potiri ...
milk to gala
mineral water to emfialomeno nero
orange juice i portokalatha
red wine to kokino krasi
rosé to rozeh
soda (water) i sotha
soft drink to anapsiktiko
sugar i zakhari
tea to tsa-i
tonic (water) to tonik
vodka i votka
water to nero
whisky to whisky
white wine to aspro krasi
wine to kras
wine list o katalogos ton krasion

another ..., please ali mia ..., parakalo

ΑΕΡΙΟΥΧΟ αεριούχο [aeriookho] fizzy

ΑΛΚΟΟΛ αλκοόλ [alko-ol] alcohol

ΑΝΑΝΑΣ ΧΥΜΟΣ ανανάς χυμός [ananas khimos] pineapple juice

ΑΝΑΨΥΚΤΙΚΟ αναψυκτικό [anapsiktiko] soft drink

ΑΠΕΡΙΤΙΦ απεριτίφ [aperitif] aperitif

ΑΣΠΡΟ ΚΡΑΣΙ άσπρο κρασί [aspro krasi] white wine

ΒΟΤΚΑ βότκα [votka] vodka

ΒΥΣΣΙΝΑΔΑ βυσσινάδα [visinatha] black cherry juice

ΓΑΛΑ γάλα [gala] milk

ΓΑΛΑ ΚΑΚΑΟ γάλα κακάο [gala kakao] chocolate milk

ΓΑΛΛΙΚΟΣ ΚΑΦΕΣ γαλλικός καφές [galikos kafes] filter coffee; French coffee

ΓΛΥΚΟ ΚΡΑΣΙ γλυκό κρασί [gliko krasi] sweet wine

ΕΛΛΙΝΙΚΟΣ ΚΑΦΕΣ ελληνικός καφές [elinikos kafes] Greek coffee

ΖΕΣΤΗ ΣΟΚΟΛΑΤΑ ζεστή σοκολάτα [zesti sokolata] hot chocolate

ΚΑΚΑΟ κακάο [kakao] cocoa

ΚΑΤΑΛΟΓΟΣ ΚΡΑΣΙΩΝ κατάλογος κρασιών [katalogos krasion] wine list

ΚΑΦΕΣ καφές [kafes] coffee

ΚΑΦΕΣ ΜΕΤΡΙΟΣ καφές μέτριος [kafes metrios] medium-sweet Greek coffee

ΚΑΦΕΣ ΒΑΡΥΣ ΓΛΥΚΟΣ καφές βαρύς γλυκός [kafes varis glikos] sweet Greek coffee

ΚΑΦΕΣ ΜΕ ΓΑΛΑ καφές με γάλα [kafes meh gala] coffee with milk

ΚΟΚΑ ΚΟΛΑ κόκα κόλα [koka kola] Coca-Cola®

ΚΟΚΚΙΝΟ ΚΡΑΣΙ κόκκινο κρασί [kokino krasi] red wine

ΚΟΚΤΕΗΛ κοκτέηλ [kokteil] cocktail

ΚΟΝΙΑΚ κονιάκ [koniak] brandy

ΚΡΑΣΙ κρασί [krasi] wine

ΚΡΑΣΙ ΑΣΠΡΟ κρασί άσπρο [krasi aspro] white wine

ΚΡΑΣΙ ΚΟΚΚΙΝΟ κρασί κόκκινο [krasi kokino] red wine

ΚΡΑΣΙ ΜΑΥΡΟΔΑΦΝΗ κρασί μαυροδάφνη [krasi mavrothafni] sweet red wine

ΚΡΑΣΙ ΡΕΤΣΙΝΑ κρασί ρετσίνα [krasi retsina] retsina

ΚΡΑΣΙ ΡΟΖΕ κρασί ροζέ [krasi rozeh] rosé wine

ΚΡΑΣΙ ΤΟΥ ΜΑΓΑΖΙΟΥ κρασί του μαγαζιού [krasi too magazi-oo] house wine

ΛΕΜΟΝΑΔΑ λεμονάδα [lemonatha] lemonade

ΛΙΚΕΡ λικέρ [liker] liqueur

ΜΕΤΑΛΛΙΚΟ ΝΕΡΟ μεταλλικό νερό [metaliko nero] mineral water

ΜΗΛΟΧΥΜΟΣ μηλοχυμός [milokhimos] apple juice

ΜΠΥΡΑ μπύρα [bira] beer, lager

ΝΕΣΚΑΦΕ νέσκαφέ [neskafeh] Nescafé®, instant coffee

ΝΕΣΚΑΦΕ ΦΡΑΠΕ νέσκαφέ φραπέ [neskafeh frapeh] iced coffee

ΝΕΡΟ νερό [nero] water

ΝΤΟΜΑΤΑ ΧΥΜΟΣ ντομάτα χυμός [domata khimos] tomato juice

ΟΥΖΟ ούζο [oozo] ouzo

ΟΥΙΣΚΥ ουίσκυ whisky, scotch

παγάκι παγάκι [pagaki] ice cube

ΠΑΓΟΣ πάγος [pagos] ice

ΠΟΡΤΟΚΑΛΑΔΑ πορτοκαλάδα [portokalatha] orange juice

ΠΟΡΤΟΚΑΛΙ ΧΥΜΟΣ πορτοκάλι χυμός [portokali khimos] orange juice

ΠΟΤΑ ποτά [pota] drinks

ΡΑΚΗ ρακή [raki] strong spirit, eau-de-vie

ΡΕΤΣΙΝΑ ρετσίνα [retsina] retsina

ΡΟΖΕ ΚΡΑΣΙ ροζέ κρασί [rozeh krasi] rosé wine

ΡΟΥΜΙ ρούμι [roomi] rum

ΣΤΑΦΥΛΙ ΧΥΜΟΣ σταφύλι χυμός [stafili khimos] grape juice

ΤΖΙΝ τζιν [tzin] gin

ΤΖΙΝ ΜΕ ΤΟΝΙΚ τζιν με τόνικ [tzin meh tonik] gin and tonic

ΤΣΑΙ τσάι [tsa-i] tea

ΤΣΑΙ ΜΕ ΛΕΜΟΝΙ τσάι με λεμόνι [tsa-i meh lemoni] lemon tea

ΤΣΙΠΟΥΡΟ τσίπουρο [tsipooro] type of ouzo

ΦΡΑΠΕ φραπέ [frapeh] iced coffee

ΧΥΜΟΣ χυμός [khimos] juice

ΧΩΡΙΣ ΚΑΦΕΪΝΗ χωρίς καφεΐνη [khoris kafeini] decaffeinated

How the
Language
Works

The Greek Alphabet

Set out below is the Greek alphabet, the names of the Greek letters, and the system of transliteration used in this book:

A, α	alfa	a as in c**a**t
B, β	vita	v as in **v**et
Γ, γ	gama	y as in **y**es, except before consonants and a or o, when it's a throaty version of the g in **g**ap
Δ, δ	thelta	th as in **th**en
E, ε	epsilon	e as in g**e**t
Z, ζ	zita	z
H, η	ita	i as in sk**i**
Θ, θ	thita	as the th in **th**eme (represented by th)
I, ι	yota	i as in b**i**t
K, κ	kapa	k
Λ, λ	lamtha	l
M, μ	mi	m
N, ν	ni	n
Ξ, ξ	ksi	x
O, o	omikron	o as in h**o**t
Π, π	pi	p
P, ρ	ro	r
Σ, σ, ς*	sigma	s
T, τ	taf	t
Y, υ	ipsilon	long i, indistinguishable from **i**ta
Φ, φ	fi	f
X, χ	khi	h as in **h**at or harsh ch in the Scottish word lo**ch** (represented by kh)
Ψ, ψ	psi	ps as in li**ps**
Ω, ω	omega	o as in h**o**t, indistinguishable from **o**mikron

* this letter is used only at the end of a word in lower case

Combinations and diphthongs:

AI, αι	e as in g**e**t
AY, αυ	av or af depending on following consonant
EI, ει	long i, exactly like **i**ta
OI, οι	long i, exactly like **i**ta
EY, ευ	ev or ef depending on following consonant
OY, ου	oo as in m**oo**n
ΓΓ, γγ	ng as in a**ng**le
ΓΚ, γκ	g as in **g**oat at the beginning of a word; ng in the middle
ΜΠ, μπ	b as in bar and sometimes mb as in e**mb**assy in the middle of a word
NT, ντ	d at the beginning of a word and sometimes nd as in e**nd** in the middle
ΤΣ, τσ	ts as in hi**ts**

Pronunciation

Throughout this book Greek words have been transliterated into romanized form (see **The Greek Alphabet** page 209) so that they can be read as though they were English, bearing in mind the notes on pronunciation given below:

a	as in c**a**t
e	as in g**e**t
eh	represents e at end of a word; should always be pronounced as in g**e**t
g	as in **g**oat
i	as in sk**i**
kh	like the ch in the Scottish way of saying lo**ch**
o	as in h**o**t
th	as in **th**en
TH	as in **th**eme

Letters given in bold type indicate the part of the word to be stressed. When two vowels (such as 'ea') are next to each other in the pronunciation, both should be pronounced, as for example in the word: amfiтнeatro (amphitheatre).

Abbreviations

acc	accusative case	neut	neuter
adj	adjective	nom	nominative case
fam	familiar	pl	plural
fem	feminine	pol	polite
gen	genitive case	sing	singular
masc	masculine		

Note

An asterisk (*) next to a word in the dictionaries means that you should refer to the **How the Language Works** section for further information.

Nouns and Articles

Articles

Greek nouns have one of three genders – masculine, feminine or neuter. The indefinite article (a, an) for each gender is:

masc	fem	neut
ένας	μία	ένα
enas	mia	ena

ένας άνδρας	μία γυναίκα	ένα παιδί
enas anthras	mia yineka	ena pethi
a man	a woman	a child

The definite article (the) is:

	masc	fem	neut			masc	fem	neut
sing	o	η	το		plural	οι	οι	τα
	o	i	to			i	i	ta

ο πατέρας	οι πατεράδες
o pateras	i paterathes
the father	the fathers

το μωρό	τα μωρά
to moro	ta mora
the baby	the babies

η χώρα	οι χώρες
i khora	i khores
the country	the countries

η μητέρα	οι μητέρες
i mitera	i miteres
the mother	the mothers

ο δρόμος	οι δρόμοι
o thromos	i thromi
the street	the streets

	το βουνό	τα βουνά
	o voono	ta voona
	the mountain	the mountains

Cases

There are three main cases in Greek – nominative, genitive and accusative. The forms of articles, nouns, adjectives and most pronouns change according to their gender, number and case. The indefinite article (a, an) declines as follows:

sing	masc	fem	neut
nom	ένας	μία	ένα
	enas	mia	ena
gen	ενός	μιάς	ενός
	enos	mias	enos
acc	ένα(ν)*	μία	ένα
	ena(n)	mia	ena

The definite article (the) declines as follows:

sing	masc	fem	neut
nom	ο	η	το
	o	i	to
gen	του	της	του
	too	tis	too
acc	το(ν)*	τη(ν)*	το
	to(n)	ti(n)	to

*The forms έναν and τον/την should be used before nouns beginning with a vowel.

plural	masc	fem	neut
nom	οι	οι	τα
	i	i	ta
gen	των	των	των
	ton	ton	ton
acc	τους	τις	τα
	toos	tis	ta

Nominative Case

The nominative case is used for the subject of sentences:

το δωμάτιό μου είναι μικρό
to thomatio moo ineh mikro
my room is small

ο Γιάννης διαβάζει ένα βιβλίο
o Yanis thiavazi ena vivlio
John is reading a book

Genitive Case

The genitive case is used to indicate possession and to translate 'of':

αυτό είναι το αυτοκίνητο του Γιώργου
afto ineh to aftokinito too Yorgoo
this is George's car

ο σκύλος του γείτονα
o skilos too yitona
the neighbour's dog

Accusative Case

The accusative case is used for direct objects:

μπορείτε να μας φέρετε το λογαριασμό, παρακαλώ;
boriteh na mas fereteh to logariasmo, parakalo?
could you bring us the bill, please?

έχασα το λεωφορείο
ekhasa to leoforio
I missed the bus

The accusative case is also used with some prepositions (to, from, with etc):

αυτή πήγε στην παραλία
afti piyeh stin paralia
she has gone to the beach

αυτός είναι από τη Σκωτία
aftos ineh apo ti Skotia
he comes from Scotland

αυτοί πηγαίνουν με τα πόδια
afti piyenoon meh ta pothia
they are going on foot

προτιμάμε να ταξιδεύουμε με το τρένο
protimameh na taxithevoomeh meh to treno
we prefer to travel by train

Vocative Case

Another case in Greek is the vocative case, which is used to
address someone directly. The vocative has the same endings
as the nominative case, apart from masculine nouns and names
where the final ς is dropped:

Μαρία, πού είναι ο Γιάννης;   Γιάννη, πού είναι η Μαρία;
Maria, poo ineh o Yanis?   Yani, poo ineh i Maria?
Mary, where is John?   John, where is Mary?

Noun Endings

The endings of nouns change according to whether they are
singular or plural and depending on whether they are in the
nominative, genitive or accusative cases.

Masculine Nouns

Masculine nouns usually have one of three endings:

	-ας	-ης	-ος
	ο χειμώνας	ο εργάτης	ο δάσκαλος
	the winter	the workman	the teacher
sing			
nom	ο χειμώνας	ο εργάτης	ο δάσκαλος
	o khimonas	o ergatis	o thaskalos
gen	του χειμώνα	του εργάτη	του δασκάλου
	too khimona	too ergati	too thaskaloo
acc	το χειμώνα	τον εργάτη	τον δάσκαλο
	to khimona	ton ergati	ton thaskalo

plural			
nom	οι χειμώνες	οι εργάτες	οι δάσκαλοι
	i khimones	i ergates	i thaskali
gen	των χειμώνων	των εργατών	των δασκάλων
	ton khimonon	ton ergaton	ton thaskalon
acc	τους χειμώνες	τους εργάτες	τους δασκάλους
	toos khimones	toos ergates	toos thaskaloos

A few masculine nouns end in:

-άς, -ές or -ούς

but for these only the plural differs from the above endings:

ο ψαράς   οι ψαράδες
o psaras   i psarathes
fisherman   fishermen

ο παπάς   οι παπάδες
o papas   i papathes
the priest   the priests

ο καφές   οι καφέδες
o kafes   i kafethes
the coffee   the coffees

ο καναπές   οι καναπέδες
o kanapes   i kanapethes
the couch   the couches

ο παππούς   οι παππούδες
o papoos   i papoothes
the grandfather   the grandfathers

Feminine Nouns

Feminine nouns either end in:

-α or -η

η γλώσσα   η νίκη
the tongue, the language   the victory

sing		
nom	η γλώσσα	η νίκη
	i **glo**sa	i **ni**ki
gen	της γλώσσας	της νίκης
	tis **glo**sas	tis **ni**kis
acc	τη γλώσσα	τη νίκη
	ti **glo**sa	ti **ni**ki

plural		
nom	οι γλώσσες	οι νίκες
	i **glo**ses	i **ni**kes
gen	των γλωσσών	των νικών
	ton glo**son**	ton ni**kon**
acc	τις γλώσσες	τις νίκες
	tis **glo**ses	tis **ni**kes

Some irregular feminine nouns ending in -η take the plural ending -εις, for example:

η λέξη	οι λέξεις
i **le**xi	i **le**xis
the word	the words

η απόφαση	οι αποφάσεις
i apo**fa**si	i apo**fa**sis
the decision	the decisions

Feminine nouns ending in -ος decline like masculine nouns. For example:

η έξοδος	η είσοδος
i **e**xothos	i **i**sothos
the exit	the entrance

Neuter Nouns

Neuter nouns have one of the following endings:

-ο, -ι or -μα

		το δέντρο the tree	το ψωμί the bread, the loaf	το όνομα the name
sing	nom	το δέντρο to thendro	το ψωμί to psomi	το όνομα to onoma
	gen	του δέντρου too thendroo	του ψωμιού too psomi-**oo**	του ονόματος too on**o**matos
	acc	το δέντρο to thendro	το ψωμί to psomi	το όνομα to onoma
plural	nom	τα δέντρα ta thendra	τα ψωμιά ta psomia	τα ονόματα ta on**o**mata
	gen	των δέντρων ton thendron	των ψωμιών ton psomi**on**	των ονομάτων ton on**o**maton
	acc	τα δέντρα ta thendra	τα ψωμιά ta psomia	τα ονόματα ta on**o**mata

Several neuter nouns end in -ος:

το είδος to **i**thos the kind	τα είδη ta **i**thi the kinds	το μέγεθος to me**ye**THos the size	τα μεγέθη ta me**ye**THi the sizes

Adjectives and Adverbs

Most adjectives also change as follows according to gender and number:

masc	fem	neut	masc	fem	neut
ακριβός expensive			γλυκός sweet		
ακριβός akriv**os**	ακριβή akriv**i**	ακριβό akriv**o**	γλυκός glik**os**	γλυκιά glik**ia**	γλυκό glik**o**
όμορφος beautiful			ελαφρύς light		
όμορφος **o**morfos	όμορφη **o**morfi	όμορφο **o**morfo	ελαφρύς elaf**ris**	ελαφριά elaf**ria**	ελαφρύ elaf**ri**

Adjective endings follow the pattern of the corresponding noun endings. Adjectives should agree with their nouns in gender, number, and case:

ο καλός φίλος	έχω μερικούς καλούς φίλους
o kal**o**s f**i**los	**e**kho merik**oo**s kal**oo**s f**i**loos
the good friend	I have some good friends

η όμορφη πόλη	είδαμε ένα ωραίο έργο
i **o**morfi p**o**li	**i**thameh **e**nah or**e**o **e**rgo
the beautiful town	we saw a good film

The most common irregular adjective is:

ο πολύς a lot of, much, many

	sing	plural
masc	ο πολύς	οι πολλοί
	o pol**i**s	i poll**i**
fem	η πολλή	οι πολλές
	i poll**i**	i poll**e**s
neut	το πολύ	τα πολλά
	to pol**i**	ta pol**a**

Comparatives

The comparative is formed by putting the word πιό [pio] 'more' in front of the adjective:

αυτό το ξενοδοχείο είναι πιό/λιγότερο ακριβό από εκείνο
aft**o** to xenothokh**i**o **i**neh pi**o**/lig**o**tero akriv**o** ap**o** ek**i**no
this hotel is more/less expensive than that one

είναι πιό ήσυχα εδώ
ineh pi**o i**sikha eth**o**
it's quieter here

Superlatives

Superlatives are formed by putting the definite article in front of the comparative:

η Ομόνοια είναι η πιό διάσημη πλατεία στην Αθήνα
i Omoni-a ineh i pio thiasimi plati-a stin ATHina
Omonia Square is the most famous square in Athens

αυτός ο δρόμος είναι ο λιγότερο επικίνδυνος
aftos o thromos ineh o ligotero epikinthinos
this road is the least dangerous

η ταβέρνα Ο Γιάννης είναι η πιο δημοφιλής ταβέρνα στη
    Μυτιλήνη
i taverna O Yanis ineh i pio thimofilis taverna sti Mitilini
the O Yanis taverna is the most popular in Mitilini

'As ... as' is translated as τόσο ... όσο:

αυτό το εστιατόριο είναι τόσο ακριβό όσο και το άλλο
afto to estiatorio ineh toso akrivo oso keh to alo
this restaurant is as expensive as that one

αυτή η πόλη δεν είναι τόσο ενδιαφέρουσα όσο νόμιζα
afti i poli then ineh toso enthiaferoosa oso nomiza
this town is not as interesting as I thought

The following common adjectives have irregular comparatives and superlatives:

κακός	χειρότερος	χείριστος
kakos	khiroteros	khiristos
bad	worse	worst
καλός	καλύτερος	κάλλιστος
kalos	kaliteros	kalistos
good	better	best
μικρός	μικρότερος	ελάχιστος
mikros	mikroteros	elakhistos
small	smaller	smallest

μεγάλος	μεγαλύτερος	μέγιστος
megalos	megaliteros	meyistos
big	bigger	biggest
λίγος	λιγότερος	ελάχιστος
ligos	ligoteros	elakhistos
few	fewer	fewest
πολύς	περισσότερος	
polis	perisoteros	
a lot of	a lot more of	

Adverbs

If the adjective ends in -ος, remove this ending and add -α to create the adverb:

adjective	adverb		adjective	adverb
καλός	καλά		ωραίος	ωραία
kalos	kala		oreos	oreh-a
good	well		nice	nicely
κακός	κακά		τυχερός	τυχερά
kakos	kaka		tikheros	tikhera
bad	badly		lucky	luckily

If the adjective ends in -ης, remove this ending and add -ως to create the adverb:

adjective	adverb
συνεχής	συνεχώς
sinekhis	sinekhos
continuous	continuously
ακριβής	ακριβώς
akrivis	akrivos
precise	precisely
διεθνής	διεθνώς
thi-eTHnis	thi-eTHnos
international	internationally

Possessive Adjectives

my	μου	moo		its	του	too
your (sing, fam)	σου	soo		our	μας	mas
his	του	too		your (pl, pol)	σας	sas
her	της	tis		their	τους	toos

Possessive adjectives do not change according to case, gender or number. They follow the noun they refer to, but note that the definite article is placed in front of the noun:

το διαβατήριό μου	τα λεφτά τους	το βιβλίο της
to thiavati**rio** moo	ta le**fta** toos	to vi**vlio** tis
my passport	their money	her book

Pronouns

Possessive Pronouns

Possessive pronouns (mine, hers etc) are formed by placing the word δικός in front of the possessive. δικός declines like an adjective, agreeing with the object possessed in case, gender and number:

	masc	fem	neut
mine	δικός μου	δική μου	δικό μου
	thik**os** moo	thik**i** moo	thik**o** moo
yours (sing, fam)	δικός σου	δική σου	δικό σου
	thik**os** soo	thik**i** soo	thik**o** soo
his	δικός του	δική του	δικό του
	thik**os** too	thik**i** too	thik**o** too
hers	δικός της	δική της	δικό της
	thik**os** tis	thik**i** tis	thik**o** tis
its	δικός του	δική του	δικό του
	thik**os** too	thik**i** too	thik**o** too
ours	δικός μας	δική μας	δικό μας
	thik**os** mas	thik**i** mas	thik**o** mas
yours (pl, pol)	δικός σας	δική σας	δικό σας
	thik**os** sas	thik**i** sas	thik**o** sas
theirs	δικός τους	δική τους	δικό τους
	thik**os** toos	thik**i** toos	thik**o** toos

Plurals take the usual adjective endings:

αυτές είναι οι δικές μας
aftes ineh i thikes mas
these are ours

Personal Pronouns

nom	gen	acc
εγώ [ego] I	μου [moo] me	με/εμένα [meh/emena] me
εσύ [esi] you*	σου [soo] you	σε/εσένα [seh/esena] you
αυτός [aftos] he	του [too] him	τον [ton] him
αυτή [afti] she	της [tis] her	την [tin] her
αυτό [afto] it	του [too] it	το [to] it
εμείς [emis] we	μας [mas] us	μας/εμάς [mas/emas] us
εσείς [esis] you**	σας/εσάς [sas/esas] you	σας/εσάς [sas/esas] you
αυτοί [afti] they (m)	τους [toos] them	τους/αυτούς [toos/aftoos] them
αυτές [aftes] they (f)	τους [toos] them	τις/αυτές [tis/aftes] them
αυτά [afta] they (n)	τους [toos] them	τα/αυτά [ta/afta] them

*   εσύ is used when speaking to one person and is the familiar
    form generally used when speaking to family, friends and
    children.
** εσείς is the polite form which can be used to address one
    person or several people.

αυτή του έδωσε τα χρήματα   εγώ τους είδα να το κλέβουν
afti too ethoseh ta khrimata   ego toos itha na to klevoon
she gave him the money   I saw them stealing it

Where two forms are given for the accusative, the second is
used after prepositions:

θα πάω μαζί με αυτές   αυτό είναι ένα δώρο γιά εσένα
THa pao mazi meh aftes   afto ineh ena thoro ya esena
I will go with them   this is a present for you

In Greek the subject pronoun (nominative) is usually omitted:

έφυγε χθές
efiyeh kh**TH**es
he left yesterday

θα ήθελα να παραγγείλω
THa **i**THela na parangilo
I'd like to order

Although it may be retained for emphasis:

αυτή ήταν πρώτη
aft**i i**tan pr**o**ti
SHE was first

εσύ φταίς
es**i** ftes
YOU are to blame

αυτός έκλεψε το πορτοφόλι μου
aft**os e**klepseh to portof**o**li moo
HE stole my wallet

Examples using pronouns in genitive and accusative:

το πήρε από την τσάντα μου
to p**i**reh ap**o** tin ts**a**nda moo
he took it from my bag

εσύ τους το έδωσες;
es**i** toos to **e**thoses?
did YOU give it to them?

την πήρα μαζί μου
tin p**i**ra maz**i** moo
I took her with me

τα αγόρασε χθες
ta ag**o**raseh kh**TH**es
she bought them yesterday

θα σου τον συστήσω
THa soo ton sist**i**so
I shall introduce you to him

την είδα
tin **i**tha
I saw her

δε σε ακούω καλά
theh seh ak**oo**-o kal**a**
I cannot hear you very well

Verbs

The form of the verb given in dictionaries is usually the first person singular of the present tense. This is the basic form (equivalent to the infinitive) and the endings are either -ω (active verbs) or -μαι (passive verbs).

Although there are two categories of Greek verbs (active and passive), many verbs that are not passive in English are considered passive in Greek.

Present Tense

Present tense endings for verbs ending in -ω depend on whether or not the stress falls on the last syllable:

	stress not on last syllable	stress on last syllable	
	αγοράζω buy	πουλώ sell	μπορώ be able
I	αγοράζ-ω	πουλ-ώ	μπορ-ώ
	agorazo	poolo	boro
you	αγοράζ-εις	πουλ-άς	μπορ-είς
	agorazis	poolas	boris
he/she	αγοράζ-ει	πουλ-ά	μπορ-εί
	agorazi	poola	bori
we	αγοράζ-ουμε	πουλ-άμε	μπορ-ούμε
	agorazoomeh	poolameh	boroomeh
you	αγοράζ-ετε	πουλ-άτε	μπορ-είτε
	agorazeteh	poolateh	boriteh
they	αγοράζ-ουν	πουλ-ούν	μπορ-ούν
	agorazoon	pooloon	boroon

πόσο το πουλάς;
poso to poolas?
how much are you selling it for?

το αγοράζω για χίλιες δραχμές
to agorazo ya hili-es thrakhmes
I am buying it for 1,000 drachmas

δεν μπορεί να περπατήσει
then bori na perpatisi
he can't walk

Passive verbs ending in -μαι take the following endings:

ντώνομαι be dressed, dress (oneself)

I	ντών-ομαι [dinomeh]
you	ντών-εσαι [dineseh]
he/she	ντών-εται [dineteh]
we	ντυν-όμαστε [dinomasteh]
you	ντών-εστε [dinesteh]
they	ντών-ονται [dinondeh]

The verbs 'to be' and 'to have' are irregular:

είμαι I am [imeh]	είμαστε we are [imasteh]
είσαι you are [iseh]	είσαστε/είστε you are [isasteh/isteh]
είναι he/she/it is [ineh]	είναι they are [ineh]

έχω I have [ekho]	έχουμε we have [ekhoomeh]
έχεις you have [ekhis]	έχετε you have [ekheteh]
έχει he/she/it has [ekhi]	έχουν they have [ekhoon]

Past Simple Tense

To describe an action that has taken place in the past, use the past simple tense in Greek. To form this, take the basic form of the verb and add the following endings. Note that in the simple past, the stress moves back one syllable and sometimes changes have to be made to the form of the verb which comes before these endings. For example, where necessary, the letter ε is added to the beginning of the verb so that the stress can move back a syllable:

ακού-ω (I hear)   κάν-ω (I do)

ακού-σ-α I heard [akoosa]	έκαν-α I did [ekana]
ακού-σ-ες you heard [akooses]	έκανες you did [ekanes]
ακού-σ-ε he/she heard [akooseh]	έκανε he/she/it did [ekaneh]
ακού-σ-αμε we heard [akoosameh]	εκάναμε we did [ekanameh]
ακού-σ-ατε you heard [akoosateh]	εκάνατε you did [ekanateh]
ακού-σ-αν they heard [akoosan]	έκαναν they did [ekanan]

The past tense of 'to be' and 'to have' is:

ήμουν I was [**i**moon]   ήμασταν we were [**i**mastan]
ήσουν you were [**i**soon]   ήσασταν you were [**i**sastan]
ήταν he/she/it was [**i**tan]   ήταν they were [**i**tan]

είχα I had [**i**kha]   είχαμε we had [**i**khameh]
είχες you had [**i**khes]   είχατε you had [**i**khateh]
είχε he/she/it had [**i**kheh]   είχαν they had [**i**khan]

πόσα χρήματα είχατε στην τσάντα σας;
p**o**sa khrimata **i**khateh stin ts**a**nda sas?
how much money did you have in your handbag?

επισκεφτήκατε το Αρχαιολογικό Μουσείο;
episkeft**i**kateh tu Arkheoloyik**o** M**oo**sio?
did you visit the Archaeological Museum?

οι τιμές ήταν πιό φτηνές πέρυσι
i times **i**tan pi**o** ftin**e**s perisi
prices were cheaper last year

υπογράψατε στο βιβλίο;
ipogr**a**psateh sto vivl**i**o?
did you sign the book?

The Indefinite

The Greek indefinite form of the verb has no direct equivalent
in English although its use often corresponds to the infinitive
used after verbs such as 'to want', 'to be able to', 'can', etc, and
has the following pattern:

να + basic form of verb + ending of the verb preceding it.

It must agree in person and number with the main verb preceding it:

θα μπορούσα να πληρώσω με επιταγή;
THa bor**oo**sa na plir**o**so meh epitay**i**?
could I pay by cheque?

The exception to this is the impersonal verb 'to have to', 'must' which always takes the same form πρέπει:

πρέπει να πηγαίνουμε τώρα
prepi na piyenoomeh tora
we must go now

Here is a list of some useful verbs with their indefinite and past simple in the first person:

present	indefinite	past simple	perfect
βλέπω see	να δω	είδα	έχω δει
vlepo	na tho	itha	ekho thi
βρίσκω find	να βρω	βρήκα	έχω βρει
vrisko	na vro	vrika	ekho vri
δίνω give	να δώσω	έδωσα	έχω δώσει
thino	na thoso	ethosa	ekho thosi
έρχομαι come	να έλθω	ήλθα	έχω έλθει
erkhomeh	na elTHo	ilTHa	ekho elTHi
κάνω do	να κάνω	έκανα	έχω κάνει
kano	na kano	ekana	ekho kani
λέω say	να πω	είπα	έχω πει
le-o	na po	ipa	ekho pi
μένω stay	να μείνω	έμεινα	έχω μείνει
meno	na mino	emina	ekho mini
παίρνω take	να πάρω	πήρα	έχω πάρει
perno	na paro	pira	ekho pari
πηγαίνω go	να πάω	πήγα	έχω πάει
piyeno	na pao	piga	ekho pa-i
πίνω drink	να πιώ	ήπια	έχω πιεί
pino	na pio	ipia	ekho pi-i
στέλνω send	να στείλω	έστειλα	έχω στείλει
stelno	na stilo	estila	ekho stili
τρώω eat	να φάω	έφαγα	έχω φάει
tro-o	na fa-o	efaga	ekho fa-i
ρωτώ ask	να ρωτήσω	ρώτησα	έχω ρωτήσει
roto	na rotiso	rotisa	ekho rotisi

αγοράζω buy	να αγοράσω	αγόρασα	έχω αγοράσει
agorazo	na agoraso	agorasa	ekho agorasi
κλείνω close	να κλείσω	έκλεισα	έχω κλείσει
klino	na kliso	eklisa	ekho klisi
κοιτάζω look	να κοιτάξω	κοίταξα	έχω κοιτάξει
kitazo	na kitaxo	kitaxa	ekho kitaxi
σταματώ stop	να σταματήσω	σταμάτησα	έχω σταματήσει
stamato	na stamatiso	stamatisa	ekho stamatisi
νομίζω think	να νομίσω	νόμισα	έχω νομίσει
nomizo	na nomiso	nomisa	ekho nomisi
γράφω write	να γράψω	έγραψα	έχω γράψει
grafo	na grapso	egrapsa	ekho grapsi

Future Tense

The simplest way to form the continuous future tense in Greek is to take the present tense forms and add the word θα in front of them:

I will be waiting	θα περιμένω	[THa perimeno]
you will ...	θα περιμένεις	[THa perimenis]
he/she will ...	θα περιμένει	[THa perimeni]
we will ...	θα περιμένουμε	[THa perimenoomeh]
you will ...	θα περιμένετε	[THa perimeneteh]
they will ...	θα περιμένουν	[THa perimenoon]

To form the simple future tense you use θα and the appropriate forms of the indefinite (without the να):

I will buy	θα αγοράσω	[THa agoraso]
you will ...	θα αγοράσεις	[THa agorasis]
he/she/it will ...	θα αγοράσει	[THa agorasi]
we will ...	θα αγοράσουμε	[THa agorasoomeh]
you will ...	θα αγοράσετε	[THa agoraseteh]
they will ...	θα αγοράσουν	[THa agorasoon]

θα σε δω το βράδυ
THa seh tho to vrathi
I'll see you tonight

Imperatives

The imperative form of the verb is used to give commands. To create the singular, familiar imperative, take the indefinite form of the verb (without the να) and change the final -ω to -ε:

κοίταξε εκεί!	πρόσεξε!
kitaxeh eki!	prosexeh!
look over there!	watch out!

Polite and plural forms of the imperative are created by changing the final -ω of the indefinite form (without the να) to -ετε or -τε :

ρωτήστε τον αστυνόμο εκεί πέρα	υπογράψτε εδώ, παρακαλώ
rotisteh ton astinomo eki pera	ipograpsteh etho, parakalo
ask the policeman over there	sign here, please

Negative imperatives are formed by placing μη or μην in front of the second person of the indefinite form (without the να) of the verb:

μην πάτε από αυτόν το δρόμο	μην πιείς αυτό το νερό
min pateh apo afton ton thromo	min pi-is afto to nero
don't go along this street	do not drink this water

Some common irregular imperatives are:

familiar	polite/plural
βρες find [vres]	βρείτε [vriteh]
δες see [thes]	δείτε [thiteh] or δέστε[thesteh]
πιές drink [pies]	πιείτε [pi-iteh] or πιέστε [pi-esteh]
πες say [pes]	πείτε [pesteh] or πέστε [pesteh]
έλα come [ela]	ελάτε [elateh]

Negatives

To form the negative, place the word δε or δεν in front of the verb:

δε μου αρέσει αυτό	δε μιλάω καλά Ελληνικά
theh moo aresi afto	theh mila-o kala Elinika
I don't like this	my Greek is not very good

δεν μπορώ να βρώ το ξενοδοχείο
then boro na vro to xenothokhio
I cannot find the hotel

Questions

The word order and intonation for questions in Greek are the same as in English:

πού είναι το γραφείο του ΕΟΤ, παρακαλώ;
poo ineh to grafio too **E**-OT, parakal**o**?
where is the tourist information office, please?

Note that in questions in Greek, a semi-colon is used instead of a question mark.

Dates

To say the date, take the ordinal number, then the genitive of the month. The exception is 'the first', when you should use the ordinal number:

σήμερα είναι εικοσιεφτά Φεβρουαρίου
simera ineh ikosi-efta Fevroo-arioo
today is the 27th of February

αύριο είναι πρώτη Ιουλίου   χθες ήταν τρεις Δεκεμβρίου
avrio **i**neh pr**o**ti Iooli-oo   khtнes **i**tan tris thekemvri**oo**
tomorrow is the 1st of July   yesterday was the 3rd of
                                           December

Πρωταπριλιά   Πρωτομαγιά
protaprilia   protoma**y**a
1st of April   1st of May

Instead of saying 'nineteen ninety-five' you literally say 'one thousand, nine hundred, ninety five':

χίλια εννιακόσια ενενήντα πέντε
kh**i**lia enniak**o**sia enen**i**nda p**e**ndeh

Days

Monday i Theftera
Tuesday i Triti
Wednesday i Tetarti
Thursday i Pempti
Friday i Paraskevi
Saturday to Savato
Sunday i Kiriaki

Months

January o I-anooarios
February o Fevrooarios
March o Martios
April o Aprilios
May o Ma-ios
June o I-oonios
July o I-oolios
August o AvGoostos
September o Septemvrios
October o Oktovrios
November o No-emvrios
December o Thekemvrios

Time

what time is it? τί ώρα είναι; [ti ora ineh?]
one o'clock μία η ώρα [mia i ora]
two o'clock δύο η ώρα [thio i ora]
it's one o'clock είναι μία η ώρα [ineh mia i ora]
it's two o'clock είναι δύο η ώρα [ineh thio i ora]
it's ten o'clock είναι δέκα η ώρα [ineh theka i ora]
five past one μία και πέντε [mia keh pendeh]
ten past two δύο και δέκα [thio keh theka]
quarter past one μία και τέταρτο [mia keh tetarto]
quarter past two δύο και τέταρτο [thio keh tetarto]
twenty past ten δέκα και είκοσι [theka keh ikosi]
half past ten δέκα και μισή [theka keh misi]
twenty to ten δέκα παρά είκοσι [theka para ikosi]
quarter to two δύο παρά τέταρτο [thio para tetarto]
at half past four στις τέσσερις και μισή [stis teseris keh misi]
at eight o'clock στις οκτώ [stis okto]
14.00 δεκατέσσερις [theka-teseris]
17.30 δεκαεφτά και τριάντα [theka-efta keh trianda]
2 am δύο η ώρα το βράδυ [thio i ora to vrathi]
2 pm δύο η ώρα το μεσημέρι [thio i ora to mesimeri]
6 am έξι η ώρα το πρωί [exi i ora to pro-i]
6 pm έξι η ώρα το απόγευμα [exi i ora to apoyevma]
noon το μεσημέρι [to mesimeri]
midnight τα μεσάνυχτα [ta mesanikhta]

an hour η ώρα [i ora]
a minute το λεπτό [to lepto]
one minute ένα λεπτό [ena lepto]
two minutes δύο λεπτά [thio lepta]
a second το δευτερόλεπτο [to thefterolepto]
a quarter of an hour ένα τέταρτο [ena tetarto]
half an hour μισή ώρα [misi ora]
three quarters of an hour τρία τέταρτα της ώρας [tria tetarta tis oras]

Numbers

0	μηδέν	[mithen]
1	ένα	[ena]
2	δύο	[thio]
3	τρία	[tria]
4	τέσσερα	[tesera]
5	πέντε	[pendeh]
6	έξι	[exi]
7	επτά	[epta]
8	οχτώ	[okhto]
9	εννιά	[enia]
10	δέκα	[theka]
11	έντεκα	[endeka]
12	δώδεκα	[thotheka]
13	δεκατρία	[theka-tria]
14	δεκατέσσερα	[theka-tesera]
15	δεκαπέντε	[theka-pendeh]
16	δεκαέξι	[theka-exi]
17	δεκαεπτά	[theka-epta]
18	δεκαοχτώ	[theka-okhto]
19	δεκαεννιά	[theka-enia]
20	είκοσι	[ikosi]
21	εικοσιένα	[ikosi-ena]
22	εικοσιδύο	[ikosi-thio]
30	τριάντα	[trianda]
31	τριανταένα	[trianda-ena]
40	σαράντα	[saranda]
50	πενήντα	[peninda]
60	εξήντα	[exinda]
70	εβδομήντα	[evthominda]
80	ογδόντα	[ogthonda]
90	ενενήντα	[eneninda]
100	εκατό	[ekato]
110	εκατό δέκα	[ekato theka]

200	διακόσια	[thiakosia]
300	τριακόσια	[triakosia]
1,000	χίλια	[khilia]
2,000	δύο χιλιάδες	[thio khiliathes]
5,000	πέντε χιλιάδες	[pendeh khiliathes]
10,000	δέκα χιλιάδες	[theka khiliathes]
20,000	είκοσι χιλιάδες	[ikosi khiliathes]
50,000	πενήντα χιλιάδες	[peninda khiliathes]
100,000	εκατό χιλιάδες	[ekato khiliathes]
1,000,000	ένα εκατομμύριο	[ena ekatomirio]

Ordinals

Ordinal numbers decline like regular adjectives:

1st	πρώτος	[protos]
2nd	δεύτερος	[thefteros]
3rd	τρίτος	[tritos]
4th	τέταρτος	[tetartos]
5th	πέμπτος	[pemptos]
6th	έκτος	[ektos]
7th	έβδομος	[evthomos]
8th	όγδοος	[ogtho-os]
9th	ένατος	[enatos]
10th	δέκατος	[thekatos]

Conversion Tables

1 centimetre = 0.39 inches   1 inch = 2.54 cm

1 metre = 39.37 inches = 1.09 yards   1 foot = 30.48 cm

1 kilometre = 0.62 miles = 5/8 mile   1 yard = 0.91 m

     1 mile = 1.61 km

km	1	2	3	4	5	10	20	30	40	50	100
miles	0.6	1.2	1.9	2.5	3.1	6.2	12.4	18.6	24.8	31.0	62.1

miles	1	2	3	4	5	10	20	30	40	50	100
km	1.6	3.2	4.8	6.4	8.0	16.1	32.2	48.3	64.4	80.5	161

1 gram = 0.035 ounces   1 kilo = 1000 g = 2.2 pounds

g	100	250	500
oz	3.5	8.75	17.5

1 oz = 28.35 g

1 lb = 0.45 kg

kg	0.5	1	2	3	4	5	6	7	8	9	10
lb	1.1	2.2	4.4	6.6	8.8	11.0	13.2	15.4	17.6	19.8	22.0

kg	20	30	40	50	60	70	80	90	100
lb	44	66	88	110	132	154	176	198	220

lb	0.5	1	2	3	4	5	6	7	8	9	10	20
kg	0.2	0.5	0.9	1.4	1.8	2.3	2.7	3.2	3.6	4.1	4.5	9.0

1 litre = 1.75 UK pints / 2.13 US pints

1 UK pint = 0.57 litre   1 UK gallon = 4.55 litre
1 US pint = 0.47 litre   1 US gallon = 3.79 litre

centigrade / Celsius $°C = (°F - 32) \times 5/9$

°C	-5	0	5	10	15	18	20	25	30	36.8	38
°F	23	32	41	50	59	64	68	77	86	98.4	100.4

Fahrenheit $°F = (°C \times 9/5) + 32$

°F	23	32	40	50	60	65	70	80	85	98.4	101
°C	-5	0	4	10	16	18	21	27	29	36.8	38.3